Webmin Administrator's Cookbook

Over 100 recipes to leverage the features of Webmin and master the art of administering your web or database servers

Michał Karzyński

PUBLISHING

BIRMINGHAM - MUMBAI

Webmin Administrator's Cookbook

First published: March 2014

Production Reference: 1190314

Published by Packt Publishing Ltd.
Livery Place
35 Livery Street
Birmingham B3 2PB, UK

ISBN 978-1-84951-584-9

www.packtpub.com

Cover Image by Michał Karzyński (michal@karzynski.pl)

Credits

Author

Michał Karzyński

Reviewers

Valerie Odolph Azar

Robert K Casto

Habyb Fernandes

Andrew Pam

Danny Sauer

Acquisition Editors

Nikhil Chinnari

Sarah Cullington

Akram Hussain

Content Development Editor

Arvind Koul

Technical Editors

Tanvi Bhatt

Neha Mankare

Shiny Poojary

Copy Editors

Roshni Banerjee

Sarang Chari

Brandt D'Mello

Project Coordinator

Priyanka Goel

Proofreaders

Bridget Braund

Ameesha Green

Lauren Harkins

Indexer

Tejal Soni

Graphics

Ronak Dhruv

Production Coordinator

Kyle Albuquerque

Cover Work

Kyle Albuquerque

About the Author

Michał Karzyński, with a scientific research background in the areas of molecular biology and bioinformatics, has been running Unix-like operating systems since 2002. He works as a web application developer, programming in dynamic languages such as JavaScript, Python, Perl, and PHP. He specializes in designing programming interfaces between servers and client applications based on the HTTP protocol. He has been using Webmin for over five years to assist in setting up and managing servers. He is currently employed as a project manager at the Gdańsk University of Technology in Poland. His blog can be found at `http://michal.karzynski.pl`.

I would like to thank my family and all my friends for their support. I would also like to express my gratitude to Jamie Cameron, the author of Webmin and all other contributors of open source projects who have made our digital revolution a fair and welcoming meritocracy.

About the Reviewers

Valerie Odolph Azar graduated from Holy Spirit University of Kaslik (USEK) in 2013 with a diploma in IT. As a part of her curriculum, she started to share her experience by working at MGG The Linux Experts company from June 2012, improving her skills in server and networking (Linux, CentOS 5, Knoppix, and Windows). She's currently a part of Microsoft Student Partner (MSP) from October 2012 at Microsoft. She develops applications in Windows 8 and Windows Phone 8 based on the C# language (using VS 2012). In addition, she's familiar with Java, HTML, VB.net, JavaScript, CS5, C++, PL/SQL, and OpenGL. She had participated in Imagine Cup 2013 where her team, M#jeur, introduced the MusicLanguage application. In May 2013, she started working at OmniSoft (IBM Partners). She learned, tested, and discovered new IBM products (TSM, TIM, TDI, WebSphere Application Server, and so on). She learned more about server hardware and maintaining teamwork by working as a technical consultant in software services. In November 2013, she started to work at Procomix Technology Group as a system developer.

Special thanks to my family and friends who support me every day, and to all my acquaintances at Procomix company who always help me upgrade my knowledge and achieve my goals.

Robert K Casto was born and raised in Columbus, Ohio where he graduated from The Ohio State University with a Computer Science degree in 1995. He has worked for companies such as Nationwide Financial Services, Amazon.com, Cornerstone Brands, PCMS, Walgreens, and Best Buy. He now lives in Cincinnati, Ohio where he started SellersToolbox in 2011 to help companies that sell on Amazon.com. He has spoken at Sellers Conference for Online Entrepreneurs (SCOE), volunteers for The Strange Loop conference in St Louis, and works on Cub Scout projects with his son. This is his first foray into the publishing world, and he would like to thank the people at Packt Publishing for making the experience an enjoyable one.

Habyb Fernandes is a senior website developer, an IT developer, and definitely a tech enthusiast based in the city of Rio de Janeiro, Brazil. He has over 12 years' experience in creating websites and belongs to a time when it was very fun to create static websites using tables, frames, and animated gifs. In all these years, he acquired a lot of experience working with a wide variety of sizes and design requirements. He has specialized in Drupal, developing solutions to medium and large customers.

Andrew Pam has been following developments in hypermedia and hypertext, content management and online publishing, file systems, distributed systems, and peer-to-peer networking for many years. He is also interested in digital information preservation and is an active advocate of free and open source software and free speech rights. His main interests are in hypermedia, computer-mediated communications technologies, media, and culture.

He is a chief scientist and system administrator of Project Xanadu, the original hypertext system that founded the field; a partner and system administrator of Glass Wings, the longest running arts website in Australia celebrating its twentieth anniversary in 2014; and a manager and system administrator of the computer consultancy Serious Cybernetics. He is a life member since the founding and ten-year board member of the online civil rights organization Electronic Frontiers Australia; a committee member of the Linux Users of Victoria user group; and currently employed as a senior software developer by Australia's leading independent digital publisher Private Media.

Danny Sauer has been a system administrator, Perl developer, security engineer, open source advocate, and general computer geek at various companies for around 20 years. His exposure to Webmin began in the late 90s, and he has written a number of custom modules over the years. When he's not building solutions in the digital world, he and his wife enjoy restoring their antique home and teaching new tricks to old cars.

www.PacktPub.com

Support files, eBooks, discount offers and more

You might want to visit www.PacktPub.com for support files and downloads related to your book.

Did you know that Packt offers eBook versions of every book published, with PDF and ePub files available? You can upgrade to the eBook version at www.PacktPub.com and as a print book customer, you are entitled to a discount on the eBook copy. Get in touch with us at service@packtpub.com for more details.

At www.PacktPub.com, you can also read a collection of free technical articles, sign up for a range of free newsletters and receive exclusive discounts and offers on Packt books and eBooks.

http://PacktLib.PacktPub.com

Do you need instant solutions to your IT questions? PacktLib is Packt's online digital book library. Here, you can access, read and search across Packt's entire library of books.

Why Subscribe?

▶ Fully searchable across every book published by Packt

▶ Copy and paste, print and bookmark content

▶ On demand and accessible via web browser

Free Access for Packt account holders

If you have an account with Packt at www.PacktPub.com, you can use this to access PacktLib today and view nine entirely free books. Simply use your login credentials for immediate access.

Table of Contents

Preface

Welcome to *Webmin Administrator's Cookbook*. This book provides over a hundred practical recipes for solving real-world system administration tasks through a convenient tool called Webmin.

Running an internet-connected private server used to be expensive and available mainly to larger companies who either hired professional sysadmins or outsourced administration. Thanks to the wide adoption of virtualization software, efficient private servers have now become available to anyone with the right skills. Whether you're a developer trying to optimize the performance of your web application or you're a startup looking to implement new software architecture for your systems, chances are you'll need to configure and run your own servers.

Few things are as valuable as having the right tools for a job, and Webmin is a great addition to your toolbox. It allows you to get your server up and running quickly, monitor its state, and be notified by e-mail when the server needs your attention. Webmin simplifies many system administration tasks by abstracting away the complexity of the system command and configuration file syntax, replacing them with a friendly graphical web interface.

Webmin is very lightweight for a GUI application because it doesn't require a desktop environment to be running on your system. You also don't need complex desktop sharing solutions to use it. Since it is a web application, all you need to make full use of Webmin is a browser. Its web nature also makes Webmin resilient to slow or unstable Internet connections. Overall, it's a great tool for administering servers remotely.

The following are just some of the things Webmin can do:

- Install software on your system
- Manage users
- Configure firewalls
- Execute commands and set commands to execute on a schedule
- Monitor and analyze system logs and send alerts

- ▶ Manage files, folders, and permissions
- ▶ Configure network disk sharing
- ▶ Perform automated backups
- ▶ Configure virtual web servers with Apache
- ▶ Manage databases with MySQL or PostgreSQL
- ▶ Set up web applications
- ▶ Configure an e-mail server

In this book, we will discuss all of the topics given in the previous list. We'll go through the process of setting up a server from a fresh installation to a full-fledged web application server that runs Apache, a database management system and e-mail software. We'll cover how to set up web applications written in a range of scripting languages. We'll also set up Webmin to monitor your system and alert you about potential problems.

What this book covers

Chapter 1, Setting Up Your System, covers the first steps that will get your Webmin up and running. In this chapter, we will discuss how to set up Webmin itself, how to monitor what it does, and how to undo changes made through Webmin. The chapter also covers the process of installing other software on your system, selecting which software gets started at boot time, and how to inspect what installation packages put on your system.

Chapter 2, User Management, deals with topics related to the users of your system. The chapter discusses adding and editing system users or groups, allowing these users access to Webmin. We'll also demonstrate how Webmin can be used to export a list of all users from one server and import their accounts into another system. We end the chapter by introducing Usermin, the user-facing companion of Webmin.

Chapter 3, Securing Your System, deals with basic system security, including locking down your system with a firewall and connecting to system services over encrypted tunnels. We'll go through a checklist of security precautions that you should take before putting your server on the Internet.

Chapter 4, Controlling Your System, demonstrates how Webmin can be used to execute commands on your system remotely through a web browser. In this chapter, we'll also discuss how to set up cron jobs to execute commands regularly, delaying command execution until a chosen time, and setting up a web panel for easy access to tasks you need to run occasionally.

Chapter 5, Monitoring Your System, discusses how Webmin can be used to watch over your system and even other servers. We'll demonstrate how Webmin can be set up to handle a situation when services on your machine crash—it can send you e-mail alerts or try to restart the services automatically. In this chapter, we'll also discuss how to analyze the state of your system through log files and configure log rotation routines.

Chapter 6, Managing Files on Your System, covers topics related to remote file management through Webmin. In this chapter, we will also cover how to set up your system as a file-sharing server (CIFS, NFS, SFTP, and FTP) and demonstrate how you can use Webmin to connect your system to remote file shares (CIFS and NFS).

Chapter 7, Backing Up Your System, deals with making copies of important files and databases for safekeeping. We'll demonstrate how Webmin can be used to automate this process, run it on a schedule, and even make off-site backups.

Chapter 8, Running an Apache Web Server, goes through topics related to administering your web server. We'll set up and configure Apache; create virtual servers, password-protected sites, HTTPS websites; and inspect incoming traffic and error logs.

Chapter 9, Running a MySQL Database Server, and _Chapter 10, Running a PostgreSQL Database Server_, cover tasks related to setting up and running your database server. We'll demonstrate how Webmin can be used to create and edit databases, back them up and manage database users. We'll also demonstrate how to connect to your database securely over an encrypted tunnel and how to install web-based database management tools.

Chapter 11, Running Web Applications, demonstrates how all the pieces come together to run web applications. We'll demonstrate how to set up your system to run web apps written in any scripting language, but we'll focus mainly on PHP and Python. We'll provide recipes for installing popular applications such as WordPress, Drupal, and Django.

Chapter 12, Setting Up an E-mail Server, covers topics related to e-mail. We'll demonstrate how to set your system up as an e-mail server for both incoming and outgoing mail. We'll also discuss dealing with spam.

What you need for this book

Throughout this book, we'll be dealing with system administration, which means you'll need a system to administer. You will get the most out of this book if you rent a **Virtual Private Server** (**VPS**) from a hosting provider and set it up with a fresh installation of Linux (preferably Debian or CentOS). VPS servers are inexpensive these days, with prices starting at $5/month. If you prefer to experiment locally, you can set up a virtual machine inside the free VirtualBox platform. You should also configure a terminal emulator or SSH client through which you can access your server to execute commands and edit files.

All instructions provided here will work on Linux, so you will get most out of this book if that is the OS you're using. Debian- or RedHat-based distributions are recommended, but other Linux flavors supported by Webmin should work as well. Many of these recipes will also work on other Unixes (such as BSD-based FreeBSD or OS X), but Webmin's support for these platforms may be limited in places. A complete list of operating systems supported by Webmin may be found online at:

```
http://www.webmin.com/support.html
```

Super users with administrative privileges

In order to perform most tasks described in this book, you will need to have administrative privileges on your system.

The main system administrator on Unix-like operating systems such as Linux is often called **root**. On some systems you can log in as this super user. When this is the case, you can do anything and everything on the system. This makes potential mistakes more dangerous. Other systems (such as Ubuntu) won't allow you to log in as root, so you will need to log in as a regular user with super user (**sudo**) privileges.

Users and groups with super user privileges are defined in the /etc/sudoers file. Throughout this book, we will mark commands that require administrative privileges by preceding them with the sudo command, for example:

```
$ sudo apt-get install webmin
```

Note that you don't need to use this additional command if you're logged in as root, but it's a good practice to stay logged in as a regular user.

If you can't find the /etc/sudoers file on your system, you will have to log in as root and install the sudo package.

Keep in mind that Webmin runs as root on your system, which means that it can break things. The recipes in this book have been tested, but every system is different and we can't guarantee that they will always work as expected. Before you implement these solutions on your production systems, you should test them in a secondary machine. Make sure you know what you're doing before changing the configuration of your production systems.

Who this book is for

This book is for people who decide to administer a Linux system and want to learn how Webmin helps to make administrative tasks easier. It is expected that you have some previous experience with Linux, but you don't necessarily need to be familiar with all of its details. If you're a novice administrator, this book is a good starting off point; if you're a professional, this book will highlight how Webmin can make your job simpler.

When working with Webmin you may find places where it does not behave as expected on your particular version of your operating system. You should report such cases to Webmin's authors via GitHub. Make sure you include the exact version numbers of Webmin, your OS and other software you're running and step-by-step instructions needed to reproduce your problem. Webmin's issues tracker on GitHub can be found at: https://github.com/webmin/webmin/issues

Conventions

In this book, you will find a number of styles of text that distinguish between different kinds of information. Here are some examples of these styles, and an explanation of their meaning.

Code words in text, database table names, folder names, filenames, file extensions, pathnames, dummy URLs, and user input are shown as follows: "The above account and privileges will allow the dbuser to connect to and have full control over the testdb database."

A block of code is set as follows:

```
create:groupname:passwd:gid:member,member,...
```

When we wish to draw your attention to a particular part of a code block, the relevant lines or items are set in bold:

```
create:username:passwd:uid:gid:realname:homedir:shell:min:max:warn:
inactive:expire
modify:oldusername:newusername:passwd:uid:gid:realname:homedir:shell:
min:max:warn:inactive:expire
delete:username
```

Any command-line input or output is written as follows:

```
$ perl -le'@chars=(a..z,A..Z,0..9,_);$p.=$chars[rand(@chars)]
while($i++<22);print $p'
```

New terms and **important words** are shown in bold. Words that you see on the screen, in menus or dialog boxes for example, appear in the text like this: "Click the **Create** button to create the account".

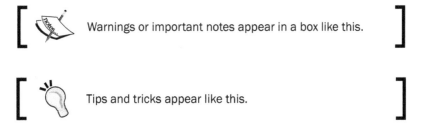

Warnings or important notes appear in a box like this.

Tips and tricks appear like this.

Reader feedback

Feedback from our readers is always welcome. Let us know what you think about this book—what you liked or may have disliked. Reader feedback is important for us to develop titles that you really get the most out of.

To send us general feedback, simply send an e-mail to feedback@packtpub.com, and mention the book title via the subject of your message.

If there is a topic that you have expertise in and you are interested in either writing or contributing to a book, see our author guide on www.packtpub.com/authors.

Customer support

Now that you are the proud owner of a Packt book, we have a number of things to help you to get the most from your purchase.

Errata

Although we have taken every care to ensure the accuracy of our content, mistakes do happen. If you find a mistake in one of our books—maybe a mistake in the text or the code—we would be grateful if you would report this to us. By doing so, you can save other readers from frustration and help us improve subsequent versions of this book. If you find any errata, please report them by visiting http://www.packtpub.com/submit-errata, selecting your book, clicking on the **errata submission form** link, and entering the details of your errata. Once your errata are verified, your submission will be accepted and the errata will be uploaded on our website, or added to any list of existing errata, under the Errata section of that title. Any existing errata can be viewed by selecting your title from http://www.packtpub.com/support.

Piracy

Piracy of copyright material on the Internet is an ongoing problem across all media. At Packt, we take the protection of our copyright and licenses very seriously. If you come across any illegal copies of our works, in any form, on the Internet, please provide us with the location address or website name immediately so that we can pursue a remedy.

Please contact us at copyright@packtpub.com with a link to the suspected pirated material.

We appreciate your help in protecting our authors, and our ability to bring you valuable content.

Questions

You can contact us at questions@packtpub.com if you are having a problem with any aspect of the book, and we will do our best to address it.

1
Setting Up Your System

In this chapter, we will cover the following topics:

- ▶ Installing Webmin on a Debian-based system
- ▶ Installing Webmin on an RPM-based system
- ▶ Installing Webmin on another system
- ▶ Connecting to Webmin
- ▶ Installing additional Webmin modules
- ▶ Monitoring what Webmin is doing
- ▶ Controlling which system services are started at boot
- ▶ Inspecting the installed software packages
- ▶ Installing software packages
- ▶ Updating the installed packages to the latest versions
- ▶ Enabling Webmin to send an e-mail
- ▶ Getting an e-mail when new versions of packages become available
- ▶ Reading the documentation of the installed software

Introduction

Webmin is an open source, web-based system configuration tool written primarily in Perl. Thanks to its web nature, Webmin can be used to control your system remotely from any computer running a browser. It allows you to control numerous aspects of your system's configuration, such as managing users, installing additional software, configuring services, controlling access, and monitoring system activity.

In this chapter, we'll focus on installing Webmin and then demonstrate how it can be used to perform the tasks related to installing, upgrading, and running other software on your system.

Installing Webmin on a Debian-based system

Installing Webmin on a Debian-based system, such as Ubuntu or Linux Mint, is easy because we can rely on the excellent package management system called **Advanced Packaging Tool** (**APT**). APT resolves and installs dependencies automatically and also ensures that Webmin will be updated automatically when you perform a system update.

How to do it...

To install Webmin, perform the following steps:

1. Webmin is not part of the standard Debian package repository, so your first step will be to add the URL of Webmin's repository to your package sources file. Open the /etc/apt/sources.list file in a text editor and add the following lines to it:

   ```
   deb http://download.webmin.com/download/repository sarge contrib
   deb http://webmin.mirror.somersettechsolutions.co.uk/repository
   sarge contrib
   ```

   On most systems, the vi text editor is installed by default, but it may be a bit tricky if you haven't used it before. If you want an easy-to-use editor, try nano. You can install it by issuing the following command:

   ```
   $ sudo apt-get install nano
   ```

   After it's installed, you can use nano to edit the sources.list file by issuing the following command:

   ```
   $ sudo nano /etc/apt/sources.list
   ```

2. We also need to add the GPG key with which Webmin's repository is signed to the list of keys used by APT to authenticate packages. This can be done by issuing the following command:

   ```
   $ wget -qO - http://www.webmin.com/jcameron-key.asc | sudo apt-key add -
   ```

3. You can now refresh the APT cache to include the contents of Webmin's repository. This is done with the following command:

   ```
   $ sudo apt-get update
   ```

4. With these preliminaries out of the way, you can install Webmin with the following command:

   ```
   $ sudo apt-get install webmin
   ```

How it works...

Webmin provides an online repository with DEB installation packages that are compatible with Debian-based systems. We need to give our system the address of this repository so that it can take advantage of it. The list of available repositories is kept in the `/etc/apt/sources.list` file as well as other `*.list` files stored in the `/etc/apt/source.list.d/` directory.

Every package is cryptographically signed to ensure that even if someone breaks into the repository and uploads a package pretending to be Webmin, we don't install it by accident. We downloaded the public GPG key needed to verify this signature by using `wget` and added it to our list of trusted keys by using the `apt-key add` command.

GNU Privacy Guard (**GPG**) is an open source alternative to **Pretty Good Privacy** (**PGP**), a cryptographic software suite that provides encryption and authentication functions. Every Webmin package contains a GPG cryptographic signature, which could only be generated using a private key that is kept secret by Webmin's author Jamie Cameron. A corresponding public key, which is made freely available, may be used to verify that the signature was generated using that private key. If even a single bit of the package code were modified after the package was signed, the signature would not match anymore. This ensures that nobody tampers with Webmin on its way between the author and your system. APT checks the signature automatically, we just need to provide it with Webmin's public key.

If you want to be extra careful, you can check whether the public key you imported is actually the one belonging to Jamie Cameron. Issue the following command and verify that its output contains the same key fingerprint:

```
$ sudo apt-key fingerprint
/etc/apt/trusted.gpg
--------------------
pub     1024D/11F63C51 2002-02-28
        Key fingerprint = 1719 003A CE3E 5A41 E2DE  70DF
D97A 3AE9 11F6 3C51
uid                     Jamie Cameron <jcameron@webmin.com>
```

By updating the APT cache, we ensure that our system becomes aware of packages available in the new repository. Then, we can install Webmin. APT not only resolves dependencies and installs more than just the Webmin package, but also other components it needs to run, including the Perl programming language and others.

There's more...

Webmin also provides a `.deb` (Debian software package) file that can be downloaded and installed manually. If you want to do it this way for some reason, you would need to follow these steps:

1. Visit Webmin's Downloads page at `http://www.webmin.com/download.html` and copy the address of the current Debian package. The package file will be named `webmin_NNN_all.deb`, where `NNN` indicates the current version number.

2. Download the package by using `wget`:

    ```
    $ wget http://prdownloads.sourceforge.net/webadmin/webmin_NNN_all.
    deb
    ```

3. First, install all the packages that Webmin depends on using the following command:

    ```
    $ sudo apt-get install perl libapt-pkg-perl libnet-ssleay-perl
    openssl libauthen-pam-perl libpam-runtime libio-pty-perl apt-show-
    versions python
    ```

4. Then, run the following command to install Webmin from the package file:

    ```
    $ sudo dpkg --install webmin_NNN_all.deb
    ```

Your system may complain that some other package needed by Webmin is missing. For instance, you could see an error message like the following:

```
dpkg: dependency problems prevent configuration of
webmin:
 webmin depends on PACKAGE-NAME; however:
  Package PACKAGE-NAME is not installed.
```

If you see this error, you should install the package designated by `PACKAGE-NAME` before installing Webmin.

See also

More information about installing Webmin on a Debian-based system and about APT package management in general can be found at the following Webmin and Debian websites:

*   `http://www.webmin.com/deb.html`
*   `http://doxfer.webmin.com/Webmin`
*   `https://wiki.debian.org/Apt`

Installing Webmin on an RPM-based system

Installing Webmin on an RPM-based system, such as RHEL, Fedora, CentOS, or openSUSE, is just as easy as on Debian-based systems. Here, we'll rely on the equally excellent package management system called **Red Hat Package Manager** (**RPM**) and the yum utility. Yum resolves and installs dependencies automatically and also ensures that Webmin will be updated automatically when you perform a system update.

On a SUSE-based system, you may use the yum utility as well, but it isn't installed by default. On these systems, it may be more convenient to use the zypper command-line utility or the YaST interface. In this recipe, we will provide zypper alternatives to yum commands to be used on SUSE.

How to do it...

To install Webmin, perform the following steps:

1. While Webmin is available in several systems, its packages are not usually kept up-to-date. We will add Webmin's repository to our system by creating a file which describes the repository. Create a file with the path /etc/yum.repos.d/webmin.repo and add the following lines to it:

   ```
   [Webmin]
   name=Webmin Distribution Neutral
   #baseurl=http://download.webmin.com/download/yum
   mirrorlist=http://download.webmin.com/download/yum/mirrorlist
   enabled=1
   ```

On most systems, the vi text editor is installed by default, but it may be a bit tricky if you haven't used it before. If you want an easy-to-use editor, try nano. You can install it by issuing the following command:

```
$ sudo yum install nano
```

After it's installed, you can use nano to edit the webmin.repo file by issuing the following command:

```
$ sudo nano /etc/yum.repos.d/webmin.repo
```

On a SUSE-based system, you don't need to edit the repository files manually. You can add Webmin's repository by issuing the following command:

```
$ sudo zypper addrepo -f http://download.webmin.com/
download/yum "Webmin Distribution Neutral"
```

2. We also need to add the GPG key with which Webmin's repository is signed to the list of keys used by RPM to authenticate packages. This is done by issuing the following commands:

```
$ wget http://www.webmin.com/jcameron-key.asc
$ sudo rpm --import jcameron-key.asc
$ rm jcameron-key.asc
```

3. You can now refresh the yum cache to include Webmin's repository. This is done by using the following command:

```
$ sudo yum makecache
```

 On a SUSE-based system, issue the following command:
```
$ sudo zypper refresh
```

4. With these preliminaries out of the way, you can install Webmin with the following command:

```
$ sudo yum install webmin
```

 On a SUSE-based system, issue the following command:
```
$ sudo zypper install webmin
```

How it works...

Installation of Webmin using yum is based on exactly the same principles as installing it using apt-get on Debian. Take a look at the *How it works...* section in the previous recipe.

There's more...

Webmin also provides an RPM package that can be downloaded and installed manually. If you wanted to do it this way for some reason, you would need to follow these steps:

1. Visit Webmin's Downloads page at http://www.webmin.com/download.html and copy the address of the current RPM package. The package file will be named webmin-NNN.noarch.rpm, where NNN indicates the current version number.

2. Download the package by using wget:

```
$ wget http://prdownloads.sourceforge.net/webadmin/webmin-NNN.noarch.rpm
```

3. Then, run the following command to install Webmin from the package:

```
$ sudo yum localinstall webmin-NNN.noarch.rpm
```

On a SUSE-based system, issue the following command:
```
$ sudo yast --install webmin-NNN.noarch.rpm
```

See also

More information about installing Webmin on an RPM-based system can be found at the following Webmin website and wiki:

- ▶ http://www.webmin.com/rpm.html
- ▶ http://doxfer.webmin.com/Webmin

Installing Webmin on another system

Even if your system doesn't use the Debian or RPM package managers, there may be a Webmin package available in your distribution repositories. For example, Arch Linux and Gentoo provide Webmin packages, while FreeBSD provides a Webmin package and port.

If your system doesn't provide a Webmin package, you may use steps outlined in this recipe to install Webmin on your Unix-like system, such as Linux, BSD, and OS X.

 A complete list of supported operating systems can be found on Webmin's website:
http://www.webmin.com/support.html

Getting ready

Before installing Webmin, make sure that you have Perl Version 5 installed on your system. You can verify this using the following command:

```
$ perl --version
```

In order to enable SSL encryption of connections, you should install the Perl module Net::SSLeay. You can verify that it's installed by using the following command. It will complain if Net::SSLeay is not installed. If it's installed, the command will generate no output.

```
$ perl -e "use Net::SSLeay"
```

How to do it...

Perform the following steps to install Webmin:

1. Go to Webmin's Downloads page at `http://www.webmin.com/download.html`.

2. Copy the link to the latest version of the Unix tar/gzip format package. The link will be similar to the following, except `NNN` will have to be substituted by the current version number: `http://prdownloads.sourceforge.net/webadmin/webmin-NNN.tar.gz`.

3. Download the package by using `wget`:

   ```
   $ wget http://prdownloads.sourceforge.net/webadmin/webmin-NNN.tar.gz
   ```

4. Extract the archive by using the following command:

   ```
   $ tar -xzf webmin-NNN.tar.gz
   ```

5. Enter the extracted directory and start the interactive installation script by using the following commands:

   ```
   $ cd webmin.NNN
   $ sudo ./setup.sh /usr/local/webmin
   ```

6. You will be asked a series of questions. You can press enter to accept the default suggested answers for the following questions. In the following prompt lines, default values are provided in brackets:

   ```
   Config file directory [/etc/webmin]:
   Log file directory [/var/webmin]:
   Full path to perl (default /usr/bin/perl):
   Web server port (default 10000):
   ```

7. Webmin will attempt to detect the name and version of your operating system. Make sure that this information is correct; otherwise, Webmin may not work correctly. Detected system version will be presented in lines similar to these:

   ```
   ****************************************
   Operating system name:    Mac OS X
   Operating system version: 10.9
   ****************************************
   ```

8. Pick a username and password for the first Webmin administrative user at the following prompts:

   `Login name (default admin):`

   `Login password:`

   `Password again:`

9. Answer yes (`y`) to the following questions:

   `Use SSL (y/n): y`

   `Start Webmin at boot time (y/n): y`

10. After installation is completed, you may delete the `webmin-NNN.tar.gz` archive and the extracted `webmin-NNN` folder from which installation was started.

How it works...

Webmin installation script is able to install it on most Unix-like operating systems.

When we were starting the installation script, we indicated that we want to install Webmin's program files in `/usr/local/webmin`. Use a different path if you want to place it elsewhere.

Webmin asks you a series of questions during installation. For instance, it asks you where to store configuration files (defaults to `/etc/webmin/`) and log files (defaults to `/var/webmin/`). These locations may be changed, but the defaults will work well on most systems.

You will also need to specify the username and password of the first Webmin user. This user will have complete control of your system through Webmin and will be able to add more user accounts.

See also

You can find more information about installing Webmin on its website at `http://www.webmin.com/tgz.html`

Look for a Webmin package for your system. Here are a few links:

- **Arch Linux**: `https://www.archlinux.org/packages/?name=webmin`
- **FreeBSD**: `https://www.freshports.org/sysutils/webmin/`
- **Gentoo**: `http://packages.gentoo.org/package/app-admin/webmin`

Connecting to Webmin

The only client software you need to start using Webmin is a web browser. You can connect to Webmin using your server's IP address or domain name. Webmin allows you to change which IP address, port, or domain name it will use for connections.

Getting ready

The first step is to check the IP address of your server. One way to do it is to run the `/sbin/ifconfig` command. It will give you lots of information about network interfaces configured on your system, including the IP number for each one under the heading **inet addr**. You will have at least two network interfaces on your system. One will be called **lo** or **lo0**, this is the local loopback interface that is used only for connections originating from the same machine. This will have the IP of 127.0.0.1. The other interface will most likely be named **eth0** or **en0** and this will be the primary network adapter of your machine. To connect from another computer, note this IP address. You can also set up a DNS entry for this IP, and then you'll be able to connect using a domain name.

How to do it...

You can connect to Webmin by performing the following steps:

1. Open your web browser and type in the following address, but substitute the words `webmin.host` with the IP address or domain name of your server: `https://webmin.host:10000`.

> If your browser reports that it could not establish a connection to the server, then you may be running a firewall on the server, which is blocking incoming connections. On most Linux systems, the default firewall is called `iptables` and you can direct it to allow all incoming TCP traffic on the port 10000 by issuing the following command:
>
> ```
> $ sudo iptables -I INPUT -p tcp --dport 10000 -j ACCEPT
> ```

2. Unfortunately, the first thing you will see after connecting successfully is a warning stating something along these lines: **This site's security certificate is not valid!** Feel free to ignore this warning and proceed to Webmin. Take a look at the *How it works...* section of this recipe for more information.

> If you receive an error stating that establishing a secure connection failed instead, try to connect to `http://webmin.host:10000` using regular HTTP.

On the next screen, you will be asked to provide the login and password of a user with administrative privileges. This is almost always either root or a user who has ALL privileges granted through `sudo`. Type the username and password and hit the button to log in.

Once you log in, Webmin will greet you with a home screen displaying an overview of your system, similar to the following screenshot:

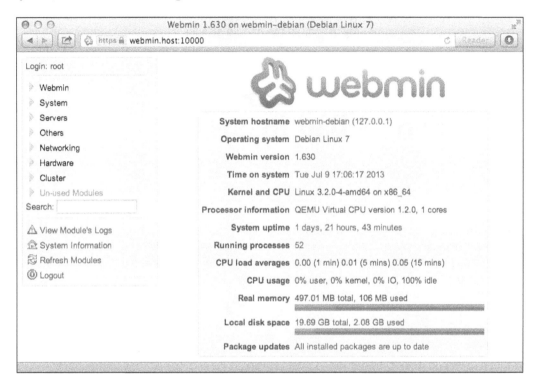

This welcome screen shows Webmin's main interface. On the left-hand side, we see a sidebar containing a hierarchical menu listing all installed modules organized into categories. To the right, we see an interface of the currently activated module (in this case, it's **System Information**).

How it works...

Webmin runs a web server on port 10000 of your server. Since browsers connect to port 80 by default (or port 443 when using HTTPS), we need to specify the port number as part of the URL.

If the Perl module Net::SSLeay is installed on your system, all connections to Webmin are encrypted to avoid eavesdropping or man-in-the-middle attacks. In order to establish an encrypted connection, we instruct the browser to connect using the HTTPS protocol. If you try to connect over regular HTTP, Webmin will provide you with a page redirecting you to the encrypted connection similar to the following screenshot:

Error - Bad Request

```
This web server is running in SSL mode.
Try the URL https://webmin-host:10000/ instead.
```

The error message we see when we establish an encrypted connection is caused by the fact that the certificate we're using to encrypt communication was generated by Webmin itself and wasn't signed by a commercial, trusted certificate authority. This is not a cause for worry. A self-signed certificate has one important advantage: it's free, and it provides the same encryption as a commercial certificate.

There's more...

Webmin uses port 10000 by default to host its web server and will accept connections coming in on any network interface. You can change these options if you wish.

Changing Webmin's listening port

Navigate to the **Ports and Addresses** configuration module by selecting the following options from the menu: **Webmin | Webmin Configuration**. Then, click the **Ports and Addresses** icon. You will get the following screen. On this screen, you can change the port on which Webmin listens for connections by specifying it in **Listen on port | Specific port**. Leave the value of the **Bind to IP address** field as **Any address** for now. Consider the following screenshot:

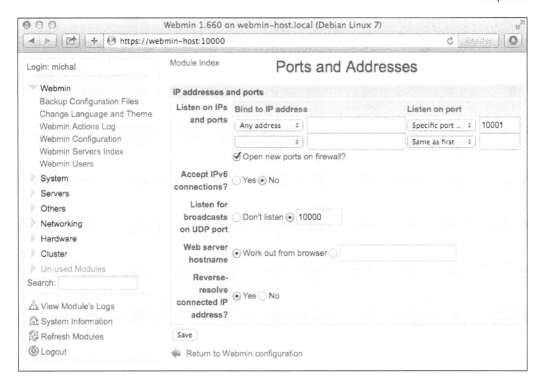

Change the port to `10001` or any unused port number you prefer and click **Save**.

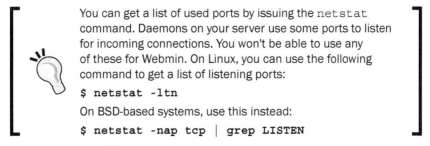

You can get a list of used ports by issuing the `netstat` command. Daemons on your server use some ports to listen for incoming connections. You won't be able to use any of these for Webmin. On Linux, you can use the following command to get a list of listening ports:

```
$ netstat -ltn
```

On BSD-based systems, use this instead:

```
$ netstat -nap tcp | grep LISTEN
```

Webmin will change its port and redirect you to the new address.

Specifying the IP address on which Webmin listens

You can use the **Ports and Addresses** screen to select on which IP address Webmin will be listening. This is useful if you have more than one network interface installed on your machine (for instance, one for accessing the Internet and one on a local network). You can also use this option to select the loopback interface and allow only connections originating from the same machine or coming in over an SSH tunnel (refer to the *Connecting to Webmin securely over an SSH tunnel* recipe in *Chapter 3, Securing Your System*). To restrict connections only to local traffic, select **Bind to IP address | Only address...** and enter 127.0.0.1 as shown in the following screenshot:

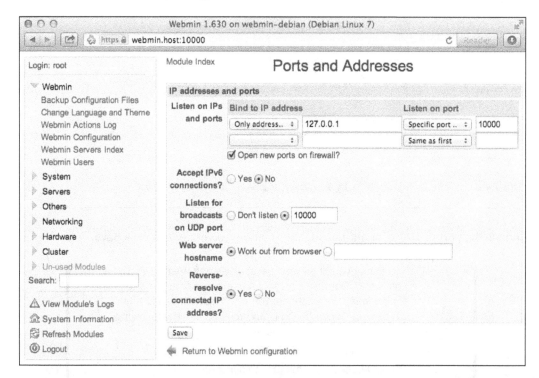

Installing additional Webmin modules

Webmin has a modular architecture and it's possible to extend it by installing additional modules. The majority of stable Webmin modules come bundled into Webmin, so in most cases you don't actually need to install them. Modules, which are installed but not active, are located in the **Un-used Modules** section of the menu. They will usually become activated automatically when you install the software that they depend on. For instance, you may see the **MySQL Database Server** module listed in this section. When you install MySQL or other supported software on your system, Webmin will detect it and move the appropriate module into its section in the menu.

After you install the additional software, you may need to click the **Refresh Modules** link at the bottom of the menu and reload the browser for this update to happen.

Getting ready

If you find a good third-party module that doesn't come bundled with Webmin, you can install it by following this recipe. Just a word of warning: a Webmin module will have privileged access to your system; you should never install modules from sources you don't fully trust.

How to do it...

To install additional Webmin modules, perform the following steps:

1. Copy the URL of a Webmin module's location. It will be in a file with the .wbm or .wbm.gz extension.

2. Navigate to the **Install** tab by going to **Webmin | Webmin Configuration | Webmin Modules**. You will get the following screen:

Module Index

Webmin Modules

Install Clone Delete Export

Webmin modules can be added after installation by using the form to the right. Modules are typically distributed in .wbm files, each of which can contain one or more modules. Modules can also be installed from RPM files if supported by your operating system.

Install Module

Install from
- From local file
- From uploaded file — Browse... No file selected.
- From ftp or http URL — ualmin.com/gpl/wbm/ruby-gems-1.4.wbm.gz
- Standard module from www.webmin.com
- Third party module from

Ignore dependencies? Yes ● No

Grant access to
- Grant access only to users and groups : root
- ● Grant access to all Webmin users

Install Module

3. Select the option to install **From ftp or http URL** and paste the module's URL in the text field provided.

4. Before you install a module, you can choose which users will be allowed to use it. Select **Grant access to all Webmin users**.

5. Click **Install Module**. The next screen will display installation progress, information about where the module was installed on disk, which section of the menu it will be available in, and a link to the module screen.

6. Reload Webmin to see the new module appear in the menu.

How it works...

Webmin will download and decompress the module archive file and place a new module folder on disk in the `/usr/share/webmin/` directory. When you reload Webmin, it will scan the modules directory, discover the new module, and add it to its menu.

Each Webmin module can be made available to all users or a selected group. This choice can be made during the installation of the module or it can be done later in **Webmin | Webmin users settings**. More information about users and access control can be found in *Chapter 2, User Management*.

There's more...

Webmin can also download module files from two repositories: the standard module repository hosted at `webmin.com` and a repository of third-party modules that may be hosted anywhere on the Internet.

Installing a module from a repository

In order to install a module from one of the repositories, perform the following steps:

1. Navigate to **Webmin | Webmin Configuration | Webmin Modules | Install**.

2. Click on the ellipsis (**...**) button at the end of the line **Standard module from www. webmin.com** or **Third party module from**.

3. Select the module you'd like to install and install as described previously.

Webmin will download the file automatically from the repository's URL.

Uninstalling a module

If you'd like to uninstall a module, navigate to **Webmin | Webmin Configuration | Webmin Modules | Delete**, select the module or modules you want to remove, and click **Delete Selected Modules**. In the next screen, you will be asked to confirm your action and the modules will be deleted.

▶   You can search a database of the third-party modules on the Webmin website at `http://www.webmin.com/third.html`

Monitoring what Webmin is doing

One useful feature of Webmin is the fact that it keeps a log of every action it performs. It's sometimes useful to refer to this history to check how users have changed your system's configuration through Webmin's interface.

Getting ready

In order to take full advantage of Webmin's logging facility, you should enable the monitoring of file changes made though Webmin. This allows you to roll back the changes later.

In order to enable this function, go to **Webmin | Webmin Configuration | Logging** and set **Yes** as the answer to these two questions: **Log changes made to files by each action?** and **Record all modified files before actions, for rollbacks?**

How to do it...

To monitor what Webmin is doing, perform the following steps:

1. To access Webmin's log, go to **Webmin | Webmin Actions Log**.
2. Select filters to narrow your search down to log entries made today only and click **Search**. You will see a table listing all actions taken today through Webmin.
3. Click on one of the actions to see a complete description of the action. This screen will inform you which user performed the action at what time, logged in from which IP, and which Webmin script was used.

4. Add an annotation to the action by writing text to the **Log entry annotation** field and clicking **Save**. You will come across something like this:

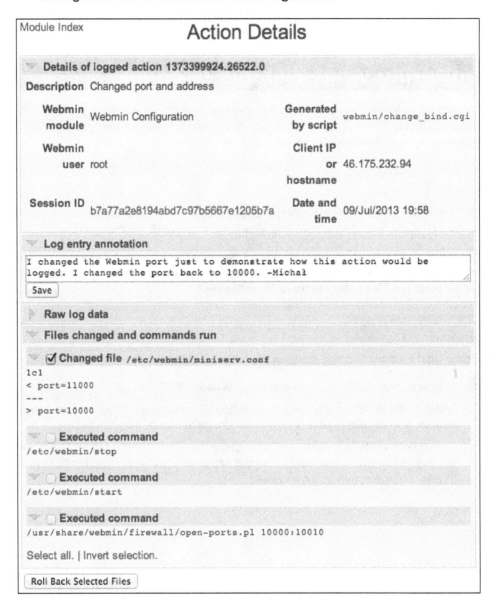

5. View all actions performed in this user session by clicking the link labeled **Session ID**. The annotated action will be visible in the list, marked with a star.

How it works...

Webmin records all actions performed by users to the log file /var/webmin/webmin.log. User annotations are stored in the /var/webmin/annotations directory. If monitoring of file changes is enabled, each change is recorded in the /var/webmin/diffs directory. Please note that these directories could potentially grow quite large over time on a busy system.

The **Webmin Actions Log** interface allows you to search these log files, display them, and use them to revert file changes.

There's more...

If you enabled monitoring of file changes as described in the *Getting ready* section of this recipe, you can use Webmin to revert the changes.

Rolling back file changes

As an exercise, go to **Webmin | Webmin Configuration | User Interface** and set the page background to a light blue color with the RGB hex value of C9DFFF. Go back to **Webmin | Webmin Actions Log**, and then find your action and view its details. In the section **Files changed and commands run**, you will see that a change to the file /etc/webmin/config was recorded, as shown in the following screenshot:

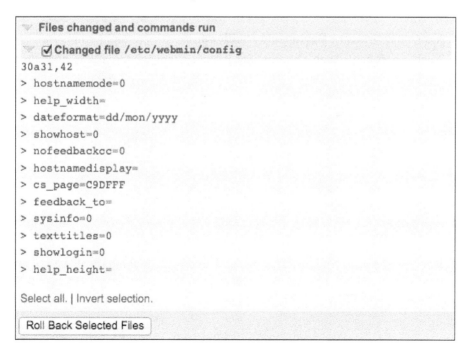

Tick the checkbox next to the file change and click the **Roll Back Selected Files** button. Confirm the rollback and go back to the **Action Details** page. Notice that the background color changes back to white.

See also

▶ For more ways to monitor what your system is doing, take a look at *Chapter 5, Monitoring Your System*

Controlling which system services are started at boot

During the boot process, your operating system should load all services that will be running in the background on your machine. This includes database servers, web servers, tools such as Webmin, and other system processes. Server distributions are very lean by default, so they will only start a handful of essential services. Webmin allows you to control which of these scripts is executed through the **Bootup and Shutdown** module.

How to do it...

Perform the following steps to check which system services are started at boot:

1. Navigate to **System | Bootup and Shutdown**.

2. Select a service to disable temporarily. If your system has the avahi daemon or the rsync service, these can probably be disabled for a minute without causing trouble. Consider the following screenshot:

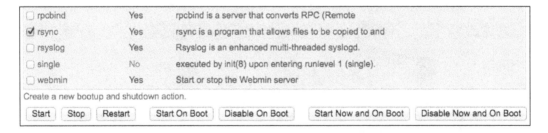

☐ rpcbind	Yes	rpcbind is a server that converts RPC (Remote
☑ rsync	Yes	rsync is a program that allows files to be copied to and
☐ rsyslog	Yes	Rsyslog is an enhanced multi-threaded syslogd.
☐ single	No	executed by init(8) upon entering runlevel 1 (single).
☐ webmin	Yes	Start or stop the Webmin server

Create a new bootup and shutdown action.

| Start | Stop | Restart | Start On Boot | Disable On Boot | Start Now and On Boot | Disable Now and On Boot |

3. Mark the checkbox next to one of these services and click the **Disable Now and On Boot** button. You will see a screen notifying you that the service was stopped and disabled from starting at the next boot.

4. Go back to the **Bootup and Shutdown** screen, select the same service again, and click the **Start Now and On Boot** button to revert your previous change.

How it works...

When your OS starts, it first loads the system kernel and then starts a process called **init** (short for initialization), which executes various init scripts that start system services. Under Linux, these scripts are stored in one directory (`/etc/init.d`) and activated by the creation of symbolic links to them in a special directory from which all scripts are executed at boot time. Webmin allows you to control which init scripts are executed by creating or removing these symbolic links or performing other activation functions specific to your system.

The init system described earlier is often referred to as **SysV-style init**. It's named after the historic UNIX System V that inspired all modern Unix-like operating systems, including Linux and BSD. Many distributions are gradually switching over to more modern alternatives such as Upstart and Systemd. The details of how these systems differ from SysV-init are beyond the scope of this book, but Webmin tries to provide a common interface to all of them. Screenshots in this recipe may differ slightly depending on which init system your distribution uses.

There's more...

Webmin also allows you to easily create your own init scripts and verify that a started service is actually running.

Creating a custom init script

Most server packages you install will come with their own init scripts and activate them in your init system. If you install a package that doesn't, you can use Webmin to create a simple init script for you.

Navigate to **System | Bootup and Shutdown** and click the **Create a new bootup and shutdown action** link.

> Depending on the init system you're using, this link may also be named `Create a new action`, `Create a new upstart service`, `Create a new systemd service`, and so on.

You will be asked to specify the name and description of the startup item as well as two commands: one for starting the service and one for shutting it down. Once you fill these out, click **Create** and Webmin will automatically create a basic init script for you.

Module Index

Create Action

Action Details

Name	custom
Description	My custom service init script.
Bootup commands	/usr/share/custom/startup
Shutdown commands	/usr/share/custom/shutdown
Start at boot time?	⦿ Yes ◯ No

Create

Inspecting active processes

Even if a service is successfully started during boot, it could potentially crash. To inspect which services are actually running, go to **System | Running Processes**. There, you will see a tree of processes sorted in the order in which another process has started them. You can also sort processes by owner or the amount of CPU or RAM they are consuming. Consider the following screenshot:

ID	Owner	Started	Command
1	root	08:09	init [2]
281	root	08:09	udevd --daemon
1616	root	08:09	/usr/sbin/rpc.idmapd
1925	root	08:09	/usr/sbin/rsyslogd -c5
2007	root	08:09	/usr/sbin/acpid
2079	root	08:09	/usr/sbin/cron
2330	Debian-exim	08:09	/usr/sbin/exim4 -bd -q30m
2383	root	08:09	/usr/bin/perl /usr/share/webmin/miniserv.pl /etc/webmin/miniserv.conf
5928	root	14:59	/usr/bin/perl /usr/share/webmin/miniserv.pl /etc/webmin/miniserv.conf
5940	root	14:59	/usr/bin/perl /usr/share/webmin/miniserv.pl /etc/webmin/miniserv.conf
5942	root	14:59	/usr/share/webmin/proc/index_tree.cgi
5952	root	14:59	sh -c ps --cols ...
5953	root	14:59	ps --cols ...

Click on a process ID for one of Webmin's processes to get more information about it, including those files or network connections the process still has open.

Inspecting the installed software packages

Webmin provides an easy-to-use interface to your system's package management system. You can use it to check what packages are installed and view the files installed by each package.

How to do it...

For checking what packages are installed, perform the following steps:

1. Go to **System | Software Packages**. Consider the following screenshot:

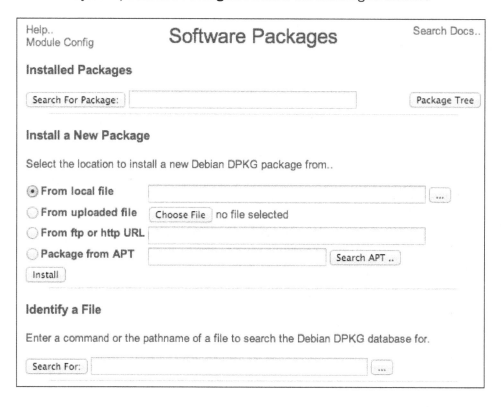

2. Search for the package you're interested in by typing the name or part of its description into the **Search For Package** form. For example, type in `webmin` and click **Search For Package**. You can also browse a listing of packages by clicking the **Package Tree** button.

3. If a package is installed, it will be visible in the package list. Click the name of the package to see a **Package Details** screen.

How it works...

Webmin is able to determine which package management system your OS is using, and provides a unified interface to common tasks such as inspecting, installing, and uninstalling packages. In the background, Webmin will execute the appropriate commands (`apt-get`, `yum`, `rpm`, `yast`, and so on) for you and display the results in the form of a web page.

There's more...

Beyond simply viewing the installed packages, it's often useful to check which files were installed by a package. You may also be interested in a particular file on disk and want to check which package installed it. Webmin allows you to gather this information easily.

Viewing the files installed with a package

To view files installed from a package, perform the following steps:

1. Go to **System | Software Packages**, type in the name of the package (webmin, for example), and click **Search For Package**.
2. In the package listing, click the name of the package to see its details.
3. To view what files were installed by this package, click the **List files** button.

Identifying which package installed a file

To identify which package has installed a file, perform the following steps:

1. Go to **System | Software Packages**.
2. In the **Identify a file** section, type in the name of a file or command or click the ellipsis (**...**) button to browse your disk.
3. Click the **Search For** button.

If the file is identified by the package management system, you will see a screen with information about the file, including the name of the package which installed it:

Module Index Help..	**File Information**		
File Information			
Path /bin/ls			
Type Regular File		**Permissions** 755	
Owner root		**Group** root	
Size 114032			

Package	Class	Description	
coreutils	A-E	amd64 GNU core utilities	

Installing software packages

Webmin is able to use your OS package management to install additional software. If you're using a Debian-based system, such as Ubuntu, you can install packages from .deb files or APT repositories. If you're using an RPM-based system, such as CentOS or openSUSE, you can install packages from .rpm files or yum repositories.

Getting ready

Many web applications depend on an image manipulation library called ImageMagick. Many programs that are used to create, edit, compose, or convert bitmap images such as PNG and JPEG use this library. In this recipe, we will install ImageMagick, but the same procedure may be applied to any other software available in your distribution's repository.

How to do it...

Follow these steps to install a software package using Webmin:

1. Navigate to **System | Software Packages**.
2. Select the **Package from Repo** radio button. Note that you won't actually see the word **Repo**, but rather the name of repository appropriate for your system (APT, YUM, Ports, and so on).

3. Click **Search Repo**, then type in the package name `imagemagick`, and click **Find packages matching** to execute the search.

4. You will be presented with a list of packages matching your search, including `imagemagick`—the package you want to install. Select the package by clicking its name.

5. You will be brought back to the **Software Packages** screen, where you can now press the **Install** button.

Webmin will download and install ImageMagick along with a long list of its dependencies. On the results screen, you can see the details for all the installed packages.

 If the software package you're installing provides a component that may be managed by Webmin (such as Apache, MySQL, PostgreSQL, and Postfix), you should take two additional steps. Click the **Refresh Modules** link in Webmin's main menu and then refresh your entire browser. This will ensure that Webmin recognizes the newly installed software and updates its menu.

How it works...

Webmin determines which package management system your OS uses. It executes the appropriate commands to search available repositories for packages matching your query and installs them along with their dependencies. The same task can be accomplished from the command line, but Webmin abstracts away the command syntax particular to your packaging system so that you can use the same interface regardless of the underlying OS.

There's more...

Webmin also allows you to install software from a package file that you may have. In order to do that, follow this recipe, but select the **From uploaded file** radio button and upload your file instead of searching the repository. If your package file is too large to upload with a browser, you can install it from its URL instead.

Please note that this method will require you to install its dependencies manually before installing the package itself.

Updating the installed packages to the latest versions

Open source communities continually release updates to the software they manage. It's very important to be up-to-date with these upgrades, because they often contain fixes for security vulnerabilities discovered in your software.

How to do it...

To update installed packages, perform the following steps:

1. Navigate to **System | Software Package Updates**. You will see a list of all packages for which updated versions are available in the repository. Consider the following screenshot:

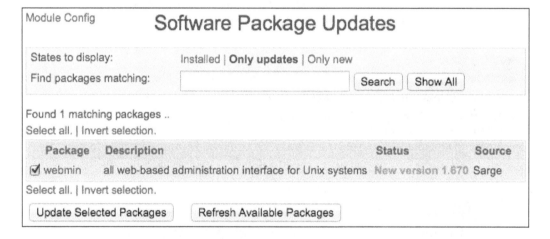

2. Before updating, you may click the **Refresh Available Packages** button to make sure that you have the most current update information.

3. Make sure that all the checkboxes next to packages with available updates are marked, and then click **Update Selected Packages**.

4. The next screen will display a list of all packages that will be updated, along with possible new dependent packages. Click **Install** to perform the updates.

5. The next screen will display progress of the update. Make sure that the page is fully loaded before navigating to another screen.

6. When you return to the package update screen, you should now see the message **No packages available to be updated were found**, informing you that all packages are up-to-date.

How it works...

Webmin determines which package management system your OS uses and queries the package repositories for information about latest available versions. You can trigger this package cache update yourself by clicking **Refresh Available Packages**. When you select to perform the update, Webmin executes the appropriate package management commands to install latest versions.

There's more...

Webmin will also notify you if updates are available for any of its own modules. This notice will appear on the **System Information** page, which is the first page displayed when you log in. If you see it, click **Install Updates Now** to install the module updates as shown in the following screenshot:

The 1 following Webmin module updates are now available ..

Module	Version	Fixes problem
Running Processes	1.632	Fixes total and free memory display on OpenVZ systems

Install Updates Now

Enabling Webmin to send an e-mail

Webmin is a good tool for monitoring the state of your server. You can set it up to send you an e-mail whenever an event that requires your attention occurs.

Getting ready

Webmin needs access to a mail server in order to send an e-mail. In *Chapter 12, Setting Up an E-mail Server,* we will cover setting one up. However, if you don't plan to set up your own mail server or you want to start monitoring your system before you do, you can use an external e-mail service.

Webmin can send e-mail over SMTP, but it doesn't support TLS/SSL encryption. You'll need an account with a provider who allows you to connect via SMTP without encryption.

How to do it...

Perform the following steps to enable Webmin to send e-mails:

1. If you want to send an e-mail via an external SMTP account, navigate to **Webmin | Webmin Configuration | Sending Email** and set the **Send e-mail using** option to **Via SMTP to remote mail server**.

2. Provide the address of the SMTP server, set **SMTP server authentication** to **Login as**, and provide your account's username and password.

3. Set the **From address for email from Webmin** option to an authorized e-mail address.

4. Click **Save** to save the settings.

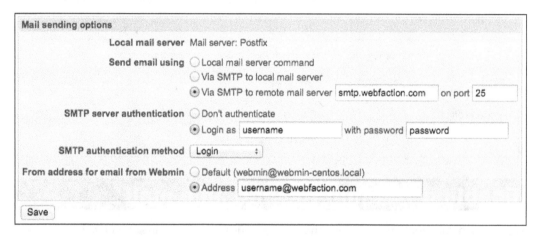

5. Go back to **Webmin | Webmin Configuration | Sending Email**, and use the **Send test message** form to test your configuration.

How it works...

Webmin is able to communicate with a remote server over unencrypted SMTP, so your mail will actually be sent from there. Please note that the configuration, including your password is saved in clear text on the server in the `/etc/webmin/mailboxes/config` file. This file is accessible to all users with administrative privileges on the server, and they will be able to read your e-mail password.

▸ Check out *Chapter 12*, *Setting Up an E-mail Server*, for information about setting up your own mail server.

Getting an e-mail when new versions of packages become available

If you have multiple servers running with different sets of installed software, it may become cumbersome to regularly check for software updates manually. Webmin allows you to schedule automatic update checking and sends you an e-mail whenever new versions of software become available.

Getting ready

Make sure that Webmin is set up for sending e-mail. Refer to the *Enabling Webmin to send an e-mail* recipe of this chapter for more information.

How to do it...

To get an e-mail notification when new versions of software become available, perform the following steps:

1. Navigate to **System | Software Package Updates** and enable **Scheduled checking options**.

2. Set **Check for updates on schedule?** to check for updates every day and provide an e-mail address to which a report will be sent in case any updates are available. Consider the following screenshot:

How it works...

cron is a system utility, which runs in the background as a daemon and starts tasks that are scheduled to execute at a specific time. When **Scheduled checking options** is enabled, Webmin adds an entry in the system's `cron` table to execute its update verification script. The `cron` daemon will then execute the script once every day (hour or week, depending on the setting). If Webmin discovers available updates, it will send you an e-mail.

There's more...

You could set up Webmin to automatically install the updates when they become available. This may not be as great idea as it seems, because every update can potentially break something on your system. This should not normally happen, but it's a good practice for a human to monitor the update process and verify that everything works as it should after updates have been applied.

Reading the documentation of the installed software

Most packages that you install on your system will come with their documentation. Webmin provides a simple utility to search through these manuals.

How to do it...

To read the documentation of the installed software, perform the following steps:

1. Go to **System | System documentation** and type in `wget` as the search term.
2. Set the **Match** option to **Name and contents**.
3. Mark checkboxes next to both **Manual pages** and **Package documentation**, and click **Search**.

Webmin will search through all available documentation and display a list of all manual pages and package notes that mention `wget`.

How it works...

Documentation accompanying a package usually consists of the program's manual pages and packaging information. The `man` pages contain instructions on using the installed software. They are stored in a special format (usually in `/usr/share/man`, `/usr/local/man` or similar locations) and displayed using the `man` command. Package information, on the other hand, may include information about how this package was prepared, how it is intended to be used, and so on. Package docs are usually stored as text or HTML files in `/usr/share/doc`.

Webmin scans the available man pages, package documentation files, and Perl module documentation for mentions of your search term. It displays all the results in the form of web pages for easy viewing.

There's more...

Webmin provides another important search form, which is located in the sidebar menu under the list of module categories. This allows you to perform a detailed search of Webmin itself, which scans both its documentation and also the elements of its user interface. For instance, if you use this form to search for the `Send test message` phrase, Webmin will display a result listing with a link to the **Sending E-mail** module that allows you to send a test e-mail.

2
User Management

In this chapter, we will cover:

- ► Creating a Webmin user
- ► Creating a Webmin group with access to specific modules and options
- ► Allowing users to log in to Webmin with the system credentials
- ► Creating Webmin users based on system accounts
- ► Controlling who is currently using Webmin
- ► Creating a system user account
- ► Modifying a user's UID and other information
- ► Temporarily disabling a user account
- ► Creating and editing a system group
- ► Changing a user's password
- ► Exporting users and importing them into another system
- ► Installing Usermin

Introduction

Webmin's user management features are quite sophisticated. You can use Webmin to manage users and groups on your system, decide which of them have access to Webmin, and which modules they will be allowed to see. You can also create special Webmin-only users, who will not have regular accounts on your system, but will still be able to access selected Webmin modules.

If you're the main administrator of a system, you can set up Webmin to allow other administrators to modify only selected parts of your system's configuration. For instance, you can allow sub-administrators to configure the Apache web server but not to change other settings. This particular workflow is so common, in fact, that a sibling product to Webmin called Usermin was developed to allow non-administrators access to a Webmin-like environment through which they can access databases, configure web hosts, set up `cron` jobs, and read local mail.

Webmin distinguishes between two types of users:

▸ **Unix users (system users)** are standard users of your system. They are usually able to log in to your system through the console or over SSH.

▸ **Webmin users** are accounts specific to Webmin itself. These type of users can log in to Webmin but may have no ability to log in to your system otherwise.

Any system user can be given the status of Webmin user. You can also configure Webmin to add and delete Webmin accounts whenever a system user is added or removed. It's up to you to decide what will suit your situation best—keeping Webmin user accounts separate from system accounts or keeping them synchronized.

Another important concept to keep in mind is a **Webmin group**. Similar to system groups, these are groups of users with specific privileges. You can decide which modules are available to all members of a Webmin group. In general, if you have more then one user with the same privileges, you should assign them to a group and then assign module permissions to the group instead of assigning them individually to each user. This will make future management easier to handle.

Creating a Webmin user

The simplest way to grant someone access to Webmin is to create a Webmin user account for him/her. You can regulate which IPs the user will be allowed to log in from and even at what times during the week the access will be open. During account creation, you can specify what modules the user will have access to or which group he/she will belong to.

In this recipe, we will create a new user with access to only one module.

Getting ready

We will create a new user account with a single-use password, which the user will have to change after the first login. In order to use this one-time password, we need to enable a feature in Webmin. Perform the following steps to set the password expiry policy:

1. Go to **Webmin | Webmin Configuration | Authentication**.
2. Set the **Password expiry policy** option to **Prompt users with expired passwords to enter a new one**.
3. Webmin's server process will restart; wait for a few seconds before continuing.

How to do it...

Perform the following steps to create a new Webmin user:

1. Navigate to the **Webmin | Webmin Users** screen, and click **Create a new Webmin user**.
2. On the user creation screen, specify a username, a password, and the real name of the user. You can set any random long string for the password, as we expect the user to change it. Note the password somewhere, so that we can use it later.

> **Strong passwords** are long strings of characters randomly selected from a large alphabet. If you use all alphanumeric characters (a-z, A-Z, and 0–9) then each character adds approximately 6 bits of entropy to the strength of the password. This means that for a 128-bit password you'd need a 22-character string, for a 256-bit strength you'd need 43 characters, and so on. You can generate a pseudo-random password using a simple Perl one-liner such as:
>
> ```
> $ perl -le'@chars=(a..z,A..Z,0..9,_);$p.=$chars[rand(@chars)] while($i++<22);print $p'
> ```
>
> If you wish to use a truly random password generated by a quantum mechanical white noise generator, visit GRC's Ultra High Security Passwords page:
>
> ```
> https://www.grc.com/passwords.htm
> ```

3. Check the **Force change at next login** option:

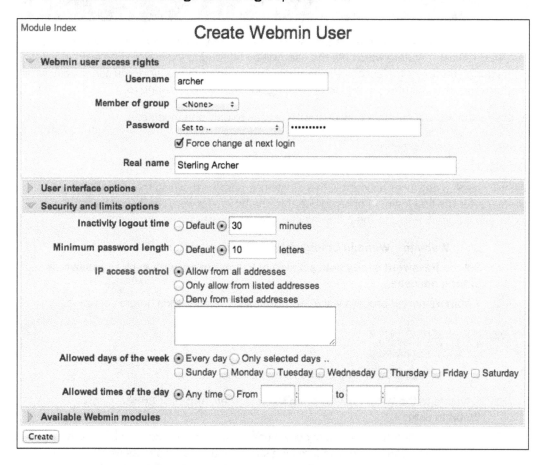

4. In the **Security and limits options** section, set **Inactivity logout time** to 30 minutes and **Minimum password length** to 10 letters.

5. In the **Available Webmin modules** section, check the box next to **Read User Mail** module in the **Servers** section.

6. Click the **Create** button to create the account.

How it works...

Webmin keeps its own database of user accounts, separate from the system user list. The list of accounts is kept by default in the `miniserv.users` file at `/etc/webmin/`. Information about which modules each account has access to is stored in the `webmin.acl` file at `/etc/webmin/` (**acl** stands for **access control list**).

When a user tries to log into Webmin, it checks those files to determine whether the login information provided is correct, if the account is active, and which modules the user has access to. Based on this information, Webmin logs the user in and creates an interface for him/her.

There's more...

Webmin provides additional features, which make account administration easier. For instance, if you find that you need to create a few similar accounts, you can create one and clone it. If you want to preview what Webmin looks like to a particular user, you can switch to that user's account without the need to know their password.

Clone a Webmin user

In order to clone an already existing user account, go to **Webmin | Webmin Users**, and click the username of the user you would like to clone. At the bottom of the **Edit Webmin User** screen, you will find a button marked **Clone**. If you click on it, you will be brought to an account creation page with options prefilled based on settings of the user you cloned.

Switch to user

If you want to check what options Webmin makes available to a particular user, you can go to **Webmin | Webmin Users**, click on the username, and then click the **Switch to User** button at the bottom of the screen. After you are finished testing, you will need to log out and log in again as yourself if this user does not have access to the **Webmin Users** module.

See also

- ► In the next recipe, *Creating a Webmin group with access to specific modules and options*, we will go into more detail about granting users access to specific module options.

Creating a Webmin group with access to specific modules and options

Webmin users should be organized into groups. If you have more then one user whom you would like to equip with the same privileges, creating a group is the way to go. Webmin provides very granular permissions, which you can grant to each group. You can set the following three types of permissions:

- ▸ Specify which Webmin modules are available to a group
- ▸ Set global permissions, which apply to all modules
- ▸ Set module-level access control settings, specifying which options of each module will be available

 Permissions for an individual account can be configured with the same level of granularity.

How to do it...

In this recipe, we will create a Webmin group with access limited to viewing log files from the `/var/log` directory:

1. To create a new Webmin group, navigate to **Webmin | Webmin Users**, and click **Create a new Webmin group**.
2. Name the new group `log_viewers`, and supply a group description.
3. In the **Available Webmin modules** section, select only **System Logs**, and click **Create**.
4. After the group is created, we can specify more detailed permissions. Go back to **Webmin | Webmin Users**, and click the name of the new group in the **Webmin Groups** section.
5. You will notice that the names of modules in the **Available Webmin modules** section are now links. Click the **System Logs** link to bring up the access control configuration for this module.
6. Set permissions, as shown in the following screenshot, to grant read-only access to the logs from `/var/log` and no other module permission:

Module Index

Module Access Control

For group `log_viewers` in `System Logs`

System Logs access control options

Can edit module configuration? ○ Yes ⦿ No

Can only view logs? ⦿ Yes ○ No   Can view any file as a log? ○ Yes ⦿ No

Can view logs from syslog? ⦿ Yes ○ No Can view logs from other modules? ○ Yes ⦿ No

Can view and configure log files ○ All logs ⦿ Only listed files and those under listed directories ..

```
/var/log/
```

Extra log files for this user

Save   Reset To Full Access

Note that full access to this module allows users to view any file as a log. This could give users unauthorized access to other files on your system.

You can reset module permissions to full access by clicking on the **Reset To Full Access** button.

Let's verify that the new group permissions work as expected:

1. Create a new user for testing according to the *Creating a Webmin user* recipe.

2. Assign him/her to the group by selecting `log_viewers` in the **Member of group** list.

3. Go to the **Edit Webmin User** screen for this new user, and click the **Switch to User** button.

You will see Webmin as the new user would see it, and you should have access limited to the **System Logs** module, within which you should only be able to view logs from `/var/log`.

How it works...

By default, Webmin keeps information about existing groups in the `webmin.groups` file at `/etc/webmin/`. Information about module-specific permissions is stored in **access control list** (**ACL**) files. Each module has its own directory in `/etc/webmin`, containing a separate ACL file for each group and user. For instance, a group of ACL files for a module named `module_name` and a group named `group_name` would be stored at: `/etc/webmin/module_name/group_name.gacl`. A similar file for a user named `user_name` would be stored in the `user_name.acl` file at `/etc/webmin/module_name/`. Webmin inspects these files whenever a user accesses a module and determines which options to make available to them.

> The exact structure of each ACL file is specific to its individual module; it may also change when upgrading Webmin to a new version. Editing these files manually requires familiarity with the module's internal code, so it's probably best to edit permissions through Webmin's interface.

There's more...

In addition to module-specific access permissions, Webmin also allows you to specify global permissions, which modify the behavior of all modules.

Permissions for all modules

In order to set Webmin-wide permissions for a group, go to **Webmin | Webmin Users**, click the name of the group, and open the **Permissions for all modules** section.

Here, you can set which files will be visible in Webmin's file chooser when a module requires the user to select a file, which users and groups will be visible in their chooser widgets, and other global options:

Permissions for all modules

Root directory for file chooser	○ User's home directory ⊙ / [ ] [...]
Other visible directories in file chooser	[ ]
Hide dot files in file chooser?	○ Yes ⊙ No
Browse files as Unix user	○ Same as Webmin login ⊙ root [...]
Users visible in user chooser	⊙ All users
	○ No users
	○ Only users [ ] [...]
	○ All except users [ ] [...]
	○ Users with UIDs in range [ ] - [ ]
	○ Users with group [ ] [...]
Groups visible in group chooser	⊙ All groups
	○ No groups
	○ Only groups [ ] [...]
	○ All except groups [ ] [...]
	○ Groups with GIDs in range [ ] - [ ]
Can send feedback email?	⊙ Yes ○ Yes, with config files ○ Yes, but not with config files ○ No
Can accept RPC calls?	○ Yes ⊙ Only for root or admin ○ No
Grant new module permissions to user?	⊙ Yes ○ No
User is in demo mode?	○ Yes (Some modules may not be available) ⊙ No
Show Webmin search field?	⊙ Yes ○ No

See also

► You can create a Webmin account for each user you wish to assign to a group, but you can also set up Webmin to create accounts automatically for all members of a system group and assign them to a Webmin group. See the recipe, *Creating Webmin users based on existing system user accounts*, for more information.

Allowing users to log in to Webmin with the system credentials

Webmin's default settings don't allow regular system users to log in to Webmin, but at least one user is allowed to log in after installation. Depending on the settings included in your Webmin package, that may be any of the following:

- The root user
- Users with unrestricted root access via `sudo` (specifically those with an `ALL=(ALL) ALL` rule)
- The user created during manual Webmin installation

In this recipe, we will allow all users of a Unix group to log in to Webmin with limited permissions.

Getting ready

We need to begin by creating a standard Webmin account, which will be shared by all system users we grant access to. Refer to the recipe, *Creating a Webmin user,* for instructions, and create a Webmin account, named `webmin_user`, for instance, with specific permissions.

How to do it...

Follow these steps to allow members of a system group to log in to Webmin:

1. Navigate to the **Webmin | Webmin Users | Configure Unix User Authentication** screen.
2. Select the **Allow Unix users listed below to login** radio button.
3. Select the options to allow **Members of group** users to log in as the Webmin user you created for this purpose.
4. If your standard user were named `webmin_user`, your screen would resemble the following screenshot:

Module Index   # Unix User Authentication

This page allows you to configure Webmin to validate login attempts against the system user list and PAM. This can be useful if you have a large number of existing Unix users who you want to give access to Webmin.

○ Only allow Webmin users to login ⦿ Allow Unix users listed below to login ..

Allow	User or Group	As Webmin user
Members of group.. ⇕	users	webmin_user ⇕
⇕		root ⇕
⇕		root ⇕

☑ Allow users who can run all commands via sudo to login as root
☐ Treat logins that only pass PAM validation as [root ⇕]

---

5. Click on the **Save** button to save your settings.

From now on, all Unix users belonging to the `users` group will be able to log in to Webmin and have the same privileges as the Webmin user you selected.

How it works...

If we use the preceding configuration, Webmin will verify login credentials against the **pluggable authentication module (PAM)** service configured on your system. In its basic setup, PAM will verify credentials against those stored in the standard system files (`/etc/passwd` and `/etc/shadow`).

 If PAM is set up differently on your system, the login information may be validated by an external service such as LDAP, NIS, Kerberos, Active Directory, or looked up in a SQL database. By default, Webmin uses your system's common configuration (`system-auth` or `common-auth`), but it can use its own separate settings.

Webmin also checks which system groups the authenticating user belongs to. If any of those groups are listed in Webmin's configuration or the user account is individually listed as allowed, the user will be logged in as if using the associated Webmin account.

There's more...

In order to allow the users with unrestricted access via `sudo` to log in to Webmin as `root`, follow these steps:

1. Navigate to **Webmin | Webmin Users | Configure Unix User Authentication**.
2. Check the box **Allow users who can run all commands via sudo to login as root**.
3. Click **Save**.

Creating Webmin users based on system accounts

In previous recipes, we talked about creating Webmin users and allowing system users to log in as a chosen Webmin account. You may choose to have a more direct, one-to-one correspondence between Webmin and system accounts. You can achieve this by creating Webmin accounts for selected existing users and setting up account synchronization for users added in the future.

Getting ready

In this recipe, we will create a Webmin account for each system user. All new Webmin accounts will be assigned to a Webmin group. Before we begin, set up a Webmin group following the recipe, *Creating a Webmin group with access to specific modules and options*.

How to do it...

Our first step will be to create Webmin accounts for existing system users:

1. Navigate to **Webmin | Webmin Users | Convert Unix To Webmin Users**.
2. Select the users you would like to add to Webmin.
3. Select the Webmin group to assign them to.
4. Click **Convert Now**.

Webmin accounts for all selected users should now be created. You can inspect them on the **Webmin Users** screen.

The second step is to instruct Webmin to create accounts automatically for all newly created system users:

1. Navigate to **Webmin | Webmin Users | Configure Unix User Synchronization**.
2. Check the boxes to create and delete Webmin accounts when system accounts are created and deleted.

3. Also, select the **Set password for new users to Unix authentication** option:

4. Select the Webmin group you would like new users to be added to, and click **Save**.

From now on, every new system account will be associated with an automatically created Webmin account.

Please note that Webmin will not synchronize accounts created at the command line or by editing system configuration files directly. Only system accounts created through Webmin will receive associated Webmin accounts.

How it works...

Webmin inspects your system configuration files (`/etc/passwd` and `/etc/group`) to find a list of system users and creates corresponding Webmin accounts based on your selection.

In reality, Webmin doesn't read the `passwd` file directly, but instead uses a system call such as `getpwent` to inspect your system's password database. This means that account information may also be read from a database or external services such as NIS or LDAP.

If you set up user synchronization, Webmin adds an additional step to its user creation functionality, which automatically sets up a new Webmin account for each new system user.

Controlling who is currently using Webmin

Webmin keeps a log of all the actions performed by users. You can inspect a list of currently open user sessions, check what actions were performed during a session, or close a session, forcing the user to be logged out.

How to do it...

Perform these steps to check which users are currently logged into Webmin:

1. Navigate to **Webmin | Webmin Users**.
2. Click the **View Login Sessions** icon.
3. To view the actions performed by the user in this session, click the **View logs** link next to any session.

You can close any session, except your own, and force the user to log in again. To do this, click the link in the **Session ID** column. The next time this user clicks a link or submits a form, he/she will be asked to log in again.

How it works...

Whenever a user logs in, Webmin creates a session for him/her. A session consists of a specific ID and associated information about who the owner of the session is and whether the session is active.

The session ID is passed to the user's browser in a secure cookie, thanks to which Webmin can identify subsequent requests coming in from the same user. This identifier is stored in Webmin's log files to group together actions performed by the user during the time between logging in and logging out. You can search Webmin's log for actions associated with any session.

If you choose to end a session, Webmin deletes its identifier from the list of active sessions. When the user makes another request to Webmin, the session identifier passed by the cookie will no longer be recognized, and the user will have to log in again, creating a new session.

Creating a system user account

Creating user accounts in Unix is a multistep process: you need to add user data to system configuration files, create a home directory, copy template files to that directory, and set ownership of those files to the new user. Webmin automates this process for you.

In addition, if you set up synchronization, a Webmin account will also be created for the new user. Refer to the recipe, *Creating Webmin users based on existing system accounts,* for more information about account synchronization.

Getting ready

We will create a new user account with a single-use password, which the user will have to change to after the first login. In order to allow the user to change the password through Webmin, go to **Webmin | Webmin Configuration | Authentication**, and set the **Password expiry policy** option to **Prompt users with expired passwords to enter a new one**.

How to do it...

Perform the following steps to create a system user account:

1. Navigate to **System | Users and Groups**, and click **Create a new user**.
2. Provide basic account information: **Username** and **Real name**.
3. Set **User ID** and **Home directory** to **Automatic**.
4. Set the user's default shell to /bin/bash.
5. For **Password**, select **Normal Password**, and type in a long, random string into the textbox. Save this string. In **Password Options**, answer **Yes** to the **Force change at next login?** question.

Take a look at the recipe, *Creating a Webmin user,* for a note about generating strong passwords.

6. Leave the primary group in **Group Membership** with system default settings.
7. Answer **Yes** to the questions about creating a home directory and copying template files in the **Upon Creation** section.
8. Also answer **Yes** to the **Create user in other modules?** question.
9. Click **Create**.
10. Send the user his/her new username and password. The user will be asked to change the password after the first login.

How it works...

Quite a bit is happening here; let's go through it step by step.

We are asking Webmin to create an account for the user whose real name we specified. The user will be able to log in using the username we provided. We told Webmin to generate **User ID** and **Home directory** automatically. The UID will be the first available integer higher than 500 or 1,000, depending on the system. The home directory will be placed in /home/ and named as the username.

We set the user's shell to /bin/bash, which is the default user shell on most modern Linux distributions. If your users prefer to use a different shell, such as ksh, zsh, or fish, you can set it here after its package is installed.

 If you wish to prevent the user from logging into the system console (or over SSH and FTP), you can set the shell to /bin/false. This will prevent shell access but will allow the user to use other system services that don't require Unix user authentication, such as e-mail or Webmin.

Next, we created a one-time password for the user. The user will be forced to change it after the first login regardless of whether he/she logs in through the console or Webmin.

During account creation, we need to assign the user to a primary group. On some systems, the default group will be named users; other systems will create a private group for the new user, named the same as the user. It's up to you as the system's administrator to decide how you wish to use these groups.

Because we answered **Yes** to questions about setting up the home directory, Webmin took care of it for us and created the new user's directory with all the required files.

Finally, by answering **Yes** to the question about creating the user account in other modules, we told Webmin to make information about the new account available to other parts of Webmin. Thanks to this, the new user will be available in configuration settings of other modules (for instance, file sharing).

Modifying a user's UID and other information

Modifying basic information about an existing user is usually quite simple. The exception to this rule is the change of a user's UID. This is sometimes necessary if a user has accounts on two different Unix systems and both systems have to identify him/her as the same person. A typical example of this situation is sharing files over NFS as we will discuss in *Chapter 6, Managing Files on Your System*.

Changing a UID requires an update of file ownership of all files belonging to that user. This can be quite tedious, but Webmin does the job for us.

How to do it...

Follow these steps for modifying a user's UID:

1. Navigate to **System | Users and Groups**, and click the username link of the account you want to edit.

2. On the next page, you will be able to edit all the basic user information, including the username, ID, home directory location, chosen default shell program, primary and secondary system groups, and so on.

3. Change **User ID** to a different value.

4. In the **Upon Save** section, answer **All files** to the **Change user ID on files?** question.

5. You can limit the update to **Home directory** if you are sure that the user owns files only in his/her home directory.

> Limiting file updates to the user's home directory will speed things up, but any files belonging to the user but located in other directories will become orphaned. If a new user is later created with the leftover UID, these files may unexpectedly change hands and belong to the new user. Choose this option only if you're sure that the user doesn't own any files outside of the home directory.

6. Click **Save**.

> You can use the same method to change the GID of the user's primary group.

How it works...

Webmin updates the user's system data with the information you provide. It then scans the disk in search of files that belong to the user and updates the file owner's UID.

Temporarily disabling a user account

If a person stops using your system, it's often a good idea not to delete their account, but rather to disable it. Perhaps you need to preserve data for forensic purposes, the user would need access to your system again in the future or is the owner of files on your system, which you don't want to delete or leave orphaned.

How to do it...

Disabling a user account through Webmin is very easy. Perform the following steps to do so:

1. Navigate to **System | Users and Groups**, and click the username link of the account you want to edit.
2. On the next page, check the box labeled **Login temporarily disabled**.
3. Click **Save**.

[You can re-enable the account by following the same procedure. Just uncheck the **Login temporarily disabled** box, and hit **Save**.]

How it works...

To disable a user account, Webmin updates the /etc/shadow file, which stores hashed user passwords. The password hash for the selected user is prepended with an exclamation point (!). This invalidates the hash and makes the password unusable, so the user can no longer log in. Removing the exclamation point re-enables the account.

Creating and editing a system group

Creating and editing system groups through Webmin is very simple; just follow the steps outlined.

How to do it...

Let's start by creating a group as follows:

1. Navigate to **System | Users and Groups**, and click through to the **Local Groups** tab.
2. Click **Create a new group**.
3. On the next page, you will be asked to specify basic group information. Set **Group name** to a chosen name, and leave **Group ID** set to **Automatic**. Ignore the password fields.

4. You can now add any user you choose to the group by moving them from the left to the right column of the **Users** widget.

5. Click **Create** to finish and create the group.

You can now edit the group by performing the following steps:

1. Go back to **System | Users and Groups**, and click the **Local Groups** tab.

2. Click the group's link in the **Group name** column.

3. You will be brought to a screen with a form similar to the one used to create a group, with one difference. If you now change a group's ID, you can tell Webmin to update files on the system with the new ID of the group.

4. Click the **Save** button to save changes.

How it works...

Depending on which operating system you're using, Webmin will either directly modify system files that store information about groups (`/etc/group`, `/etc/gshadow`), or use a dedicated utility to update group information (such as the `dscl`—Directory Service command-line utility on OS X).

When you change a group's GID, Webmin will also scan your filesystem and update all the files owned by the group with its new GID.

Changing a user's password

When a user forgets his/her password, he/she will contact you as the system's administrator and request a password reminder. For security reasons, passwords are stored on your system only in the form of cryptographic hashes, not plain text. Because of this, you cannot send passwords to users, but you can reset a password and send the new one to the user. The best practice in such a case is to make the new password usable only once, allowing the user to log in, but requesting that he/she immediately change it to a password of his/her own choice.

In this recipe, we will describe how to reset a user's password to a one-time value.

Getting ready

In order to use single-use passwords in Webmin, we need to enable this feature. Go to **Webmin | Webmin Configuration | Authentication**, and set the **Password expiry policy** option to **Prompt users with expired passwords to enter a new one**.

How to do it...

Perform the following steps to change the user's password:

1. Navigate to **System | Users and Groups**, and click the username link of the account you want to change the password for.

2. In the **Password** section, choose **Normal password**, and enter a long, random string of characters. Make a note of this string, as we will send it to the user as a one-time login password afterward.

 Take a look at the recipe, *Creating a Webmin user*, for a note about generating strong passwords.

3. In the **Password Options** section, answer **Yes** to the **Force change at next login?** question.

4. Click **Save** to commit changes.

5. Send the new single-use password to the user.

How it works...

Webmin modifies your system's passwords file (/etc/shadow), updating the user's stored password hash with the new string we provided.

Your system also stores the information about when the password was last changed. Webmin changes this setting to 0 (equivalent to January 1, 1970). This causes your system to request a password change next time the user logs in. Webmin also respects this setting and will ask the user to change the password when he/she logs into Webmin. Note the steps described in the *Getting ready* section.

Exporting users and importing them into another system

When you're setting up another server for your organization, you may need to recreate accounts of multiple users on the new system. Webmin's user management module has the ability to export data about existing user accounts to a special **batch file**, which you can then import into any other system that also runs Webmin. This allows you to recreate multiple accounts quickly and easily.

How to do it...

In this recipe, we will export selected users from one system (source) and import them into a second system (destination).

Let's start by exporting users as follows:

1. On your source system, navigate to **System | Users and Groups**, and click the link marked **Export to batch file**.

2. Set **Batch file format** to **Standard passwd and shadow files**.

 Note that you should use an export format compatible with the destination operating system. Use the **Standard** format if you're exporting to Linux, but use the BSD, Mac OS, or AIX specific formats if you're exporting to those systems. Always test on a small number of users' accounts before importing a large batch.

3. Set **Batch file destination** to **Display in browser**.

4. Set **Users to export** to **Only users**, and click the ellipsis (...) at the end of the line.

5. A new user-chooser window will pop up, in which you can select the names of accounts you want to export.

6. Select accounts by clicking their usernames on the left-hand side of the screen. If you make a mistake, you can remove an account by clicking its name listed among **Selected Users** on the right-hand side of the screen. After you make your selection, click **OK**.

7. Back in the **Export Batch File** screen, click **Export Now**.

8. The resultant batch file will be displayed as text in your browser; copy this to your clipboard or save it to a local file.

You can now import the accounts on another machine.

1. On your destination system, navigate to **System | Users and Groups**, and click on the link marked **Run batch file**.

2. Set **Batch data source** to **Text in box**, and paste the exported batch file content into the provided text area.

3. Answer **Yes** to the following questions:

- ❑ **Create, modify or delete users in other modules?**
- ❑ **Create home directories for created users?**
- ❑ **Copy files to home directories of created users?**
- ❑ **Passwords are already encrypted?**

4. Your screen should resemble the following screenshot:

Module Index	**Execute Batch File**

▷ Instructions and batch format

Batch user creation, update and deletion options

Batch data source	○ Upload file [Browse...] No file selected.
	○ File on server [ ] [...]

	⊙ Text in box `create:archer:$6$75375200$dsEHLzaDR3KtVU`
	`Ra2.nBpu6fGmjzTOuoCm/fq3K36VNSWbUd4C`
	`/RDakhK3DjY4pD5ct0DrCGAy5HKa8gle Zzc1:501`
	`:502:Sterling Archer:/home/archer:`
	`/bin/bash::::::`

Create, modify or delete users in other modules? ⊙ Yes ○ No

Only update users file when batch is complete? ○ Yes ⊙ No

Create home directories for created users? ⊙ Yes ○ No

Copy files to home directories of created users? ⊙ Yes ○ No

Rename home directories of modified users? ⊙ Yes ○ No

Change UID on files of modified users? ○ No ⊙ Home directory ○ All files

Change GID on files of modified users? ○ No ⊙ Home directory ○ All files

Delete home directories of deleted users? ⊙ Yes ○ No

Passwords are already encrypted? ⊙ Yes ○ No

[Execute batch]

5. Click **Execute batch** to import the accounts.

How it works...

Webmin uses a simple but powerful file format to describe its operations on users and groups. Each line in this file describes a single operation, which may be either `create`, `modify`, or `delete`. Fields in each line are separated by colon characters (`:`), similar to the format of the Unix user file (`/etc/passwd`). The first field is the name of the operation, the second field contains the name of the user or group we want to perform the operation on, and the following fields contain additional data.

The following is a brief explanation of the format for Webmin's batch files:

Webmin's batch file format for operations on users

Webmin's batch instructions are written as text with one operation described in each line. The following standard format is used in operations on system users in Linux:

```
create:username:passwd:uid:gid:realname:homedir:shell:min:max:warn:
inactive:expire
modify:oldusername:newusername:passwd:uid:gid:realname:homedir:shell:
min:max:warn:inactive:expire
delete:username
```

The fields used in Webmin's batch instructions are similar to fields stored in standard Unix system files. Following are various fields used in Webmin's batch instruction:

- username: This is the username of the account we want to perform our operation on (for example, archer).

- oldusername and newusername: These fields are used in a **modify** operation. The username field is used twice in case we want to change its value. The first instance is the current username, and the second is the value we want to change it to. You can leave newusername blank if you don't want to make a change.

- passwd: This is the password that may already be encrypted into a hash or provided in plain text (for example, myVeryLongPassword123456789). If this field contains just an x character, the account will be locked.

- uid: This is the user ID represented as a number (for example, 500). If this field is left empty, Webmin will assign an ID automatically.

- gid: This is the ID of the user's primary group (for example, 500). If this field is left empty in a create operation, Webmin will automatically create a new group named the same as the user.

- realname: This is the real name of the user (for example, Sterling Archer).

- homedir: This is the home directory of the user (for example, /home/archer).

- shell: This is the user's default shell program (for example, /bin/bash).

- min: This is the minimum number of days until the system allows the user to change his/her password. You can set this to 0 to remove this limitation.

- max: This is the maximum number of days after which the system will force the user to change his/her password. Set this to 0 to remove this feature.

- warn: This is the number of days before the password expires, during which the user will be warned about the upcoming password change.

- inactive: This is the number of days after the password expires, during which the user will still be able to log in and change the password. After this time passes, the user will not be able to log in.

▶ `expire`: This is the date when the password will expire, expressed as the number of days since January 1, 1970.

 If you're performing the `modify` operation, you can leave all fields empty, except for the ones you want to change.

Webmin's batch file format for operations on groups

The following format is used in operations on system groups:

```
create:groupname:passwd:gid:member,member,...
modify:oldgroupname:newgroupname:passwd:gid:member,member,...
delete:groupname
```

The following fields are used:

▶ `groupname`: This is the name of the group we want to perform an operation on (for example, `users`).

▶ `oldgroupname` and `newgroupname`: These fields are used in a **modify** operation. The group name field is used twice in case we want to change its value. The first instance is the current name of the group, and the second is the value we want to set it to.

▶ `passwd`: Group passwords are not in common use. They may be used to password-restrict a user's ability to add himself or herself to a group. Set this field to an asterisk or exclamation point (`*` or `!`) to disable this functionality.

▶ `gid`: This is the group's ID (for example, `100`). If this field is left empty, Webmin will set it automatically to the next available value.

▶ `member`: This is the username of a user account that should be a member of this group (for example, `archer`).

There's more...

Webmin's batch file format can be used to perform operations on both system users and groups. This functionality is not limited to exporting and importing data between systems. Batch files can also be used to quickly modify or delete multiple accounts.

Export and import system groups

In order to export a list of system groups from one system to another, you can follow this recipe, but when you navigate to **System | Users and Groups**, switch to the **Local Groups** tab before performing the import and export.

Batch update user accounts

Let's say you find yourself in a situation that calls for a change in all system user accounts. Let's also say, for example, that we decide to switch the default shell program of all accounts to `zsh`. In order to do that, you should prepare a batch file with the following line for each user, where `username` is substituted by the username of each account:

```
modify:username:::::::/bin/zsh:::::
```

Next, navigate to **System | Users and Groups**; click on the link marked **Run batch file**, provide your batch file, and execute it. This will update all user accounts with the new default shell program.

The same method can be used to update the values of any standard account field.

Batch delete user accounts

If you need to delete a large number of users, you can create a batch file with the following line for each user, where `username` is substituted by the name of each user:

```
delete:username
```

We run the file in the same way as described previously.

 You can use the same method to delete multiple groups; just use group names instead of a username, and switch to the **Local Groups** tab before executing the batch file.

▶ You can find more information about using Webmin's batch formats on its wiki: `http://doxfer.webmin.com/Usermin/Introduction`.

Installing Usermin

If you would like to make the basic functionality of your system available to its users through an interface similar to Webmin, you can use Webmin's companion product called Usermin. This environment is just as easy to use as Webmin and provides a number of features that do not require administrative privileges:

▸ Reading e-mails

▸ Setting up mail forwarding and auto-replies

▸ Setting up scheduled e-mails

▸ Changing passwords

▸ Executing system commands

▸ Opening an SSH session in the browser

▸ Configuring Apache virtual hosts

▸ Configuring MySQL or PostgreSQL databases

▸ Setting up CRON jobs or scheduled command execution

How to do it...

Installation of Usermin is very simple and using it is analogous to using Webmin. The main difference is that you connect over a different port; the default port for Usermin is 20000.

Let's start by installing Usermin:

1. If you've installed Webmin from its repository, follow the recipe, *Installing software packages* from *Chapter 1, Setting Up Your System*, and install the package called `usermin`.

 If you've installed Webmin from a package file instead of a repository, navigate to **Un-used Modules | Usermin Configuration**, and click on the button marked **Install Usermin** package.

2. After installing the package, click **Refresh Modules** in Webmin's sidebar menu and reload Webmin.

After installation, Usermin will be automatically activated. The usage of Usermin is analogous to the way you use Webmin. Usermin's default port is 20000, so you can connect to it using your web browser and the following address; just substitute the words `webmin.host` with the IP address or domain name of your server:

```
https://webmin.host:20000
```

You can now log in as any user of your system and explore Usermin's features.

Usermin's configuration is done through Webmin and is available in the **Webmin | Usermin Configuration** module. Notice that this screen is similar to Webmin's main settings screen. Configuration options are analogous but limited to the features of Usermin.

First of all, let's decide which of our users will have access to Usermin:

1. Navigate to **Webmin | Usermin Configuration | Allowed Users and Groups**.

2. In the **Usermin login access control** section, select **Only allow listed users**.

3. You can now provide a list of usernames of users whom you wish to grant access to Usermin. If you want to add all members of a group, add the group name to the list preceded by an @ sign, that is, `@groupname`.

Second, let's decide which Usermin modules to make available:

1. Navigate to **Webmin | Usermin Configuration | Available Modules**.

2. Check the boxes next to each module that you wish to make available to users. If you're not sure what a module does, it's probably best to leave it unavailable until you decide you need it.

3. In order to configure options specific to each module, navigate to **Webmin | Usermin Configuration | Usermin Module Configuration**.

4. Click the name of the module and set its options.

5. You will be able to set modules' global options (**Global module configuration** tab) and default values, which the user will be able to override (**Default user preferences** tab).

How it works...

Usermin is a companion package to Webmin, which is installed by default in the directory, `/usr/share/usermin`. It functions in much the same way as Webmin, but is focused on providing access to basic functions that don't require root privileges.

See also

Because Usermin's functionality is similar to Webmin's, you can refer to other recipes in this book to get an idea about its usage and configuration. In particular, take a look at the following chapters:

- ▶ *Chapter 1, Setting Up Your System*
- ▶ *Chapter 8, Running an Apache Web Server*
- ▶ *Chapter 9, Running a MySQL Database Server*
- ▶ *Chapter 10, Running a PostgreSQL Database Server*

You can find more information about Usermin online at the following URL:
`http://doxfer.webmin.com/Usermin/Introduction`

3
Securing Your System

In this chapter, we will cover the following topics:

- ▶ Setting up a Linux firewall
- ▶ Allowing access to a service through the firewall
- ▶ Verifying your firewall by port scanning
- ▶ Turning off unnecessary services
- ▶ Verifying the strength of passwords
- ▶ Disabling root login over SSH
- ▶ Restricting Webmin access to a specific IP
- ▶ Connecting to Webmin securely over an SSH tunnel
- ▶ Closing inactive Webmin sessions automatically

Introduction

Some people say that the only secure machine is one that is switched off. This may be true, but that machine is not very useful. If you want to make your server more functional, you'll have to turn it on and most likely expose it to the curious eyes of the Internet.

Online computer security is a topic large enough to deserve its own book. In fact, a whole shelf of such books is readily available. In this chapter, we will learn basic techniques, which will allow you to secure your server before putting it up online. If your server is exposed to the Internet, it will be a good idea to follow up by doing more in-depth security research and monitor what's happening to your machine on a day-to-day basis. Because this is a book on Webmin, we will only address topics in which Webmin can assist you.

This chapter is divided into three parts:

- We'll begin by running through a basic checklist of security issues that every system administrator should keep in mind. We'll point to the recipes in this book if Webmin can assist you with these topics.
- The first six recipes in this chapter cover topics related to general system security.
- The remaining recipes refer to securing Webmin itself.

Server security checklist

There are a number of basic security precautions that you should undertake on any computer system exposed on the Internet. This list is not comprehensive; there are other things you might probably want to do, but it's a good starting point and you shouldn't be ignoring these areas.

Keeping your system up-to-date

Software is never perfect and mistakes are discovered every day. Some of these mistakes are merely inconvenient, but others have the potential to be exploited by nefarious people to break into your machine. It's a critical part of an online system's maintenance to be up-to-date with security patches and system updates. Refer to the *Updating the installed packages to the latest versions* and *Getting an e-mail when new versions of packages become available* recipes from *Chapter 1, Setting Up Your System*, for information about keeping yourself updated.

Turning off unnecessary services

A security flaw in your FTP server software will not be very dangerous if this service is not running. It's a good idea to switch off all the unessential services to minimize your system's exposure. Refer to the *Turning off unnecessary services* and *Verifying your firewall by port scanning* recipes in this chapter for more information on this topic.

Building a firewall around your system

You can use packet-filtering software to restrict access to your system. You can decide whether you want to allow only people from certain parts of the Internet to connect, which ports should accept connections, or whether some services will be available only locally. Refer to the *Setting up a Linux firewall* and *Allowing access to a service through the firewall* recipes in this chapter for more information.

Performing backups

In case something does go wrong, it's important to keep a backup copy of all your essential data, preferably on another system in another location. Refer to *Chapter 7, Backing Up Your System*, for more information.

Monitoring your system

If something goes wrong on your server, it's important that you are the first one to know about it. Keep an eye on your system's logs and set up your system to send you automated e-mails with log updates. If someone breaks into your system, they may tamper with the logs. So, it's a good idea to keep logs on a separate dedicated logging server. For more information, look at *Chapter 5, Monitoring Your System*.

Verifying the strength of your passwords

No matter how tight your security is otherwise, if you leave your root password set to root or admin, your server is sure to get hacked. Likewise, the strength of your users' passwords should be periodically verified. See the *Verifying the strength of passwords* recipe in this chapter. It's actually a good idea to disable root's login over SSH altogether. For this, take a look at the *Disabling root login over SSH* recipe.

Verifying the system security and setting up intrusion detection and prevention software

The following topics go beyond the scope of this book. However, if you want to make sure that your server is as secure as possible, you should implement the following processes:

- Perform regular security audits (using tools such as Nessus).
- Set up intrusion detection and prevention systems (OSSEC, Bro Network Security Monitor, or Snort).
- Scan for viruses and malware (ClamAV and Linux Malware Detect).
- Check for rootkits (chkrootkit and rkhunter).

> More information about the following systems can be found on their web pages:
>
> **Nessus**: http://www.tenable.com/products/Nessus.
>
> **OSSEC**: http://www.ossec.net.
>
> **Bro**: http://www.bro.org.
>
> **Snort**: http://www.snort.org.
>
> **ClamAV**: http://www.clamav.net.
>
> **Linux Malware Detect**: https://www.rfxn.com/projects/linux-malware-detect/.
>
> **chkrootkit**: http://www.chkrootkit.org.
>
> **rkhunter**: http://rkhunter.sourceforge.net.

Backtrack is a Linux distribution that comes with a wide range of preinstalled security tools. It's a good starting point for security testing and auditing your servers. More information is available online at http://www.backtrack-linux.org.

Setting up a Linux firewall

Linux systems have a firewall software built right into the kernel. This packet-filtering framework is called **netfilter** (since Linux 2.4). It is controlled by a tool called iptables, which instructs the kernel what to do with incoming and outgoing network packets.

In this recipe, we will begin with an empty iptables configuration (firewall disabled) and configure it to drop any incoming packets except those we specifically allow. Before we set up a firewall, we should review some basic concepts related to network communication and the organization of iptables.

The following are some basic packet-filtering concepts:

- ▶ **Packets**: The Internet is a packet-switched network. This means that all communication is facilitated by breaking up the content into small blocks called packets, which are routed from one computer on the network to another.

- ▶ **IP address**: The adresses of machines on the Internet are specified by numerical IP addresses, such as 93.184.216.119 (IPv4) or 2606:2800:220:6d:26bf:1447:1097:aa7 (IPv6).

- ▶ **Port number**: Most common applications use the TCP or UDP transport protocols that require a specific port number to distinguish between different services running on the same machine.

- ▶ **Packet header**: Each packet passing through the network contains a header, which specifies where it is coming from and where it's travelling. This allows routers on the Internet to guide the packets in the right direction or send error messages back to the sender.

- ▶ **Packet filtering**: The firewall software is able to inspect packet headers and decide whether a particular packet should be allowed to proceed on its way or should be dropped.

Some iptables terminology

The iptables tool is capable of performing quite a complex set of operations on packets. The rules used to make decisions about a packet's fate are grouped into several levels of organization, which are as follows:

- ► **Table**: This is the highest level of organization. The `iptables` tool allows you to filter network packets (using the `filter` table), set up a network address translation system (using the `nat` table), or modify the packets (using the `mangle` table). We will focus only on the packet filtering functionality (`filter`) to create a firewall.

- ► **Chain**: Each table contains a number of chains of rules, which are applied in specific situations. The chains that are built into the `filter` table are called `INPUT` (applied to the packets coming into our system), `OUTPUT` (applied to the packets originating on our system), and `FORWARD` (applied to the packets coming into our system, but which are destined for another system). In this recipe, we will focus on incoming traffic and the `INPUT` chain.

- ► **Rule**: Any packet that passes through the firewall is compared to the rules in the appropriate chain. The rules may be configured to match a specific source or destination IP addresses or port numbers. They may also match packets on a specific network interface, protocol, or connection state. Rules are tried in a specific order and the first rule that matches the packet can decide if the packet is accepted or dropped.

- ► **Default policy**: If the packet doesn't match any rules, its fate will be decided by the chain's default policy.

Getting ready

In this recipe, we will set up a firewall configuration from scratch and reset any configuration that your system may have come with. This is not necessary, and if you know how `iptables` work, you may build on your system's default firewall configuration. In this case, you may wish to skip ahead to the recipe *Allowing access to a service through the firewall*.

Webmin also provides a series of predefined configurations that you may use to initialize your firewall. These configurations will become available after enabling the firewall or by navigating to **Networking | Linux Firewall** and clicking **Reset Firewall**. Webmin's predefined firewall configuration choices are shown in the following screenshot:

The following table describes what Webmin's predefined firewall configurations do:

Option	Description
Allow all traffic	This is a configuration without any rules, which allows all traffic by default.
Block all incoming connections on external interface	This prevents connections to your server from the network and allows only established connections and basic DNS and ICMP packets through.
Block all except SSH and IDENT on external interface	This is the same as *Block all incoming connections on external interface*, but allows incoming SSH connections and, unfortunately, requests of the **Identification Protocol** (**IDENT**). Permitting the latter is not recommended.
Block all except SSH, IDENT, ping and high ports on interface	This is the same as *Block all except SSH and IDENT on external interface*, but also allows your server to respond to the ping command and allows requests to most ports in the range 1024 to 65535. These high ports may be used to accept connections by processes started by non-root users. This configuration should not be used on the open Internet.
Block all except ports used for virtual hosting, on interface	This allows incoming connections to most commonly used services, such as SSH, HTTP, mail, FTP, and DNS. This also allows connections to Webmin, Usermin, and unfortunately IDENT.
Do network address translation on external interface	This sets the Masquerade rule on the POSTROUTING chain. This allows your server to act as a network gateway for other computers on your network.

How to do it...

Perform the following steps to set up a firewall:

1. Check if your system already has an `iptables` firewall set up. This can be done by navigating to **Networking | Linux Firewall**.

2. If your firewall is set up, you will see a list of rules in the chains of the filter table. Create a new firewall configuration by clicking **Reset Firewall**.

3. Select the option **Allow all traffic**, check the **Enable firewall at boot time?** box, and click **Setup Firewall**.

4. Make sure that Webmin is showing the table for **Packet filtering (filter)** and that no rules are set up yet. Your screen should resemble the following screenshot:

Help..
Module Config

Linux Firewall
Rules file `/etc/iptables.up.rules`

Search Docs..

Showing IPtable:

Add a new chain named:

Packet filtering (filter) ⇕

Incoming packets (INPUT) - Only applies to packets addressed to this host

There are no rules defined for this chain.

Set Default Action To: | Accept ⇕

Add Rule

Forwarded packets (FORWARD) - Only applies to packets passed through this host

There are no rules defined for this chain.

Set Default Action To: | Accept ⇕

Add Rule

Outgoing packets (OUTPUT) - Only applies to packets originated by this host

There are no rules defined for this chain.

Set Default Action To: | Accept ⇕

Add Rule

Apply Configuration

Click this button to make the firewall configuration listed above active. Any firewall rules currently in effect will be flushed and replaced

Revert Configuration

Click this button to reset the configuration listed above to the one that is currently active.

Activate at boot ⦿ Yes ◯ No

Change this option to control whether your firewall is activated at boot time or not.

Reset Firewall

Click this button to clear all existing firewall rules and set up new rules for a basic initial configuration.

5. We will now create the basic set of rules that will allow your firewall to function properly. The first rule will allow incoming packets that are part of an already established connection. Add the first rule to the INPUT chain by clicking **Add Rule** in the **Incoming Packets** section.

   Set the following options:

   - Set **Action to take** to **Accept**
   - For **Connection states**, select **Equals** and both **ESTABLISHED** and **RELATED**

   Then, click the **Create** button.

6. The second rule will allow incoming network diagnostics (ICMP) packets (ping, traceroute, and so on). Click **Add Rule** again and set the following options before clicking **Create**:

   - Set **Action to take** to **Accept**
   - For **Network protocol**, select **Equals** and **ICMP**

7. The third rule will allow any connection originating from our own machine via the local loopback interface. Create the rule as described in the preceding step:

   ❑ Set **Action to take** to **Accept**

   ❑ For **Incoming interface**, select **Equals** and **lo**

8. The preceding rules are sufficient to make your network interface behave properly in most cases. We can now add rules that are specific to our particular needs. Let's make a rule to allow incoming SSH connections. Create a rule with the following options:

   ❑ Set **Action to take** to **Accept**

   ❑ For **Network protocol**, select **Equals** and **TCP**

   ❑ For **Destination TCP or UDP port**, select **Equals** and set **Port(s)** to 22

   ❑ For **Connection states**, select **Equals** and **NEW**

9. Our final rules will allow incoming Webmin connections. Create a rule with the same options as for SSH. However, instead of 22 select port 10000.

> Webmin also uses UDP port 10000 to discover other servers that are running Webmin on your network. If you plan to use Webmin's clustering functions, you should also add a rule for port 10000 and **Network protocol UDP**.

10. Finally, let's set the chain's default policy to drop packets that don't match any of our rules. Select the default action to **Drop** and click the **Set Default Action To** button.

> You may choose to *drop* or *reject* packets. When packets are dropped, your server sends no response, and when they are rejected, it sends a friendly *port closed* response.

11. At this stage, your firewall configuration should resemble the following screenshot. Verify that you haven't made any mistakes.

Help..
Module Config

Linux Firewall
Rules file `/etc/iptables.up.rules`

| Showing IPtable: | Packet filtering (filter) ⬍ | Add a new chain named: |

Incoming packets (INPUT) - Only applies to packets addressed to this host

Select all. | Invert selection.

Action	Condition	Move	Add
☐ Accept	If state of connection is **ESTABLISHED,RELATED**	↓	⬇ ⬆
☐ Accept	If protocol is **ICMP**	↓↑	⬇ ⬆
☐ Accept	If input interface is **lo**	↓↑	⬇ ⬆
☐ Accept	If protocol is **TCP** and destination port is **22** and state of connection is **NEW**	↓↑	⬇ ⬆
☐ Accept	If protocol is **TCP** and destination port is **10000** and state of connection is **NEW**	↑	⬇ ⬆

Select all. | Invert selection.

| Set Default Action To: | Drop ⬍ | Delete Selected | Move Selected | Add Rule |

A firewall configuration that allows incoming SSH and Webmin connections, but drops all others.

12. To activate your new firewall, click the **Apply Configuration** button.

Modifying the firewall configuration using a network tool such as Webmin is a little tricky; if you make a mistake, you could potentially lock yourself out. In case of emergency, you can disable the firewall temporarily by logging in through the system console and issuing the following commands:

```
$ sudo iptables -F INPUT
$ sudo iptables -P INPUT ACCEPT
```

The first command flushes (removes) all rules from the INPUT chain and the second sets its default policy to ACCEPT incoming packets. These changes will be temporary and the default configuration will be reset after a system reboot.

How it works...

Webmin really helps us out here, especially if your system doesn't come with a default firewall configuration. Webmin issues a long series of commands to create an empty but valid `iptables` configuration. It then saves this configuration to a file and allows us to add rules to it. When we ask Webmin to enable the firewall at boot time, it also adds the appropriate commands to the system's network configuration scripts.

There's more...

There is quite a bit more that `iptables` can do for you. For instance, it would be a good idea to limit access to Webmin only to yourself and perhaps some of your administrator colleagues. Other people on the Internet don't even need to know that you are running Webmin. In order to achieve this, you can restrict access to a list of IP addresses or Internet subnets.

Go back to the rule you created for Webmin access and add another condition. Set source address or network to the IP of the machine you're connecting from. If you'd like to grant access to the whole network segment, also specify the subnet mask after a slash character (/). For instance, if you would like to restrict the access to requests coming from IPs in the range 10.10.10.0 to 10.10.10.255, use the following address and mask: `10.10.10.0/255.255.255.0`

In this recipe, we only set up rules that filter incoming network traffic. Firewalls can also control outgoing traffic from your server to the Internet. It may be a good idea to block outgoing connections on machines that could potentially be compromised by user-installed malware.

See also

▶ You can verify that your firewall works as expected by scanning the ports. Refer to the *Verifying your firewall by port scanning* recipe for more information.

▶ If you're interested in learning more about what `iptables` can do, check out its documentation at `http://www.netfilter.org/documentation/`.

▶ For more information about Webmin's firewall module functions, take a look at its Wiki page at `http://doxfer.com/Webmin/LinuxFirewall`.

Allowing access to a service through the firewall

Once your firewall is set up, all unauthorized traffic coming into your server will be dropped. If you decide to add a service to your server, you'll need to add another firewall rule to allow the incoming traffic to reach the service. Otherwise, external users will not be able to access the new service. In fact, they will not even be able to see that the service is running and their connections will simply time out.

Getting ready

Make sure that your firewall is set up. Refer to the *Setting up a Linux firewall* recipe for more information. Make sure you know which port numbers and protocols are used by the service to which you want to allow access. Common port numbers such as 80 and 443 for a web server and 20 and 21 for FTP are listed in the file `/etc/services`. Usermin uses the port 20000 by default.

How to do it...

Perform the following steps for accessing a service through firewall:

1. Navigate to **Networking | Linux Firewall**.
2. Click the **Add rule** button in the **Incoming packets (INPUT)** section.
3. Set the following options:
   - Set **Action to take** to **Accept**
   - For **Network protocol**, select **Equals** and **TCP** (or **UDP** if your service requires it)
   - For **Destination TCP or UDP port**, select **Equals** and set **Port(s)** to the port number required
   - For **Connection states**, select **Equals** and **NEW**
4. Click **Create**.

 The `iptables` rules are applied in a specific order. This is the order in which the rules are listed in Webmin from top to bottom. If a rule to accept or drop matches a packet, other rules further down the list will have no effect. When you make a rule to accept a certain type of packet, make sure it's placed before a more general rule that would cause this packet to be dropped or rejected. Use the grey upward arrows to move rules up the chain.

5. Click the **Apply Configuration** button to activate the changes.

How it works...

We created a new firewall rule that allows packets to come in if, and only if, they are using the protocol we specified (TCP or UDP), the port number we selected, and they are packets initiating the connection (NEW state).

Webmin adds our rule to the `iptables` configuration file and loads the new firewall configuration. From now on, packets with the specified port will be allowed a safe passage into your system.

There's more...

You may wish to run services on your system that will only be accessible internally from the same machine. A database server for your web application may be a good example of such a case. If you wish to allow access to a service only locally, you can create a firewall rule that will allow incoming request only if they are coming in over the local loopback interface.

Creating a service accessible only from the internal network

In order to create a local-only service, follow the same steps as described in this recipe, but add another condition to the rule. Under **Incoming Interface**, select **Equals** and **lo** (the name of the local loopback interface).

 Our default firewall configuration, which is described in the *Setting up a Linux firewall* recipe, allows all locally initiated requests to come in. You may disable this behavior by removing its rule and allow local access to specific services only.

See also

▶ For more information about how the `iptables` firewall works, refer to the *Setting up a Linux firewall* recipe of this chapter

Verifying your firewall by port scanning

After your firewall is configured, you may wish to check that you haven't unintentionally left any unnecessary open doors. A good way to do this is to initiate a scan from another machine that will tell you what open ports it discovered on your server. Only ports associated with services that you want to make publicly accessible should be found.

Getting ready

We will be using two machines in this recipe. One will be the scanner machine and the other will be the server we want to scan.

Nmap is a great and widely available port scanner. Let's start by installing it on the scanner machine. You can install it from the repositories of most Linux distributions, from ports on BSD and from Homebrew on OS X. You can also download an installer for Windows from `http://nmap.org/download.html`.

How to do it...

Perform the following steps to verify your firewall by port scanning:

1. On your scanner machine, open up a terminal window and type the following command (here, `webmin.host` is the IP address or domain name of the server you wish to scan):

   ```
   $ nmap -sT webmin.host
   ```

   You should see the following output:

   ```
   Starting Nmap 6.25 ( http://nmap.org ) at 2013-08-13 21:42 CEST
   Nmap scan report for 37.139.1.192
   Host is up (0.039s latency).
   Not shown: 998 filtered ports
   PORT        STATE SERVICE
   22/tcp      open  ssh
   10000/tcp open    snet-sensor-mgmt


   Nmap done: 1 IP address (1 host up) scanned in 17.65 seconds
   ```

2. The output lists the open ports discovered on your server. Among them, you will find port 22 for SSH connections and port 10000 for Webmin. If you find ports that you didn't expect in the scan, you may need to go back to the firewall configuration to close them down.

Some ISPs may block outgoing scan packets before they reach the server that you're testing. For instance, packets addressed to port 25 are quite commonly blocked to fight against spam e-mail.

You can verify that the scan you're performing is actually working by running it against the server with its firewall temporarily disabled. When the server has no active firewall, your remote scan should give results similar to executing the following command on the server itself. This `netstat` command enumerates the open ports on the server.

```
$ netstat -ltn
```

Take a look at the *Turning off unnecessary services* recipe in this chapter for more information about using `netstat`.

How it works...

With its default options, Nmap scans will send a SYN packet (the first part of an initial connection handshake) to the 1,000 most commonly used ports on the machine you specify. If the machine is accepting connections on any port, it will send an SYN/ACK packet back, acknowledging that it is ready to open a connection. From this, Nmap can determine that the port is open.

Connections to those ports that your firewall is set to drop will be marked as `filtered` because they don't return any information at all. Ports that your firewall is set to reject will return a port unreachable message and will be marked as `closed` in your scan.

There's more...

Nmap has a wide variety of options. It can be used to perform a scan of the whole network, scan every port of a machine, or perform a scan that doesn't require administrative privileges on the scanning machine.

Host discovery with Nmap

If you want to know what computers are active on your segment of the network, type in the following command, specifying the range of IP addresses that you want to scan:

```
$ nmap -sn 10.10.10.0-255
```

Scanning all ports

By default, Nmap scans only the 1,000 most commonly used port numbers. If you want to be more thorough and scan every single port, use the following command (with the `-p-` argument). Note that such a scan may take a few minutes.

```
$ sudo nmap -sT -p- webmin.host
```

Scanning without administrative privileges

Nmap's standard port scanning technique requires administrative access on the scanning computer, because it uses raw sockets to perform only the first part of a connection (sending the SYN packet). If you don't have administrative privileges, you can perform a different type of scan that initiates a normal connection by issuing the following command (with the `-sP` argument):

```
$ nmap -sP webmin.host
```

▸ For more information, take a look at the Nmap Reference Guide on `http://nmap.org/book/man.html`

Turning off unnecessary services

The best way to avoid potential security issues with services you're not actively using is to disable them. This recipe will list the steps to identify the running system services that have open network ports and disable them.

How to do it...

Let's start by identifying the processes that open network ports on your systems. This can be done with the help of the following steps:

1. Navigate to **Others | Command Shell**.
2. Type in the command `netstat -tulpen` and click **Execute command**.

You will see a list of server processes with active network connections.

In the `Local Address` column, you will see entries such as `0.0.0.0:22`. This means that a process is listening on port 22. The `PID/Program name` column will tell you which process is responsible for opening this port.

If you identify a process that you are not using and you know that it isn't essential to your system, you can disable it with the help of the following steps:

1. Navigate to **System | Bootup and Shutdown**.
2. Find the startup entry associated with the process and check the box next to its name.
3. Click the **Disable Now and On Boot** button.
4. Go back to **Others | Command Shell**.
5. Execute the `netstat -tulpen` command again and check that the process no longer appears on the list.

How it works...

The `netstat` command allows you to display information about the network connections. The arguments written as `-tulpen` are a mnemonic (*tulpen* means tulips in German) for the options that you need to verbosely list the servers with open ports listening for connections. The parameters serve the following functions:

- ▸ `-t` lists TCP connections
- ▸ `-u` lists UDP connections
- ▸ `-l` lists only connections that are listening (servers)
- ▸ `-p` will display the process ID and program name
- ▸ `-e` will give you extended information
- ▸ `-n` will display data as numbers instead of resolving it to names

Verifying the strength of passwords

If you allow administrative users to log into your system using their username and password, your system is only as secure as the passwords used by those users. It's a good idea to periodically attempt to crack all the passwords on your system. If you find passwords that are easy to guess or crack through brute force, you should ask users to change them.

Getting ready

For this recipe, we will be using the password-cracking program called John the Ripper. Start by installing the package named `john`. Refer to the *Installing software packages* recipe from *Chapter 1, Setting Up Your System*, for more details.

How to do it...

John the Ripper tries to crack passwords by brute force, which means it will try every word and combination of characters. If any user on your system has a strong password (long and complex), John will not be able to crack it in a reasonable amount of time. You should let the cracking run for a couple of days and then decide that the remaining passwords are strong enough.

> John the Ripper tries to be a good system citizen and uses only spare CPU cycles that would otherwise go unused. It may nevertheless reduce the responsiveness of your system. So, if your system is under heavy load or its speed is mission critical, you may choose to crack passwords on a different machine.

Perform the following steps to identify weak passwords:

1. Navigate to **System | Scheduled Commands** and create a new command to run as root 5 minutes from now in the /root directory. Set the john /etc/shadow command for execution. Refer to the *Setting a command to be executed in the future* recipe in *Chapter 4, Controlling Your System*, for more information.

2. After a couple of hours, you can check how many passwords were cracked. Navigate to **Others | Command Shell** and execute the following command:

   ```
   john -show /etc/shadow
   ```

3. This command will show you any passwords that are already cracked and the information about how many John the Ripper is still trying to guess. You can go back to the second step at any time to check the progress in cracking.

4. You should reset the passwords for users whose passwords were cracked and inform them about the situation. Refer to the *Changing a user's password* recipe in *Chapter 2, User Management*, for details.

If some passwords remain uncracked after a couple of days, you may decide that they are strong enough and stop John the Ripper with the help of following steps:

1. Navigate to **System | Running Processes**.

2. Click the **CPU** option to **Display** processes ordered by processor usage.

3. On the top of the list, you will see john. Click its PID.

4. On the **Process Information** screen, click the **Terminate** button to stop this cracking session.

>
> You may resume the stopped cracking session by issuing the following command:
>
> ```
> john -restore
> ```
>
> Use the same procedure as in the first step to schedule its execution in the background.

5. When you decide to finish password cracking, you should remove files created by John the Ripper. They will be stored in the /root/.john directory. It's especially important to remove the john.pot file as it contains all the passwords that were cracked and can be read by all users who have administrative privileges.

How it works...

You provide John the Ripper with password hashes of your system users. The `john` program first determines which hashing techniques and salts your system uses. It then proceeds to apply the same hashing algorithm to every word in a wordlist file. If a hash it generates is identical to a password hash stored for one of your users, then this particular word was used as the password—the password is cracked. After trying every word in the wordlist, John the Ripper proceeds to try every letter combination possible. This part of the process takes a long time and uses a lot of CPU power. If you find that John is taking a very long time (more then a few days) to crack your passwords, you may decide that they are strong enough and stop.

Disabling root login over SSH

Allowing the root user to log in over SSH is a potential security vulnerability. An attacker may try to break into your system by trying every password for the root user. It's recommended to disallow the root user's access over SSH and to log in as another user with the `sudo` privileges to perform administrative tasks.

How to do it...

Perform the following steps to disable root login:

1. Navigate to **Servers | SSH Server | Authentication**.
2. Answer **No** to the **Allow login by root?** question.
3. Click **Save**.
4. Back on the **SSH Server** module screen, click **Apply Changes**.

How it works...

Webmin updates the SSH configuration file (`/etc/ssh/sshd_config`) by setting `PermitRootLogin` to `no`. From now on, SSH will treat every password entered for the root user as incorrect.

Restricting Webmin access to a specific IP

The firewall is your first line of defense, but you should take additional precautions while running Webmin on an Internet-connected server. Webmin allows you to restrict access to a list of specific IP addresses and networks. It's a good idea to protect Webmin this way; otherwise, an attacker can try to guess your password and take over your system.

In this recipe, we will configure Webmin to accept connections only from your IP address.

Getting ready

Before you start, you should determine the IP address you are currently using to connect to Webmin. In order to do this, log into Webmin and navigate to **Webmin | Webmin Users | View Login Sessions**. Your active login session will be marked in bold and your address will be listed in the **IP address** column.

How to do it...

For restricting Webmin access, perform the following steps:

1. Navigate to **Webmin | Webmin Configuration | IP Access Control**.
2. Set **Allowed IP addresses** to **Only allow from listed addresses**.
3. Enter your IP address in the text area below.
4. Click **Save**. Webmin will save changes and restart.

From now on, you will be able to connect from the specified IP. However, users trying to connect to Webmin from other computers will receive an **HTTP 403 error (Access denied)**.

How it works...

Webmin stores information about which hosts are allowed to connect in its server configuration file (`/etc/webmin/miniserv.conf` by default). The line that allows host access starts with the keyword `allow`, and specifies a list of IP addresses and ranges separated with a space character. For instance, it may look like the following:

```
allow=93.184.216.119 192.0.2.0/24
```

Whenever a client tries to connect, Webmin consults this configuration to determine whether to allow the incoming connection or not.

There's more...

Webmin's IP access control module is quite flexible and allows you to specify sets of IP addresses in a number of ways.

Allowing access from multiple IP addresses

The simplest way to allow access to Webmin from multiple locations is to add multiple IP addresses to the text area in the **IP Access Control** module. You can add as many IP addresses as needed, just place each one on a separate line.

Allowing access from a dynamically allocated IP

Many Internet providers allocate IP addresses dynamically. This type of address may change at some point in the future, which could leave you unable to connect to Webmin. If you're using a dynamic IP, you may consider signing up for dynamic DNS. A dynamic DNS service will provide you with a hostname that automatically updates to match your changing IP. Keeping this information up-to-date requires the setting up of a daemon process on your computer or network router.

> There are many providers of dynamic DNS; some also offer a basic free service. Take a look at the following or search for Dynamic DNS Providers:
>
> **DynamicDNS**: `http://dyn.com`.
>
> **NoIP**: `http://noip.com`.
>
> **FreeDNS**: `http://freedns.afraid.org`.

For Webmin to grant access to your dynamically allocated IP address, go to the **IP Access Control** module and enter the hostname provided by your dynamic DNS provider.

Allowing access from an IP range

If all your Webmin users use the same Internet provider, they are probably using a shared network. If you know the range of IP addresses shared by this subnet, you can specify the range by using the subnet address/mask or address/mask bits format:

```
192.0.2.0/24
192.0.2.0/255.255.255.0
```

> Both of the preceding lines are equivalent and specify all IP addresses between `192.0.2.0` and `192.0.2.255`. Don't be overly broad while specifying the IP range. Using the entire range of public IPs that is used by your Internet provider would not be a very good idea, because a potential attacker may have control of a computer connected to the Internet from the same provider.

Allowing access from the local network

If your server is available via your local network, you can tell Webmin to allow all the connections coming from within the LAN. In order to do this, follow the steps in this recipe, but also check the box marked as **Include local network in list**.

Connecting to Webmin securely over an SSH tunnel

If your server is connected to the Internet and you use SSH to connect to it, you can secure it by disallowing Webmin from accepting any remote connections. You can then use an SSH tunnel to connect to Webmin. This lowers the potential attack surface of your machine and protects you against possible security vulnerabilities in Webmin itself. Any attacker would have to break into your SSH account or otherwise gain local access to your system to connect to Webmin.

Getting ready

Before you begin, you should follow the *Restricting Webmin access to a specific IP* recipe of this chapter and add the IP address `127.0.0.1` to the list of hosts allowed to connect to Webmin.

In this recipe, we'll be using the command line version of SSH that is available on most systems, but it is not available on Windows. Look in the *There's more...* section of this recipe for instructions specific to Windows.

How to do it...

Perform the following steps to securely connect to Webmin:

1. On the client machine, open a terminal window and issue the following command. However, substitute `username` with your username and `webmin.host` with the IP address or host name of your server:

   ```
   $ ssh -L 15000:localhost:10000 username@webmin.host
   ```

2. Enter your SSH username and password to establish the connection.

3. On the client machine, open a browser and navigate to the URL `https://localhost:15000`.

You should now be able to use Webmin through an SSH tunnel.

How it works...

You can open an SSH tunnel by issuing the following command:

```
$ ssh -L client_port:remote_host:remote_port username@ssh_host
```

An SSH tunnel connects machines as listed in the following diagram:

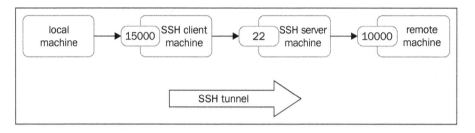

When you open a tunnel, the SSH client opens a network port on the machine on which it is running (`client_port`). This port will now accept connections and all incoming packets will be intercepted by the SSH client program. The SSH client will encrypt them and send them using the SSH protocol to the SSH server machine. The SSH server will decrypt the packets and forward them to the remote machine (`remote_host:remote_port`). Responses sent by the remote machine will also be encrypted and traverse the tunnel in the opposite direction.

The tunnel we use to connect to Webmin is simpler because only two machines are involved. The local machine is also the SSH client machine, while the remote machine is also the SSH server.

When we issue the command

```
$ ssh -L 15000:localhost:10000 username@webmin.host,
```

we are opening port 15000 on our computer and the SSH server on `webmin.host` will forward all the packets to its own machine's Webmin port (`localhost:10000`). In effect, by connecting to our own computer's port 15000, we will have access to the remote Webmin interface as if we were connecting to that machine directly.

There's more...

We will cover two more things in this recipe: giving access to the SSH tunnel to other machines and creating an SSH tunnel on Windows using Putty.

Sharing the SSH tunnel with other machines

By default, the SSH client will only allow tunneling of connections originating on the same machine. You can override this by using the -g option:

```
$ ssh -g -L 15000:localhost:10000 username@webmin.host
```

This command will allow all the computers that can connect to the SSH client machine on port 15000 access to Webmin on the remote machine.

Creating a tunnel on Windows using Putty

If you're running Windows, download the Putty SSH client from `http://www.chiark.greenend.org.uk/~sgtatham/putty/`.

1. In order to create an SSH tunnel on Windows, start Putty.

2. In the **Session** section, provide the hostname or IP address of your Webmin host machine in the **Host Name (or IP address)** field as shown in the following screenshot:

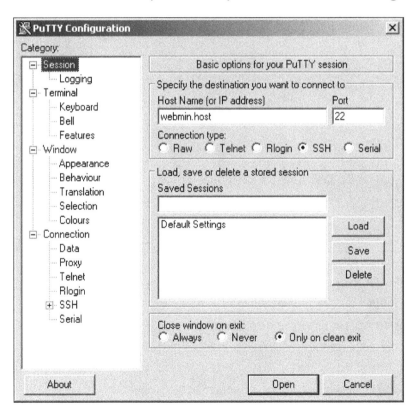

3. Open the configuration section by navigating to **Connection | SSH | Tunnels**.

4. Specify port `15000` as **Source port**.

5. Specify `localhost:10000` as **Destination**.

6. Select the radio button labelled as **Local** as shown in the following screenshot:

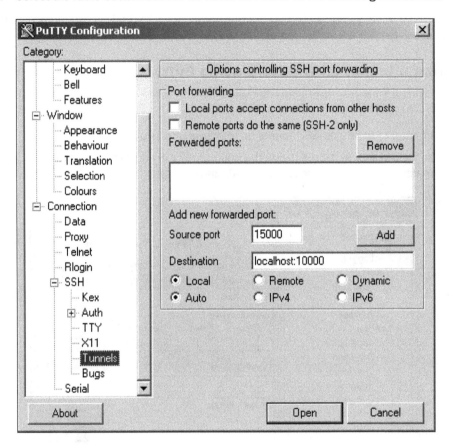

7. Click **Add**.

8. Click **Open** to open the connection.

9. Provide your SSH username and password.

10. On the client machine, open a browser and navigate to `https://localhost:15000`.

You should now be able to use Webmin through an SSH tunnel.

See also

Once you are able to establish tunneled connections to Webmin, you will no longer need to provide remote access to it. You can remove Webmin's entry from the firewall configuration and instruct Webmin to listen for connections only on the local IP 127.0.0.1.

- ▶ Refer to the *Setting up a Linux firewall* recipe of this chapter
- ▶ Refer to the *Specifying the IP address on which Webmin listens* section of the *Connecting to Webmin* recipe from *Chapter 1, Setting Up Your System*

Closing inactive Webmin sessions automatically

Webmin's login sessions are not set to expire by default. This causes a potential security risk. If a user leaves his or her computer unattended while logged into Webmin, an attacker could potentially use the situation to harm your system or disable its security. Fortunately, this situation is easily remedied by changing a Webmin setting.

How to do it...

Perform the following steps to close inactive Webmin sessions automatically:

1. Navigate to **Webmin | Webmin Configuration | Authentication**.
2. Tick the checkbox marked as **Auto-logout** and set the automatic logout to happen after 10 minutes of inactivity.
3. Click **Save**.

How it works...

Webmin stores authentication options in its server configuration file (`/etc/webmin/miniserv.conf` by default). The line defining inactivity time after which users will be automatically logged out starts with the keyword `logouttime` and specifies the time in minutes. For instance, it may look like this:

```
logouttime=10
```

Whenever a client tries to connect, Webmin checks in the session database when this user was last connected. Webmin consults its configuration to determine whether the time elapsed is not higher then allowed. If the user wants to perform an action after the allowed inactivity time elapses, he or she is asked to log in again.

4

Controlling Your System

In this chapter, we will cover the following topics:

- ▸ Executing a command on the server
- ▸ Executing a command as another user
- ▸ Setting a command to be executed in the future
- ▸ Scheduling a command to run regularly with cron
- ▸ Creating a panel for the commands that you execute often
- ▸ Creating a panel with the database commands that you execute often
- ▸ Running a terminal emulator in the browser

Introduction

Webmin allows you to control your system remotely using only the browser. Whether you need to execute a single command or have full terminal access, Webmin provides convenient tools for each job. In order to make your life easier, Webmin also allows you to set up a control panel for each task you execute more than once. In the cases where you need to run commands repeatedly, Webmin gives you an easy-to-use interface for creating cron jobs.

Executing a command on the server

The simplest way to execute commands on your server that uses Webmin is the **Command Shell** module. In this recipe, we will execute a command that lists all network services running on our machine.

How to do it...

Perform the following steps to execute a `netstat` command:

1. Navigate to **Others | Command Shell**.

2. Type in a command in the textbox. To list all active network servers on your system, use the `netstat -tl` command.

3. Click the **Execute** button.

You will be presented with a page showing the output of your command. At the bottom of the screen, you will see a form that allows you to execute another command. You can clear the command output by clicking the **Clear history** button:

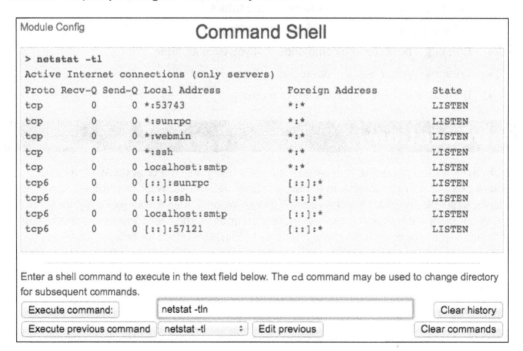

How it works...

Webmin executes every command you type in as the root user by default, and saves each command into a history file for the currently logged in user. Webmin also keeps track of the directories you move into using the `cd` command, but other environment variables will not be preserved between command executions.

There's more...

Sometimes, you may need to execute multiple commands that depend on one another. It's possible to do this in Webmin's basic command shell by combining multiple commands into a single execution.

Executing a series of commands

The most basic way to run a series of commands is to separate commands using the semicolon (`;`) character. Perform the following steps to do so:

1. Navigate to **Others | Command Shell**.
2. Type in the following two commands (separated by a semicolon):

   ```
   export MESSAGE="Hello from Webmin!" ; echo $MESSAGE
   ```

3. Click the **Execute** button.

The first command (`export`) sets a variable in the environment where your commands are being executed. The second command (`echo`) sends the value of this variable to the standard output. Consequently, you should see the message displayed on screen. If you executed these commands separately, the environment variable would not be preserved between executions.

Executing commands conditionally

If you want to execute a series of commands in which the second command should only be executed (in case the first one is completed without problems), you may chain them using the logical AND operator (`&&`). This will cause the second command to be executed only if the first one completes successfully (returns an exit code value of `0`). Perform the following steps:

1. Navigate to **Others | Command Shell**.
2. Type in the following two commands (separated by `&&`):

   ```
   /bin/true && echo "Last command exited cleanly"
   ```

3. Click the **Execute** button.

You should see the message, **Last command exited cleanly**, appear on the screen.

If the previous command returned an exit code indicating an error, the message would not appear. Try it yourself by executing the following commands:

```
/bin/false && echo "Last command exited cleanly"
```

You will not see any output because the second command does not get executed.

This method is useful for commands such as `make && make install` that are used during compilation and installation of software, where the second command should not be executed if the first one fails.

Executing a command from history

Because Webmin keeps a history of all the commands you execute, you can re-run previous commands by selecting them from a list instead of typing them in again.

You will see the list of previous commands appear under the command textbox after you execute your first command:

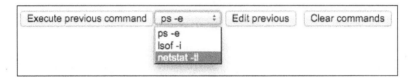

To execute a command from history, select it from the list and click **Execute previous command**. You can also change the command by clicking the **Edit previous** button. If you wish to clear the command history, click the **Clear commands** button.

Executing a command as another user

Sometimes, it's useful to execute commands as another user. For instance, management commands for some services are, by default, accessible to the system user associated with the service. You may also wish to test whether a user account is configured correctly and execute a command as another user to check if it will work as expected.

Getting ready

In this recipe, we will create a new PostgreSQL database named `testdb` by issuing the `createdb` command that is available to the `postgres` user. If you do not have PostgreSQL installed yet, you may refer to *Chapter 10, Running a PostgreSQL Database Server*, for information about installing and running this database system.

How to do it...

To execute a command as another user, we will use the **Running Processes** module:

1. Navigate to **System | Running Processes**.
2. Select **Run..** in the **Display** line.
3. Enter `createdb testdb` in the **Command to run** textbox.
4. Select **Wait until complete** as **Run mode**.
5. Enter `postgres` in the **Run as user** textbox.
6. Click the **Run** button.

You will be redirected to a page that shows the output messages of your command. If the command executes silently, you will be informed that no output was generated.

How it works...

Webmin executes the command you pass to it using a system call. It collects all the command outputs and displays it on the next screen. Because the Webmin process itself runs as `root`, it can impersonate any user when executing commands.

There's more...

Webmin offers a few more options for issuing commands in this module.

Passing input to a command

If you wish, you can put input data for the command in the **Input to command** text area. The data that is provided will be passed to the program that is executed by your first command over **standard input (STDIN)**:

1. Navigate to **System | Running Processes**.
2. Select **Run..** in the **Display** line.
3. Enter sort in the **Command to run** textbox.
4. Select **Wait until complete** as **Run mode**.
5. Enter a list of words in the **Input to command** text area, each on a separate line.
6. Click the **Run** button.

The output screen will present you with a sorted list of the words you provided.

This functionality is also useful for executing short programs written in scripting languages:

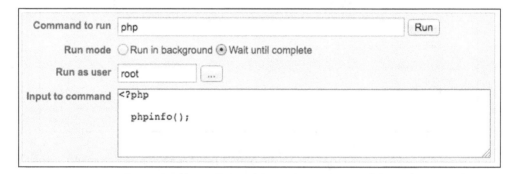

Running tasks in background

If a task takes a long time to complete, you may execute it in the background. This option will not present you with the output of the command, but you may safely disconnect from Webmin without interrupting command execution.

Setting a command to be executed in the future

It is sometimes useful to schedule a command to run at some point in the future. For instance, you may want to update or synchronize your database or restore files from a backup during the night, when your system is not heavily used. You may decide not to wait until a convenient time, but instead ask your system to execute a command automatically at a specific moment. Webmin gives you access to your system's command scheduling functionality and makes it easy to set up and remove scheduled commands.

Getting ready

For this recipe, I will assume that you have an installation of MediaWiki (the software which runs Wikipedia) installed on your server and you want to schedule the execution of its checkUsernames script at 2:30 a.m. on a Sunday.

Before you begin, you should make note of the following:

► The name of the maintenance script you wish to execute (in this example, I will assume it's called checkUsernames.php)

► The directory in which the script should be executed (in this example, /var/www/mediawiki/maintenance)

► The interpreter that should execute the script (php)

> We are assuming that the PHP command-line package is installed on your system and the php binary is placed within the binary search path. The default search path usually includes locations such as /bin, /sbin, /usr/bin, and /usr/local/bin. If the binary you wish to execute is not located in one of the default search paths, you should use an absolute path to the binary, that is, one which starts with /, for example, /usr/bin/php.

► The user who should execute the script (root)

How to do it...

For setting a command that will be executed, perform the following steps:

1. Navigate to **System | Scheduled Commands**.

2. Enter the name of the user who will execute the script (root) in the **Run as user** textbox.

3. Enter the desired future date and time in the fields provided. Set it to 2:30 a.m. next Sunday.

4. In the **Run in directory** textbox, enter the name of the directory (/var/www/mediawiki/maintenance) from which the script should be executed.

5. Enter the command you wish to execute—usually consisting of the name of the script interpreter and the name of the script in the **Commands to execute** field. In our example, it would be php checkUsernames.php.

6. Answer **Yes** to the **Send email on completion?** question.

7. Click the **Create** button.

On the screen that follows, you will see your command on a list of currently scheduled commands. Consider the following screenshot:

New scheduled command

Run as user	root `...`
Run on date	8 / Sep ÷ / 2013 `...`
Run at time	02 : 30
Current date	07/Sep/2013
Current time	13:00
Run in directory	/var/www/mediawiki/maintenance
Commands to execute	php checkUsernames.php

Send email on completion? ⦿ Yes ◯ No

[Create]

How it works...

Webmin uses your system's command scheduling facility (called at on Unix systems) that allows users to postpone the execution of a command until a specified future time.

The steps we took in this recipe could also be performed at the command line by issuing the following commands:

```
$ su root
# cd /var/www/mediawiki/maintenance
# echo 'php checkUsernames.php' | at -m 02:30 8.9.2013
```

The at command wraps commands (that are passed through standard input) into script files that are stored in a directory (usually in /var/spool/at or /var/spool/cron/atjobs/). The atd daemon waits until the time specified for execution and runs the scripts at the appropriate moment.

Webmin also allows you to list and delete scheduled jobs. Take a look at the *There's more...* section of this recipe. Listing of jobs can be done at the command line using the `atq` command, and deleting a particular job can be done using the `atrm` command that takes the job's number as a parameter.

There's more...

To see a list of commands scheduled for execution on your system, navigate back to **System | Scheduled Commands**. Consider the following screenshot:

	Job ID	Run as user	Run at	Created on	Commands to execute
Select all.	Invert selection.				
☐	1	root	Sep 8 02:30:00 2013	Sep 7 13:00:00 2013	php checkUsernames.php
Select all.	Invert selection.				

Cancel Selected Commands

To cancel any of these commands, check the box next to its ID and click the **Cancel Selected Commands** button.

See also

▸ If you would like to execute the same command repeatedly, take a look at the next recipe, *Scheduling a command to run regularly with cron*

Scheduling a command to run regularly with cron

Many tasks need to be executed repeatedly on a regular schedule. These include housekeeping jobs such as backing up important files, checking for software updates, deleting old temporary files, and checking logs for unusual messages to alert administrators.

Your applications may have additional tasks that should also be run on a regular schedule, and Webmin provides an interface that is more intuitive than the command-line `crontab` utility to create and manage cron jobs.

Getting ready

In this recipe, I will assume that you have a site powered by Drupal hosted under the URL, `http://example.com/`. Drupal has a series of tasks that it should execute regularly (updating caches, checking for updates, and so on). In order to trigger these tasks, we will set up a cron job which regularly connects to the following URL: `http://example.com/cron.php?cron_key=XYZ`.

How to do it...

To add a command to the cron schedule, follow these steps:

1. Navigate to **System | Scheduled Cron Jobs**.
2. Click the link marked **Create a new scheduled cron job**.
3. Specify your username in the textbox marked **Execute cron job as**.
4. Answer **Yes** to the **Active?** question.
5. Specify the following command in the **Command** textbox:

```
curl -s 'http://example.com/cron.php?cron_key=XYZ'
```

 `curl` is a widely available command to transfer data with URL syntax over various network protocols. We use the preceding command to connect to and download a webpage from our web server. This strategy is used by Drupal to trigger maintenance tasks. The `-s` parameter passed to `curl` prevents it from outputting a progress meter or error messages.

6. Give the job a **Description**, for example, `Drupal periodic tasks for Example.com`.
7. Now, specify how often you want the task to be executed. We'll need to specify a particular minute after the hour at which the task will be executed: Under **Minutes**, pick **Selected...** and choose a minute at random, for example, `19`. We'd like the task to run twice a day. So, under **Hours**, pick **Selected...** and choose `0` and `12`. We want the task to run every day, so we'll pick **All** under **Days**, **Months**, and **Weekdays**.
8. Click the **Save** button.

How it works...

Webmin adds the task we specified in the `crontab` (cron table) file for the user we selected. These files are usually stored in the `/var/spool/cron/crontabs` directory.

The time is specified in terms of minutes, hours, days of month, months, and weekdays. The scheduled command will execute at the exact time that matches these settings. For instance, if we specified the time as 19 minutes, 0 and 12 hours, and all days, months, and weekdays, the command will be executed every day at 0:19 and 12:19. The `cron` daemon waits until the appropriate time and then executes the scheduled commands.

You should not start all jobs on the full hour because you may create unnecessary system load spikes. Jobs should be spread out over the hour. If you don't have many jobs scheduled yet, you can pick a time at random. If your cron does a lot of work, you should probably check when fewest jobs are scheduled.

There's more...

Webmin's interface allows us more control over cron jobs.

Disabling a cron task temporarily

If we want to disable a cron job temporarily, we can edit the `crontab` and comment the job's line out by prepending it with a hash symbol (#). Webmin makes this simpler by providing a graphical interface to the task.

1. Navigate to **System | Scheduled Cron Jobs**.
2. Click the command you would like to disable.
3. Select **No** as the answer to the **Active?** question.
4. Click the **Save** button.

Cloning a cron task

If you would like to create another cron task similar to one that already exists, use Webmin's cloning function.

1. Navigate to **System | Scheduled Cron Jobs**.
2. Click the command you would like to replicate.
3. Click the **Clone Job** button.
4. A prefilled job creation screen will be open. Modify the job settings as needed.
5. Click the **Create** button.

Specifying which users can schedule tasks with cron

For security reasons, you may wish to restrict which users have the ability to schedule cron jobs. You may choose to allow all users access, choose to select users who have access, or select users for whom access will be denied.

 If you allow certain users to create cron jobs, all other users will be prevented from doing so. Conversely, if you deny some users the ability to create cron jobs, you are implicitly granting this possibility to everyone else.

1. Navigate to **System | Scheduled Cron Jobs**.
2. Click the link marked **Control user access to cron jobs**.
3. Select the **Allow only listed users** checkbox.
4. Click the ellipsis (**...**) in the same line and use the user chooser to select which users will be allowed to create cron jobs.

Creating a panel for the commands that you execute often

There are some commands that you will find yourself running over and over again. In such cases, you may wish to use Webmin's **Custom Commands** module to create a convenient control panel from which you can run your command with the click of a button.

 Using this feature, you can also allow some users to run a command as a different user. It's also useful as an alternative to creating scripts and a way to store the syntax of long or complicated commands.

Getting ready

In this recipe, we will create a custom button that uses the `drush` command to clear caches of a Drupal site. You will probably want to use a different command, so make a note of its syntax and the directory you want to execute it in before you begin.

How to do it...

In order to create a custom command button, follow these steps:

1. Navigate to **Others | Custom Commands**.
2. Click the link marked **Create a new custom command**.

3. Provide a short **Description** of the command, for instance: `Clear caches`.

4. Provide a longer description in the **HTML Description** field, for instance: `Clear Drupal caches for Example.com`.

5. Input the command in the **Command** text area. In our example, the command is `drush cache-clear all`.

6. Specify the directory in which the command will be executed in the **Run in directory** field. In our case, we'll specify the directory in which the Drupal site is installed: `/var/www/drupal`.

7. Specify the username of a user who has the ability to execute your command in the **Run as user** field.

8. Click the **Save** button.

You will be brought back to the **Custom Commands** module where a new command button will be presented. Click the button to execute your command. You can come back to **Others | Custom Commands** at any time to run your command by pressing this button.

How it works...

Webmin stores the custom command configurations in the `/etc/webmin/custom` directory. Whenever you visit the **Custom Commands** module, Webmin reads these configuration files and dynamically builds an administrative panel for you. When you press a button associated with a command, Webmin executes it for you.

There's more...

There are quite a few other options associated with Webmin's custom commands functionality.

Cloning a command

If you would like to create another custom command similar to one that already exists, use Webmin's cloning function.

1. Navigate to **System | Custom Commands**.

2. Click the **Edit command** link under the command you wish to replicate.

3. Click the **Clone** button.

4. A new command screen will be open. Modify settings as needed.

5. Click the **Create** button.

Specifying command arguments

If your command takes arguments, you can build a more complex user interface that will ask you to specify the values of these parameters.

In our example, we set up a control panel entry to execute the following command:

```
drush cache-clear all
```

The last argument (`all`) specifies which caches should be cleared. Other possible values of this parameter include: `theme-registry`, `menu`, `css-js`, and so on. Let's expand our control panel to ask the user for this parameter:

1. Navigate to **Others | Custom Commands**.
2. Click the **Edit command** link under the command we created in this recipe.
3. Change the command to `drush cache-clear $cacheType`. `$cacheType` will be a placeholder for our argument value.
4. Now, let's add the parameter to the command form and specify how it should be displayed. Specify `cacheType` as **Parameter name**, add **Description**, specify **Type** as **Menu..**, and type in the following command:

   ```
   printf "all\ntheme-registry\nmenu\ncss-js"  |
   ```

 Do not forget to add the pipe (|) character at the end or the menu will fail to appear properly.

The command line outputs possible values of the parameter on separate lines. Consider the following screenshot:

Parameter name	Description	Type		Quote?	Required?
cacheType	Which cache?	Menu.. ⇕	printf "all\ntheme-registry\nmenu\ncss-js" |	◯ Yes ◉ No	◉ Yes ◯ No

5. Click the **Save** button.

 In this example, we specified the possible parameter values by using the `printf` command and separating each value by a new-line character (`\n`).

Another way of specifying possible parameter values is to save them to a file (also one value per line) and specify the pathname of the file in the textbox.

In effect, you would have created a custom command form that allows you to specify a parameter value before execution. Consider the following screenshot:

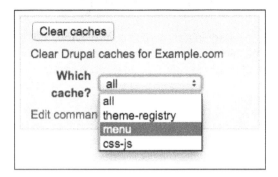

Making the command available in Usermin

You may decide to make your custom control panel command available to your non-administrative users through Usermin. This is quite simple. Perform the following steps:

1. Navigate to **Others | Custom Commands**.

2. Click the **Edit command** link under the command you would like to make available in Usermin.

3. Answer **Yes** to the **Available in Usermin?** question.

4. Now, log in to Usermin and navigate to **Others | Custom Commands** to see the available commands.

See also

▶ Webmin's online help has additional tips and tricks about creating custom commands. Click the **Help..** link on each Webmin screen to access this information.

▶ For more information about setting up Usermin, refer to the recipe, *Installing Usermin*, in *Chapter 2, User Management*.

Creating a panel with the database commands that you execute often

In the previous recipe, we created an easy-to-use control panel that allows you to execute custom commands with the click of a button. Webmin allows you to extend this functionality by adding custom commands that execute SQL queries on MySQL and PostgreSQL databases.

Getting ready

In order to follow this recipe, you will need to have a MySQL or PostgreSQL database installed and set up. Refer to *Chapter 9, Running a MySQL Database Server*, and *Chapter 10, Running a PostgreSQL Database Server*, for information on how to do this.

In this recipe, I will assume that you are running a web application that uses a database called `django` and stores its caches in the database table called `cache`. We'll create a custom command that empties (truncates) the `cache` table. Your situation will probably be different. So, before beginning, make a note of the following:

- Name of the database that you want to run your query on
- Syntax of the SQL command that you want to execute
- Name and password of the database user with appropriate privileges
- Location of the database server (if different than localhost)
- Type of the database to which you're connecting (MySQL or PostgreSQL)

How to do it...

In order to create a custom database command button, follow these steps:

1. Navigate to **Others | Custom Commands**.
2. Click the link marked **Create a new SQL command**.
3. Provide a short **Description** of the command, for instance: `Clear cache`.
4. Provide a longer description in the **HTML Description** field, for instance: `Clear Django DB cache for Example.com`.
5. Select **Type** of database you're using: either MySQL or PostgreSQL.
6. Enter **Database name**; in our example, it's `django`.
7. Enter the SQL command that will be executed, in our example, it would be:

```
TRUNCATE TABLE cache;
```

8. Enter the username and password of the database user with appropriate permissions to execute the SQL command.

9. Specify which server the database is hosted on if it's different than the localhost, or choose **This server as Database server host**.

10. Click the **Create** button.

How it works...

Webmin stores the custom command configurations in the `/etc/webmin/custom` directory. Whenever you visit the **Custom Commands** module, Webmin reads these configuration files and dynamically builds an administrative panel for you. When you press a button associated with a command, Webmin connects to the database server and executes the SQL commands for you.

See also

▶ There are additional options for setting up custom commands. Refer to the previous recipe, *Create a panel for commands you execute often*, for more information and examples.

▶ Webmin's online help has additional tips and tricks about creating custom commands. Click the **Help..** link on each Webmin screen to access this information.

Running a terminal emulator in the browser

Despite the wide range of options that Webmin allows you to control, you will find yourself in situations that require more direct access to your system. For such situations, you should equip yourself with a full-fledged terminal emulator and SSH client. If you need to perform a quick operation on your server through the terminal but don't have access to your tools, Webmin will allow you to open a simple terminal emulator in the browser.

How to do it...

To run a server terminal in your browser, follow these steps:

1. Navigate to **Others | Text login**.

2. Log in to the system using the username and password of a user with SSH access.

3. Perform your command-line tasks.

4. Type `exit` and press *Enter* to close your terminal session.

How it works...

Webmin uses a component called Ajaxterm that connects to your system over SSH, passes your commands to the server, and displays terminal output in the web browser.

For more information, visit the Ajaxterm website at `https://github.com/antonylesuisse/qweb`.

There's more...

There is another component that allows you to access your computer's terminal through Webmin. You can find it by navigating to **Others | SSH login**. This component has similar features. However, it requires running Java in your browser, which isn't recommended for security reasons.

5

Monitoring Your System

In this chapter, we will cover the following topics:

- ▸ Viewing and searching through system logfiles
- ▸ Saving Syslog messages to a file
- ▸ Adding other logfiles to Webmin
- ▸ Configuring logfile rotation
- ▸ Listing recent logins
- ▸ Receiving an e-mail when a service stops running
- ▸ Automatically restarting a service that goes down
- ▸ Monitoring a remote server

Introduction

While your server is running, it keeps a record of the actions it performs. A log entry is made whenever a service is started or stopped, a cron job runs, a mail message is sent and especially whenever some action produces an unexpected result or error.

Log messages help you fix problems on your server. If something isn't working, there is probably a log message somewhere explaining what's happening and what the problem is. Log messages also allow you to detect unusual situations, such as attempts to break into your server. It's important to review your system logs regularly.

Each log message is useful for a limited time. After a couple of weeks or months, old log messages can be removed to prevent logs from growing too large and filling up your disk space.

In this chapter, we will demonstrate how Webmin can be used as a convenient tool for viewing your system logfiles, how it can assist you in rotating logs to keep an archive and delete old entries. We will also demonstrate how Webmin can monitor your system by performing regular tests and how it can alert you to problems or even try to fix some of them automatically.

Viewing and searching through system logfiles

You can configure Webmin's System Logs module to be a one-stop source for all logging information about your system. In this recipe, we'll demonstrate how easy it is to quickly view and scan through logfiles using Webmin's interface. In the two recipes following this one, we'll show you how to add other logfiles to this module to create a comprehensive overview of your system's activity.

Getting ready

In this recipe, we'll inspect the `auth.log` file at `/var/log/`, which keeps a log of messages related to authentication and authorization. This file is present by default on most systems from the Debian family, but if you're using a different system, you may not find it. You can add this file to your system by following the recipe, *Saving Syslog messages to a file*.

You can, of course, follow the same steps to view any other file listed in the System Logs module.

How to do it...

Follow these steps to view log messages:

1. Navigate to **System | System Logs**. You will be presented with a list of logfiles available through Webmin.

2. Click the **View...** link in the line for the `/var/log/auth.log` file.

3. By default, Webmin will display the last 20 messages (lines) from this logfile. To view more lines, type in `40` in the field, **Last [ ] lines of file**, and click the **Refresh** button.

4. The `auth.log` file will show you information about users logging in. We can filter the display to show only messages associated with Webmin. Type `webmin` in the field, **Only show lines with text**, and click **Refresh**:

Module Index

View Logfile

`/var/log/auth.log`

Last `10` lines of `/var/log/auth.log` Only show lines with text `webmin` [Refresh]

```
Feb 14 15:25:15 webmin-host sshd[2173]: Server listening on 0.0.0.0 port 22.
Feb 14 15:25:15 webmin-host sshd[2173]: Server listening on :: port 22.
Feb 14 15:25:16 webmin-host perl: pam_unix(webmin:auth): authentication failure; logname=
Feb 14 15:25:18 webmin-host webmin[2387]: Webmin starting
Feb 14 15:25:18 webmin-host sshd[2173]: Received signal 15; terminating.
Feb 14 15:25:18 webmin-host sshd[2471]: Server listening on 0.0.0.0 port 22.
Feb 14 15:25:18 webmin-host sshd[2471]: Server listening on :: port 22.
Feb 14 15:25:34 webmin-host login[2419]: pam_unix(login:session): session opened for user
Feb 14 15:26:06 webmin-host perl[2512]: pam_unix(webmin:session): session opened for user
Feb 14 15:26:06 webmin-host webmin[2512]: Successful login as root from 10.10.20.147
```

Last `10` lines of `/var/log/auth.log` Only show lines with text `webmin` [Refresh]

---

5. You can now test that new messages appear in the log. Use another browser to log into Webmin, and then come back and click **Refresh** again to see a new message about the login attempt appear in the log.

How it works...

Behind the scenes, Webmin uses the `tail` command to display the last lines of your system log. If you want to achieve a similar view at the terminal, you could use the following command:

```
$ sudo tail -n 40 /var/log/auth.log
```

If you want to filter the log to include only lines containing the word, `webmin`, combine the `tail` command with `grep`, as follows:

```
$ sudo grep webmin /var/log/auth.log | tail -n 40
```

There's more...

When debugging a problem on your system, it's often useful to watch the logfile messages appear as you're performing the task, which ends in an error. Webmin can automatically refresh the log display to show new messages as they come in.

Configuring system logs to refresh automatically

Perform the following steps to configure system logs to refresh automatically:

1. Navigate to **System | System Logs**.
2. Click the **Module Config** link in the top-left-hand side corner.
3. Set **Seconds between log view refreshes** to `10`, and click **Save**.

Now, when you display a log, it will automatically refresh your view, filters and all, every 10 seconds. You can keep this window open while you're performing a debugging task, and watch as messages are output to the log.

> Depending on your browser, Webmin's automatic refresh functionality may be disabled by a security mechanism, which checks each incoming HTTP request for a correct referrer header. You can disable this mechanism by following these steps:
> - Navigate to **Webmin | Webmin Configuration | Trusted Referrers**.
> - Answer **No** to **Referrer checking enabled?**.
> - Click **Save**.

You can also follow the output as it is added to a file by using the `tail` command's `-f` option, as follows:

```
$ sudo tail -f /var/log/auth.log
```

See also

> ► In this recipe, we discussed how to view and filter a logfile. In the following two recipes: *Saving Syslog messages to a file* and *Adding other logfiles to Webmin*, we will demonstrate how you can add other log messages to this interface.

Saving Syslog messages to a file

The standard logging protocol on Unix and related systems is called Syslog. Most modern Linux distributions use an implementation such as **Rsyslog** or **Syslog-NG**. They all perform the same tasks:

> ► Allow software running on your system to send Syslog messages
> ► Separate incoming messages by type and priority and save them to different files

Most system utilities send log messages to Syslog, but other server software (such as Apache, MySQL, or PostgreSQL), by default, save messages directly to files on disk.

Webmin allows you to control Syslog and decide which messages get saved to which files. In order to understand how Syslog separates messages, we need to explain two concepts: **facilities** and **priorities**.

Each message sent to Syslog is described by a facility level and priority level. Based on these properties, you can decide which messages to discard, which to save, and where.

A facility level describes what type of message this is. Since programs usually send all messages with the same facility, it usually specifies what type of program sent the message. The following table lists various facility levels:

Facility	Associated messages
`auth` and `authpriv`	Messages associated with user authorization or security. These may contain sensitive information (especially `authpriv`) and should be accessible only to trusted system users.
`cron`	Messages associated with the execution of scheduled commands.
`daemon`	Messages output by background processes (system daemons).
`ftp`	Messages associated with the FTP server.
`kern`	Messages generated by the system kernel.

Facility	Associated messages
`local0` to `local7`	You can configure your local programs to send log messages to Syslog using these facilities.
`lpr`	Messages associated with printing.
`mail`	Messages associated with the mail server.
`mark`	A special facility, which generates a timestamp at regular intervals.
`news`	Obsolete.
`syslog`	Messages associated with Syslog itself.
`user`	Messages associated with user processes. This is also the default facility if no other was specified when sending the message.
`uucp`	Obsolete.
`*`	All of the above.

The priority (severity) level describes how important a log message is. You can use this description to specify which messages to discard and which to keep. Priority levels have a specific order, so you can choose, for example, to log all messages with the priority, `warning`, and above. The following table lists priority levels from highest to lowest:

Priority	Description
`emerg`	Emergency—system is unstable. This is the highest possible priority level.
`alert`	Alert—action must be taken immediately.
`crit`	Critical—system is in a critical condition. Action should be taken.
`err`	Error—an error occurred and should be fixed.
`warning`	Warning—something is not working as expected. Check configuration.
`notice`	Notice—system performed a significant action.
`info`	Information—messages with information about the system's normal functions.
`debug`	Debugging—verbose messages used primarily for setting services up and debugging problems.

Getting ready

In this recipe, we will use Webmin to instruct our Syslog daemon to save all log messages associated with user authorization to the file, `auth.log` at `/var/log/`. If you're using a Debian-based system, you will probably already have this file on your system. In this case, you can save these messages to a second file called `auth2.log` for practice and remove the configuration later.

How to do it...

Follow these steps to save Syslog messages to a file:

1. Navigate to **System | System Logs**.
2. Click the **Add a new system log** link.
3. Choose **Log to File**, and specify `/var/log/auth.log` as the filename.
4. Verify that **Logging active?** is set to **Yes**.
5. Under **Facilities**, choose **Many**, and enter both facility names associated with authentication (separated by a comma): `auth,authpriv`.
6. Under **Priorities**, choose **All**:

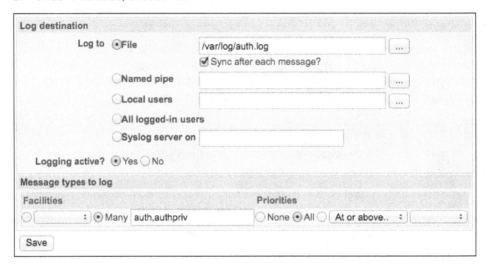

7. Click the **Save** button.
8. Click the **Apply Changes** button at the bottom of the **System Logs** module screen.

On some systems, the **Apply Changes** button may not be visible or will have no effect. In this case, you'll need to restart the Syslog service manually.

If your system uses Rsyslog, you can restart it with this command:

```
$ sudo service rsyslog restart
```

Refer to the recipe, *Executing a command on the server,* in *Chapter 4, Controlling Your System* for information about executing commands via Webmin.

You can now view the `/var/log/auth.log` file as described in the recipe, *Viewing and searching through system logfiles.*

How it works...

Based on the choices you make, Webmin updates your Syslog configuration file and restarts the service. Your Syslog daemon reads in the new configuration; if necessary, creates a new output file for log messages; and sends the selected messages there.

There's more...

After you change your Syslog configuration, you may want to check if log messages are routed correctly to their intended destinations. You can send a log message to Syslog by executing the logger command. The command's syntax is this:

```
logger -p facility.priority "The message text"
```

For instance, if you want to send a message `Hello Syslog` with a priority `info` and facility `auth`, use the following command:

```
$ logger -p auth.info "Hello Syslog"
```

Check the `auth.log` file to see your log entry.

Adding other logfiles to Webmin

Server daemons, which do not use Syslog, save their log messages directly to files on your disk. Webmin allows you to view, search, and monitor all logfiles in ways described in this chapter's first recipe. For easy reference, you can add commonly viewed logfiles to the list in System Logs module.

Getting ready

Log messages you need to debug your problem are in there somewhere; you just need to know where to look. Before you can add them to Webmin, you need to find the logfile's full path.

On Linux, logs are typically stored in the `/var/log` directory. The following table lists the default locations of log messages of some commonly used services:

Daemon	Default log file location
Apache 2	Messages may be output to: `/var/log/apache2/access.log`, `/var/log/apache2/error.log`, and so on.
MySQL	Messages may be output to: `/var/log/mysql/mysql.log`. or go to Syslog with the `daemon` facility.
PostgreSQL	Messages may be output to: `/var/log/pgsql_log`. or go to Syslog with the `local0` facility.

Daemon	Default log file location
PHP	PHP does not specify a default log location. If PHP is running as an Apache module, messages may appear in Apache logs. Check your `php.ini` file to see if logging is enabled.
Webmin	Messages may be output to: `/var/webmin/webmin.log` and other files in `/var/webmin`.

Because every system distribution may configure your services in a slightly different way, check your service's configuration file to determine the location of its logs if you cannot find it in its default place.

In this recipe, we'll add the Apache access log (`/var/log/apache2/access.log`) and error log (`/var/log/apache2/error.log`) to Webmin's System Logs module.

How to do it...

To monitor additional logfiles through Webmin, follow these steps:

1. Navigate to **System | System Logs**.
2. Click the **Module Config** link in the top left-hand side corner.
3. Add the path to each logfile followed by a space and description in the **Other log files to show** field. Place each entry on a separate line as follows:

   ```
   /var/log/apache2/access.log Apache access log
   /var/log/apache2/error.log Apache error log
   ```

Other log files to show (With optional descriptions)	`/var/log/apache2/access.log Apache access log` `/var/log/apache2/error.log Apache error log`

4. Click the **Save** button.

The files you added will now appear in the System Logs list.

How it works...

The additional file definitions are stored in a configuration file (`/etc/webmin/syslog/config`). Webmin inspects this file each time it prepares the System Logs module page and adds the files to its listing.

There's more...

You can also use Webmin to check a logfile once, without adding it to System Logs permanently. The following are the steps to do so:

1. Navigate to **System | System Logs**.
2. Enter the path to the logfile into the **View log file** field. You can also use the file chooser by clicking on the ellipsis (**...**) button.
3. Click the **View** button.

Configuring logfile rotation

Log messages are very useful for debugging problems, analyzing usage patterns of your system, and checking if attempts were made to compromise your server. Each message is useful for a limited time, however, and old logs can be deleted to reclaim disk space.

Log rotation is a strategy that ensures that the most recent log messages are always readily available while older messages are stored in separate files, which can be compressed to save space. After a few weeks or months, depending on the log type, the oldest messages can be deleted.

Webmin allows you to control the `logrotate` utility that performs automatic logfile rotation for you. Most packages that you will install will come with their own `logrotate` configuration files, which they will place in the `/etc/logrotate.d` directory. Placing a configuration file in this directory ensures that files will fall under log rotation control. Webmin gives you a graphical interface to easily create and modify these files.

Getting ready

Before creating a log rotation routine, make sure that the `logrotate` package is installed on your system. Refer to the recipe, *Installing software packages* in *Chapter 1, Setting Up Your System*, for more information.

In this recipe, we will create a `logrotate` configuration for a logfile called `custom.log`, which contains the log output of a daemon called `customd`. We will schedule a weekly rotation of the logfile, storing four weeks worth of past logs, and compressing all but the latest log archive. We will instruct Webmin to restart the daemon after log rotation, so it starts writing to the new file.

When creating a `logrotate` configuration, you will need the logfile path as well as the syntax of the command, which restarts the logging daemon. Some software have a special command designed to inform the daemon that logs were rotated, which does not require a full restart. Refer to the daemon documentation to find it.

How to do it...

Follow these steps to create a `logrotate` configuration:

1. Navigate to **System | Log File Rotation**.

2. Click the link marked **Add a new log file to rotate**.

3. In the **Log file paths**, enter the full path to the file you want to rotate. You can specify multiple files on separate lines or include the content of a whole directory by specifying the directory path followed by an asterisk. In our case, we want to rotate one file, so we should enter: `/var/log/custom.log`.

4. Specify the **Rotation schedule** as **Weekly**.

5. Set **Number of old logs to keep** to **4**.

6. Answer **Yes** to the **Compress old log files?** question.

7. Answer **Yes** to the **Delay compression till next cycle?** question. This will ensure that the most recent archival logfile is not compressed, which makes it easier to view at the expense of some disk space.

8. Answer **Yes** to the **Re-create log file after rotation?** question. If you leave the **mode**, **owner**, and **group** fields blank, `logrotate` will create the file with the same ownership and permissions as the original logfile.

9. In the **Commands to run after rotation** field, enter the command to restart the service, which writes to the logfile. In our contrived example, it would be: `service customd restart`.

10. Click the **Create** button.

How it works...

Webmin creates a `logrotate` configuration file in the `/etc/logrotate.d` directory, which places the logfiles you specify under rotation.

There's more...

Webmin's interface has a number of other features to control `logrotate`.

Rotating logfiles on demand

Rotation of logfiles is triggered by a command scheduled with cron to run once a day. If you wish to rotate the logfiles sooner, you can trigger rotation manually at any time:

1. Navigate to **System | Log File Rotation**.

2. Click the button marked **Force Log Rotation**.

Editing default options

Webmin allows you to set the default options, which apply to all log rotation routines if not overridden. Perform the following steps to do so:

1. Navigate to **System | Log File Rotation**.
2. Click the button marked **Edit Global Options**.

Sending logfiles by email when rotating

`logrotate` can be set to send you a copy of your logfile when rotating it:

1. Navigate to **System | Log File Rotation**.
2. Click on the link with the name of the file under rotation. This will allow you to edit an existing log rotation configuration.
3. Answer **Yes** to **Email log file before deleting?** and specify an e-mail address.

You could specify whether you wanted to be e-mailed the newest logfile archive, which was just created, or the oldest archive, which was about to be deleted.

Listing recent logins

Every time a user logs into your system or logs out, information about this is stored in a log of interactive login sessions. You can use Webmin to inspect this log.

How to do it...

Follow these steps to list recent logins:

1. Navigate to **System | Users and Groups**.
2. Use the form at the bottom of the screen. Select the radio button marked **Only user**, and enter the username of the user whose logins you're interested in. You can also select **All** to list logins by all users.
3. Click the button marked **Displays Logins By**.

You will see a list of logins by the selected user since the logfile was last rotated.

How it works...

Webmin inspects the standard Unix file named `wtmp`, usually stored in `/var/log/wtmp`, which stores the history of all logins and logouts on the system. This is a binary file, so you can't inspect it using standard text log parsing tools. If you wanted to view login history at the command line, you would use the `last` command, for example, `last root` to show logins of the root user.

You can also use the other related commands as listed:

- The `lastlog` command displays a list of all users along with the time they last logged in
- The `sudo lastb` command displays information about failed login attempts
- The `who` command displays a list of currently logged in users.

There's more...

Webmin also allows you to check which users are logged in currently:

1. Navigate to **System | Users and Groups**.
2. Click the button marked **Show Logged In Users**.

Receiving an e-mail when a service stops running

You put your server up to perform a specific service: running a website, hosting a database, or exchanging e-mail. If that service stops working, your visitors, clients, or co-workers will complain, so in case of problems you should always be the first to know.

Webmin provides a capable monitoring system, which can periodically check the status of your server and send you an e-mail if something is out of the ordinary.

Getting ready

Webmin's monitoring service will send an e-mail alert using your local e-mail server. Refer to *Chapter 12, Setting Up an E-mail Server* for instructions on setting it up.

Before you can use Webmin's monitoring functionality, you'll need to activate it. Follow these steps to do it:

1. Navigate to **Others | System and Server Status**.

2. Click the button marked **Scheduled Monitoring**.

3. Answer **Yes** to the **Scheduled checking enabled?** question.

4. Set **Send email when** to **When a service goes down** to receive a single message when a monitor test fails. If you prefer to be spammed, you can choose to receive an e-mail **Any time service is down**.

5. Select the option **E-mail status report to**, and provide your e-mail address:

Scheduled background monitoring options	
Scheduled checking enabled? ⦿ Yes ◯ No	Send one email per service? ◯ Yes ⦿ No

Check every `5` `minutes ÷` with offset `0`

Run monitor during hours
```
00:00  06:00  12:00  18:00
01:00  07:00  13:00  19:00
02:00  08:00  14:00  20:00
03:00  09:00  15:00  21:00
04:00  10:00  16:00  22:00
05:00  11:00  17:00  23:00
```
Run monitor on days
```
Sunday
Monday
Tuesday
Wednesday
Thursday
Friday
Saturday
```

Send email when ◯ When a service changes status ⦿ When a service goes down ◯ Any time service is down

Email status report to ◯ Don't send email ⦿ Email status report to `krieger@isis.net`

From: address for email ⦿ Default (webmin) ◯

Send mail via ⦿ Local mail server ◯ SMTP server

Page status report to number ⦿ Don't send pages ◯

Send SMS to ⦿ Nobody ◯ Phone on carrier `Alltel ÷` with number `___`

Save

6. Click the **Save** button.

You should receive e-mail alerts when a monitor has something to report. You should set up a test monitor, which you know will fail to check whether these e-mails reach you.

In this recipe, we'll set up a monitor that checks whether the Apache web server is running. Refer to *Chapter 8, Running an Apache Web Server*, for information about setting up Apache.

How to do it...

Follow these steps to receive e-mail alerts when a service stops running on your server:

1. We will use a monitor, which checks if a service started by a given command is still running. The first thing to check is the name of the command that started the service. We can do this by navigating to the **System | Running Processes** module. In case of Apache on Debian, the command is: `/usr/sbin/apache2 -k start`. The string `apache2` is unique and appears only in processes associated with this server, so we'll set up our test to scan for this string in the table of running processes. If no process matching this string is found, our test will fail. Make a note of how many processes Apache is running. In my configuration, there are six processes associated with the web server.

2. Navigate to **Others | System and Server Status**.

3. From the drop-down list, select **Check Process** as the monitor type, and click the **Add monitor of type:** button.

4. Specify `Apache Process` as the description.

5. Answer **Yes** to the **Check on schedule?** question, and select when you want to be notified, for example, **Yes, and report on status changes**.

6. Check the box marked **Email** in the **Notification methods** section.

7. In the **Command to check for** text field, enter a regular expression that matches the name of the command that started Apache. The string, `apache2`, will work, but you have the power of Perl regular expressions if you want to be more precise.

8. Enter the number from step 1 in the field marked **Number of process that must exist for monitor to consider them running**. In our configuration, Apache is running six processes, so that is the number we'll specify. If any of these processes fail, we'll be notified.

9. Click the **Create** button.

You should now receive an e-mail if any of Apache's processes stop running. To test the monitor, stop Apache for five minutes, and check if you received an e-mail report.

How it works...

When you activate Webmin's monitoring facility, it creates a cron job, which runs the monitor scripts on a schedule. Each monitor test can return a success or failure status. If a failure status is returned by a test, Webmin will send out alert e-mails to the address specified in the Scheduled Monitoring configuration.

There's more...

Webmin's monitoring is quite feature rich, and we will cover aspects of it in this section and in the following dedicated recipes.

Inspecting monitor history

Webmin keeps a history of the status of all monitors, allowing you to check when a given monitor passed and when it failed its test:

1. Navigate to **Others | System and Server Status**.

2. Click the name of a chosen monitor, for example, the **Apache Webserver** monitor.

3. Unfold the **Status history** section at the bottom of the screen.

 If your monitor just started running, you may not have a history to inspect yet. Check back after a few monitoring cycles have been completed. If the history fails to appear at all, it suggests that your monitor is not set up correctly.

Using predefined monitors

In this recipe, we created a custom monitor, which checked whether the Apache process was running. In fact, Webmin has quite a few predefined monitor types that require no configuration, they only need to be activated. For instance, to use a predefined monitor for Apache, follow these steps:

1. Navigate to **Others | System and Server Status**.

2. From the drop-down list, select **Apache Webserver** as the monitor type, and click the **Add monitor of type:** button.

3. Customize the reporting settings as required.

4. Click the **Create** button.

Monitoring system load

In addition to checking if a given piece of software is running, Webmin can also monitor other system resources. For instance, you can be notified when your system is pegging its CPU. This could indicate heavy traffic on your server, but may also indicate a runaway process stuck in an infinite loop, which should probably be killed, or an on-going denial of service attack. Perform the following steps to monitor system load:

1. Navigate to **Others | System and Server Status**.

2. From the drop-down list, select **Load Average** as the monitor type, and click the **Add monitor of type:** button.

3. Customize the reporting settings as required.

4. Select 15 minute for **Load average to check**, so we don't get information about short bursts of normal activity.

5. As a rule of thumb, the value for **Maximum load average** should be the number of CPU cores your machine has.

> If you have a single CPU, a load average higher then 1 for the last 15 minutes indicates that your system is overloaded. On a 2-core machine, a load below 2 indicates that the system is not overloaded. Different operating systems calculate this value in slightly different ways, so you may need to test your server with the `uptime` command during normal operation to check what load average is normal for your system.
>
> You may find more information about system load on Wikipedia: `http://en.wikipedia.org/wiki/Load_(computing)`.

6. Click the **Create** button.

Monitoring disk space

Your server will come to a screeching halt if it completely runs out of disk space. Because this situation must be avoided, you should monitor your system and react if file space usage reaches a high value, such as 90 percent. Perform the following steps to monitor disk space:

1. Navigate to **Others | System and Server Status**.

2. From the drop-down list, select **Disk Space** as the monitor type, and click the **Add monitor of type:** button.

3. Select the root filesystem (/) from the **Filesystem to check** drop-down.

4. Select the option, **Percentage of total**, and set it to 90 percent.

5. Click the **Create** button.

See also

▶ Beyond sending you an e-mail when a system monitor test fails, Webmin can also try to react automatically. Take a look at the next recipe, *Automatically restarting a service that goes down*, for more information.

▶ More information about Webmin's monitoring capabilities may be found on its wiki: `http://doxfer.webmin.com/Webmin/SystemAndServerStatus`.

Automatically restarting a service that goes down

Webmin's monitoring functionality can alert you to problems detected on your system, but it can also automatically react to detected problems by executing commands. For instance, if a service goes down, you can try to restart it automatically.

Getting ready

This recipe is an extension of the previous one, *Receiving e-mail when a service stops running*. Make sure you follow the setup steps in that recipe before you start this one.

In this recipe, we'll tell Webmin to monitor Apache and restart it automatically if it stops running.

How to do it...

Follow these steps to automatically restart a service that goes down:

1. Navigate to **Others | System and Server Status**.
2. Click the link for the **Apache Webserver** monitor.
3. In the **Commands to run** section, enter the command to start Apache in the **If monitor goes down, run command** text field. The command on most Linux distributions is `service apache2 start`.
4. Click the **Save** button.

How it works...

Webmin creates a cron job, which runs its monitors on a regular schedule. If a monitor changes state from success to failure, Webmin will execute any commands you preset. The commands may be used to restart a service that stopped running, thus automatically reacting and correcting your system's state.

This is a good strategy for services such as a web server, mail server, or application server. This may not be the best idea for a service such as a database, which may require your intervention when restarting to fix problems such as corrupt database tables.

Monitoring a remote server

You may use Webmin's monitoring facility to periodically check the state of a remote server that does not run Webmin itself. Since we only have limited access to a remote server, we can only test its externally visible state. Nevertheless, this is a very useful tool, which can tell us whether any other server is up and running a network service on a specific port. If a service on the remote server goes down, Webmin will notify us by an e-mail.

Getting ready

This is an extension of the recipe, *Receiving e-mail when a service stops running*. Make sure you follow the setup steps in that recipe before you start this one.

In this recipe, we'll tell Webmin to periodically check if a remote web server is running and returning an expected HTML page.

How to do it...

Follow these steps to monitor a remote server:

1. Navigate to **Others | System and Server Status**.
2. From the drop-down list, select **Remote HTTP Service** as the monitor type, and click the **Add monitor of type:** button.
3. In the **URL to request** field, enter the URL of a webpage you expect to find on the remote server, for instance: `http://example.com/index.php`.
4. Set the **HTTP request method** to **GET**.
5. In the **Page must match regexp** field, enter a string containing a fragment of the HTML code you expect the web server to respond with. This could be the page title or other text that does not change frequently on the remote website.

> For example, if we were to monitor `https://en.wikipedia.org/wiki/Main_Page`, we could check for the string, `Wikipedia, the free encyclopedia`, which we expect to appear as the title of a properly generated page.

6. Click the **Create** button.

How it works...

Webmin creates a cron job, which runs its monitors on a regular schedule. The remote HTTP service monitor tries to establish a connection to the web server configured to respond under a given URL. If the connection is established, Webmin requests the specified web page and scans it in search of our regular expression.

If the monitor cannot establish a connection, or the returned webpage does not match our regular expression; the test will fail; and the monitor will change its state and send an e-mail alert message.

There's more...

Webmin is able to monitor remote web servers, but it can also be used to monitor other services remotely.

Checking that a remote server is up

The remote server you are running may be a firewall or another piece of network infrastructure that does not expose any network services. Even such a secure server should still respond to ICMP ping echo requests. Webmin can send ping packets to the remote server to determine that it is reachable via the network. Perform the following steps to check if a remote server is up:

1. Navigate to **Others | System and Server Status**.
2. From the drop-down list, select **Remote Ping** as the monitor type, and click the **Add monitor of type:** button.
3. In the **Host to ping** field, enter the IP address or domain name of the remote server.
4. Click the **Create** button.

Checking that a remote server is running a network service

You can use Webmin to test virtually any network service on the remote server if you know the port number it's supposed to be listening on. Webmin will send a TCP connection request to the remote server on a specific port. If the remote server responds, Webmin will immediately close the connection. If the server fails to respond, an alert message will be sent.

1. Navigate to **Others | System and Server Status**.
2. From the drop-down list, select **Remote TCP Service** as the monitor type, and click the **Add monitor of type:** button.
3. In the **Host to connect to** field, enter the IP address or domain name of the remote server.
4. Specify the service port in the **Port to connect to** field.
5. Click the **Create** button.

6
Managing Files on Your System

In this chapter, we will cover:

- ▶ Downloading files from the server
- ▶ Uploading files to the server
- ▶ Managing files and directories on the server
- ▶ Changing file ownership and permissions
- ▶ Setting up network-shared folders for Windows
- ▶ Mounting a Windows-shared folder
- ▶ Setting up an NFS-shared volume
- ▶ Mounting a remote NFS volume
- ▶ Giving users access to your server via SFTP
- ▶ Giving users access to your server via FTP

Introduction

Webmin provides facilities to transfer files to and from your server, as well as a full-fledged file manager, which can be run in your browser as a Java applet. In this chapter, we will go over using these functionalities to manage files on your server from Webmin without the need for additional tools.

The second half of the chapter will demonstrate how you can use Webmin to set up file sharing on your local network using **Windows networking** (**CIFS**), **Network File System** (**NFS**), and **File Transfer Protocol** (**FTP**). If you would like to access your files from the Internet, the best solution would be to use the **Secure File Transfer Protocol** (**SFTP**) functionality, which is also covered in this chapter.

The two recipes *Mounting a Windows-shared folder* and *Mounting a remote NFS volume* in this chapter demonstrate how Webmin can help you set up a CIFS or NFS client and make remote file resources available on your system.

Downloading files from the server

You will often run into a situation where you need to view the contents of a file or download a file from your server. Webmin's **Upload and Download** module makes these tasks very easy.

In this recipe, we'll inspect your system's hostname database file to check if you defined any local hostname entries that override domain names resolved by DNS. This file is stored in /etc/hosts on most systems.

How to do it...

Follow these steps to download a file from the server:

1. Navigate to **Others | Upload and Download**.
2. Select the **Download from server** tab.
3. Click the ellipsis (**...**) button in the **File to download** line.
4. Select the file hosts located in the /etc directory in the file browser.
5. Answer **Yes** to the question **Show in browser if possible?**.
6. Click **Download**.

The hosts file will be displayed in your browser. If you would prefer to download your file to disk, simply answer **No** in step 5.

How it works...

Webmin accesses the file you select from your system disk. If the file contains text, it will be displayed directly in your browser. If you choose to download the file, Webmin will add HTTP headers (such as Content-Disposition: Attachment) to the response to force your browser to display a save dialog, which allows you to save the file on disk instead of displaying it.

See also

> ▶ If you would like to download an entire directory including its content, take a look at the *Downloading a directory and its content* section in the *Managing files and directories on the server* recipe later on in this chapter.

Uploading files to the server

Webmin's graphical interface allows you to easily upload files from your local computer to your server. Webmin also allows you to transfer files from a web URL directly onto your server, without the need to download them to your local computer first.

Getting ready

In this recipe, we'll upload a default welcome message to be served by your Apache web server. Refer to *Chapter 8, Running an Apache Web Server*, for information about setting up Apache.

If you would like to perform the same task, start by preparing a simple HTML file on your local system and saving it as `index.html`. You can of course follow the same steps to upload any other file to any location on your server.

How to do it...

Follow these steps to upload your files on the server:

1. Navigate to **Others | Upload and Download**.
2. Select the **Upload to server** tab.
3. Click one of the four buttons in the **Files to upload** section and select your file from your local disk. Select additional files using the other buttons if needed.
4. Click the ellipsis (**...**) button to the far right of the **File or directory to upload to** field and use the file browser to select the directory into which you wish to upload your files. Choose `/var/www` for the default root directory from which Apache serves files.
5. Set the user who will own the file on disk, or leave the field **Owned by user** set to `root`.

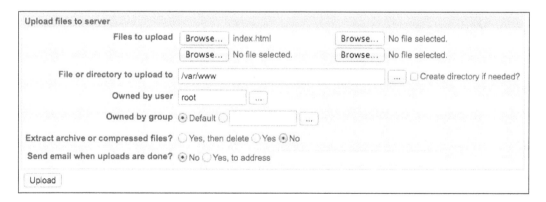

6. Click the **Upload** button.

An upload progress window will pop up to inform you about the status of the upload. After the upload is complete, Webmin will display a screen informing you about how much data was uploaded onto your server.

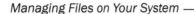
How it works...

Webmin uses the HTTP protocol to transfer files onto your server. Uploaded files will belong to the user selected as owner. This functionality eliminates the need for any additional tools for simple tasks such as uploading a small number of files onto your server.

There's more...

Webmin also allows you to transfer files from a web URL directly onto your server without the need to download them to your local computer first.

Downloading files from the Web directly onto your server

Let's say that you'd like to use jQuery on your welcome webpage. You can download the library directly onto your server if you know its URL. In case of jQuery, you can download it from `http://code.jquery.com/jquery-1.10.0.min.js`.

1. Navigate to **Others | Upload and Download**.
2. Select the **Download from web** tab.
3. Paste the required URLs in to the **URLs to download** text field.
4. Click the ellipsis (**...**) button to the far right of the **Download to file or directory** field and use the file browser to select the directory into which you wish to upload your files. Choose `/var/www` for the default root directory from which Apache serves files.
5. Set the user who will own the file on disk, or leave the field **Owned by user** set to `root`.
6. Set **Download mode** to **Immediately, and show progress**.
7. Click the **Download URLs** button.

A download progress screen will appear, informing you about the status of the download.

Downloading files from the Web in the background

If you want to download a large file from a slower server, Webmin allows you to schedule the download to be executed in the background.

In order to accomplish this, follow the steps in the *Downloading files from the Web directly onto your server* section, but set the **Download mode** field to **In background**. You can set the download time to the current time or later. If you configured Webmin to send mail, as discussed in *Chapter 1, Setting Up Your System*, you can instruct Webmin to notify you when the transfer is complete.

Managing files and directories on the server

Webmin provides a simple but capable file manager, which you can access directly in the browser.

Getting ready

Webmin's file manager runs as a Java applet. In order to use it, you will need to install Java on your local machine and enable its use in the browser. You do not need to install Java on your server.

How to do it...

In this recipe, we'll discuss basic functions of the file manager, such as copying and moving files on your server.

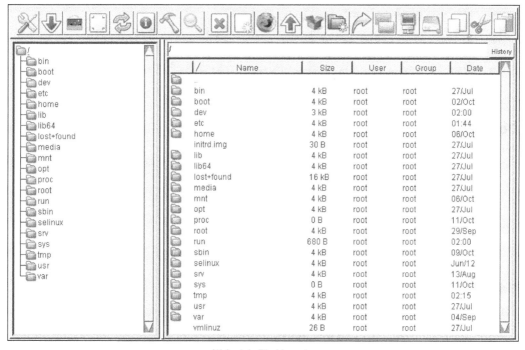

Webmin's File Manager

Copying or moving a file or directory

Perform the following steps to create or move a file or directory:

1. Navigate to **Others | File Manager**.
2. Browse the filesystem to a directory that contains a file or directory you wish to manipulate and click the file to select it.
3. Click the **Copy** button in the toolbar to copy the file or the **Cut** button to move it.
4. Browse the filesystem to the destination directory.
5. Click the **Paste** button.

The file will be transferred from source directory to the destination directory. If the destination directory already contains a file with the same name, a dialog will appear in which you can specify an alternate name or the same name to overwrite the destination file.

Renaming a file or directory

Perform the following steps to rename a file or directory:

1. Navigate to **Others | File Manager**.
2. Browse the filesystem to the directory, which contains the file or directory you wish to rename and click the filename to select it.
3. Click the **Rename** button and provide the new filename in the pop-up dialog.
4. Click the **Rename** button in the pop-up dialog.

Deleting a file or directory

Perform the following steps to delete a file or directory:

1. Navigate to **Others | File Manager**.
2. Browse the filesystem to the directory, which contains the file or directory you wish to delete and click the filename to select it.
3. Click the **Delete** button.
4. Confirm by clicking the **Delete** button in the pop-up dialog.

Editing a file on the server

Perform the following steps to edit a file on the server:

1. Navigate to **Others | File Manager**.
2. Browse the filesystem to the directory, which contains the file you wish to edit and click the filename to select it.
3. Click the **Edit** button.
4. Edit the file content in the pop-up dialog.
5. Click the **Save and close** button in the pop-up dialog to finish editing.

Creating a directory on the server

Perform the following steps to create a directory on the server:

1. Navigate to **Others | File Manager**.
2. Browse the filesystem to the directory in which you wish to create a subdirectory.
3. Find the **New** button with an icon of a directory and click it.
4. Provide the full path for the new directory by appending the name of the new directory to the path in the pop-up window.
5. Click the **Create** button in the pop-up dialog.

Creating a new file on the server

Perform the following steps to create a new file on the server:

1. Navigate to **Others | File Manager**.
2. Browse the filesystem to the directory in which you wish to create a new file.
3. Find the **New** button with an icon of a blank file and click it.
4. Provide the full path for the new file by appending the name of the new file to the path provided in the **Filename** field in the pop-up window.
5. You can optionally place initial content in the file by entering it in the large text area.
6. Click the **Save and close** button in the pop-up dialog to create the new file.

Creating a symbolic link on the server

In many instances, you will find it useful to create symbolic links to files or directories in another location. For most practical purposes, symbolic links behave like the objects they link to, but they are only pointers to the original location. This means that you can have access to a single directory or file from many filesystem paths. Perform the following steps to create a symbolic link on the server:

1. Navigate to **Others | File Manager**.
2. Browse the filesystem to the directory in which you wish to create a new symbolic link.
3. Find the **New** button with an arrow icon, which symbolizes the link.
4. In the **Link from** field, enter the full path of the link you wish to create.
5. In the **Link to** field, enter the full path of the file or directory you're creating a link for.
6. Click the **Create** button to create the link.

Symbolic links can reference absolute paths (those starting with the root directory /), but they can also reference relative paths. In relative paths, two dots denote the parent of the directory in which the link is placed. For instance, if we have `file` in directory A and want to make a link to it in a sibling directory B, we could make a link to `../A/file`. This way, we can move both directories A and B together to another location and the symbolic link would still point to the same file.

Downloading a directory and its content

Webmin's file manager allows you to download an entire directory, including its content, as a compressed archive file, as shown in the following steps:

1. Navigate to **Others | File Manager**.
2. Browse the filesystem to the parent directory of the directory you would like to download.
3. Click the name of the directory to select it.
4. Click the **Save** button in the toolbar.
5. In the pop-up dialog, click the **TAR.GZ** button to download the directory as a tape archive file compressed by GZIP.

The tape archive (TAR) file format is able to preserve most metadata about the files you're downloading, such as ownership, permissions, and extended file attributes (although not SELinux contexts or POSIX ACLs).

You can also choose to download the file in a ZIP format, which may be easier to extract on some systems, but metadata about the files will be lost.

6. Save the file on your local computer.

Extracting files from a compressed archive

If you have a compressed archive on your server in the ZIP, TAR, or GZIP format, Webmin's file manager will allow you to extract its content by performing the following steps:

1. Navigate to **Others | File Manager**.
2. Browse the filesystem to the directory that contains the archive file.
3. Click the name of the archive file to select it.
4. Click the **Extract** button in the toolbar.
5. Click **Yes** in the pop-up dialog.

Please note that if your directory already contains files with the same names as files in your archive, they will be overwritten without further confirmation prompts.

How it works...

Webmin's file manager runs in the Java Virtual Machine on your local PC. The Java applet is embedded in Webmin's webpage and can be accessed in the browser. Whenever you perform an action in the file manager, the Java applet sends a request to your server with instructions about what actions should be performed.

File manager requests are sent using the HTTP protocol. The instructions will be encrypted by SSL if you enabled HTTPS support in Webmin.

Webmin performs those instructions on the server and sends back information about their effect along with other information needed to display on the next screen in the file manager window.

See also

▸   For more information about the functioning of Webmin's file manager, refer to the _Changing file ownership and permissions_ recipe in this chapter.

Changing file ownership and permissions

Webmin's file manager allows you to manipulate standard POSIX file ownership and permissions. The user interface for this function is easy to use and powerful, allowing you to modify files recursively, but distinguish between files and directories.

Every filesystem node (file, directory, and so on) on a UNIX-like system is owned by a single user and a single group. The system also stores permission information for each node with separate permissions for the file owner, group, and everybody else. Standard permissions are listed in the following table:

Binary notation	Octal notation	Permission name	Description
000	0	None	No permission of any kind.
001	1	Execute	Execute a program file or traverse a directory. In most cases, read permission is also needed.
010	2	Write	Write to file or create file entries in directory.

Binary notation	Octal notation	Permission name	Description
100	4	Read	Read file content or list directory content.
011	3	Write and execute	
101	5	Read and execute	
110	6	Read and write	Combinations of the mentioned permissions.
111	7	Read, write, and execute	

The octal notation is commonly used as it is the most concise. For instance, commonly used permissions for files are denoted as 644, which specify 6 (read and write bits) for the file owner, 4 (read bit) for the file's group and all other users. We could specify the permissions as 640 to deny access to any user from outside our group.

The standard permissions for a directory, on the other hand, are denoted as 755, which is similar to 644 but adds the execute bit to all permissions allowing everyone to enter the directory.

[Be careful when setting the third permission for others as this applies to everyone with access to your system.]

If you copy a directory from another system to your server, the ownership and permission information can be lost or improperly set. In this recipe, we'll edit a directory recursively to change the owner and permission for the directory and its content. We'll set the permission to 644 on all files and 755 on all subdirectories.

Getting ready

In this recipe, we'll be using Webmin's file manager, which runs as a Java applet. In order to use it, you will need to install Java on your local machine and enable its use in the browser. You do not need to install Java on your server.

How to do it...

Let's begin. Perform the following steps to change the file ownership and permissions:

1. Navigate to **Others | File Manager**.
2. Browse the filesystem to the directory, which contains a file or directory you wish to manipulate and click the directory name to select it.

3. First, we'll set the permission `755` on the directory and all of its content.

   1. Click the **Info** button in the toolbar.

   2. Mark the checkboxes next to **Read** and **List** for all types: **User**, **Group**, and **Other**.

   3. Mark the checkbox next to **Write** only for **User** (owner) and make sure that **Write** permission is not marked for **Group** and **Other**.

   4. Set the **Apply changes to** option to **This directory and all subdirectories and files**.

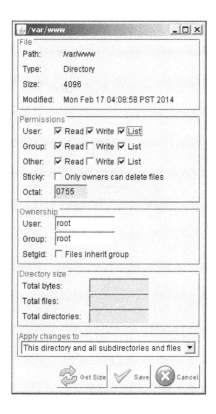

   5. Click the **Save** button.

4. Next, we'll set the permission `644` only on files in the directory and its subdirectories.

   1. Click the **Info** button in the toolbar.

   2. Uncheck the **List** permissions of all types: **User**, **Group**, and **Other**.

   3. Set the **Apply changes to:** option to **Files under this directory and subdirectories**.

   4. Click the **Save** button.

How it works...

Webmin's file manager runs in the Java Virtual Machine on your local PC. The Java applet is embedded in Webmin's webpage and can be accessed in the browser. Whenever you perform an action in the file manager, the Java applet sends an HTTP request to your server with instructions on what actions should be performed. Webmin performs those instructions on the server and sends back information about their effect along with the other information needed to display on the next screen in the file manager window.

There's more...

Webmin's file manager has a number of other options related to file permissions.

Enabling the setuid bit on an executable file

Normally, when a user executes a program from a file, that program will run with the permissions of that user. In special cases, when an executable file is marked with the `setuid` (set user ID upon execution) bit, then the executed program will run with the permissions of the owner of the executable, not the user who is running the program. This is useful in situations where a user has to write something to a file he or she would not normally have access to. For example, when a user updates his or her password, they change the `shadow` file in the `/etc` directory, which normal users don't have access to. Follow these steps to set the setuid bit on a file:

1. Navigate to **Others | File Manager**.
2. Browse the filesystem to the directory, which contains the file you wish to manipulate and click the filename to select it.
3. Click the **Info** button in the toolbar.
4. Mark the checkbox labeled **Setuid** under **Ownership**.
5. Click the **Save** button.

Setting the sticky bit on a directory

The `sticky` bit is a useful feature of directories on modern UNIX-like systems. If a directory has the `sticky` bit set, then files contained within the directory can only be edited or deleted by their respective owners or the root user, regardless of what the other file permissions dictate. A good example of this is the `/tmp` directory, where every user may create files, but they can only delete and rename files they own.

Webmin's file manager allows you to set the `sticky` bit on directories by performing the following steps:

1. Navigate to **Others | File Manager**.
2. Browse the filesystem to the directory, which contains the directory you wish to manipulate and click the directory name to select it.
3. Click the **Info** button in the toolbar.
4. Mark the checkbox labeled **Sticky** under **Permissions**.
5. Click the **Save** button.

Changing ACLs on a directory

If your system supports filesystem **Access Control Lists** (**ACLs**), you can use them to specify additional permissions on files and directories. For example, you may choose to set default permissions which will be applied to all new files created in a directory. If you have a directory where Webmin places backup files, you may choose to make backups inaccessible to other users by default.

You can use Webmin to manipulate ACLs by using the following steps:

1. Navigate to **Others | File Manager**.
2. Browse the filesystem to the directory, which contains the directory you wish to manipulate and click the directory name to select it.
3. Click the **ACL** button in the toolbar.
4. From the dropdown, select **Default Others** and click the **Add ACL of type** button.
5. Uncheck all boxes for **Read**, **Write**, and **Execute**.

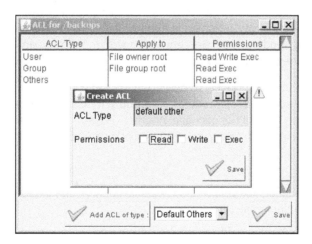

6. Click the **Save** button in the **Create ACL** window and the **Save** button in the main ACL window.

Setting up network-shared folders for Windows

A server running on a local area network can be quite useful as a repository of shared files. If other computers in your local network are running Microsoft Windows, your best choice for setting up a network file server is the Windows standard **Common Internet File System** (**CIFS**) protocol. Webmin can assist you with setting up network shares of this type by installing and helping you configure the Samba package utilities.

It wouldn't be a good idea to use Windows file sharing on the open Internet. Computers out in the open are regularly scanned for vulnerabilities of the Windows file sharing protocol and you could fall victim to an attack if an exploit becomes widespread before a security patch is developed and applied on your system.

Make sure that your firewall blocks incoming external network traffic on **User Datagram Protocol** (**UDP**) ports 137, 138, and 139 as well as TCP ports 137, 139, and 445. All of these ports are used by Windows file sharing and should only be accessible to trusted computers on your local network.

If you need to make network assets available via the Internet, a better choice would be to use the SFTP or FTP protocols, described later in this chapter.

Getting ready

In order to set up Windows file sharing on your server, you need to install the Samba package from your distribution repository. If Samba is already installed, you will find the **Samba Windows File Sharing** module in the **Servers** section of Webmin's main menu; otherwise, you will find it in the **Un-used Modules** section.

On most systems, Webmin will be able to download the Samba package and its dependencies automatically. Navigate to **Un-used Modules | Samba Windows File Sharing** and click the link to download and install the package. Alternatively, you can follow the *Installing software packages* recipe from *Chapter 1, Setting Up Your System*, and install the package named samba.

 At the time of this publication, Webmin supports Samba Version 3 series, not yet the newer Samba 4.

After installation, follow the *Allowing access to a service through the firewall* recipe from *Chapter 3, Securing Your System*, to unblock TCP ports 137, 139, and 445 and UDP ports 137-139.

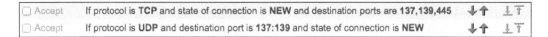

Follow the *Controlling which system services are started at boot* recipe from *Chapter 1, Setting Up Your System*, to make sure that services nmb, smb, and winbind are started and set to start automatically at boot time.

Finally, we can set how our server will be visible on the network. Navigate to **Servers | Samba Windows File Sharing | Windows Networking** and set **Workgroup** to WORKGROUP or another name used in your organization. Set **Server description** to the name by which you want the server to be visible on the network. You can set the description field to %h, which will cause Samba to use the server's default hostname.

How to do it...

In this recipe, we will create a shared network folder available to the users of Windows. Linux and OS X are also capable of accessing CIFS servers, so this type of network-attached storage will be broadly available on your local network.

Creating a UNIX pseudo user

We will create a shared network folder accessible to multiple users. This shared resource must be stored on our server's disk and will have to belong to a UNIX user. In order to simplify management of file ownership and permissions, we will create a special pseudo user named samba. This user will not be associated with any one person and the account will not have the ability to log into our system. The user will simply own all files in the shared directory, which we'll create in /srv/samba. Follow the *Creating a system user account* recipe from *Chapter 2, User Management*, to create a pseudo user. Use the following settings:

- **Username**: samba
- **Real name**: Samba Network Pseudo-user
- **Home directory**: /srv/samba
- **Shell**: /usr/sbin/nologin

 The nologin binary may be placed under another path, such as /sbin/nologin, on your system. You may also use /bin/false, which will not return a polite message to the user but also prevents logging in.

- ▸ **Password: No login allowed**
- ▸ **Primary group: New group with same name as user**
- ▸ **Copy template files to home directory?: No**
- ▸ **Create user in other modules?: No**

These settings are shown in the following screenshot:

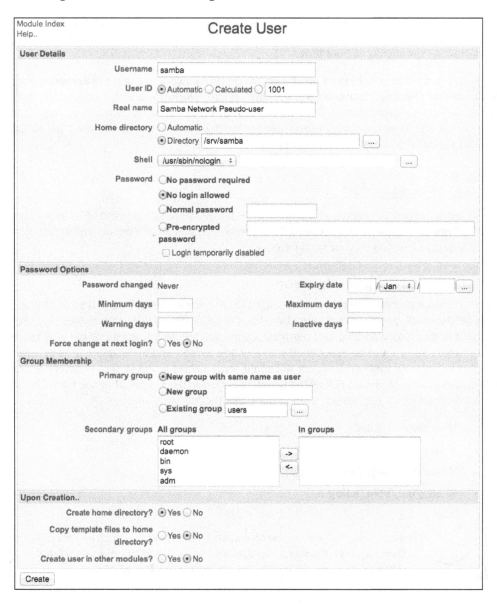

Creating a Samba shared network folder

The next step is creating the actual shared network resource. Webmin makes this part quite easy. Perform the following steps to create a shared network folder:

1. Navigate to **Servers | Samba Windows File Sharing**.
2. Click the **Create a new file share** link.
3. Set **Share name** to `SharedFolder` or a more appropriate description.
4. Set **Directory to share** to `/srv/samba`.
5. Since we already created the directory when setting up a pseudo user account, answer **No** to **Automatically create directory?**.
6. Set both **Available** and **Browseable** to **Yes**.
7. Click the **Create** button.

Creating Samba user accounts

Samba stores its own list of users separate from your system's user list. Webmin allows you to easily create Samba user accounts for system users by performing the following steps:

1. Navigate to **Servers | Samba Windows File Sharing**.
2. Click **Convert Users** in the **Samba Users** section.
3. Set **Unix users to convert** to **Only listed users or UID ranges** and use the ellipsis button (**...**) to bring up the user-selector pop up and select a user you wish to grant Samba access to.
4. Set **For newly created users, set the password to** to **Use this password** and type in a password for the user.
5. Click the **Convert Users** button.

The user may change his or her password through Usermin. Refer to the *Installing Usermin* recipe in *Chapter 2, User Management*, for information about setting up Usermin.

If the user's name and password on your Samba server matches their username and password on Windows, they should be able to authenticate transparently, without retyping their password when accessing shared folders.

Granting Samba users access to the shared folder

The final part of the process is to grant Samba users access to the shared folder we created. We'll also inform Samba that it should set UNIX ownership of all incoming files to the pseudo user `samba` created in the preceding section. Perform the following steps to grant Samba users access to the shared folder:

1. Navigate to **Servers | Samba Windows File Sharing**.
2. Click the name of the share we just created.
3. On the **Edit File Share** screen, click the **Security and Access Control** icon.
4. Set **Writable?** to **Yes**.
5. Set **Read/write users** to a list of users who should have write access to the shared folder. Use the ellipsis (**...**) button to bring up the helpful user-selector pop up.
6. Click the **Save** button.
7. Back on the **Edit File Share** screen, click the **File Permissions** icon.
8. Set **Force Unix user** and **Force Unix group** to `samba`.
9. Click the **Save** button.

> If you're running **Security Enhanced Linux (SELinux)**, you may run into a problem wherein your users are able to access shares but cannot list, read, or write files. This is caused by SELinux blocking what it considers unauthorized access to the underlying directory. You may overcome this problem by either disabling SELinux or configuring a SELinux security context for `/srv/samba`. Take a look at this link for more information: `http://fedoraproject.org/wiki/SELinux/samba`.

After a moment, you should be able to access your shares from other computers on the network. Look for your server in the Windows network `WORKGROUP` or in the **Shared** sidebar of Finder on OS X.

How it works...

Samba's configuration is stored in `/etc/smb.conf` or `/etc/samba/smb.conf` depending on the operating system. Webmin's graphical interface allows you to edit options stored in this and associated files to modify Samba's configuration without learning this file's complex syntax. Samba automatically re-reads its configuration quite often, so there should be no need to restart `smb` and associated daemons after making most common configuration changes.

There's more...

There is quite a lot more you can do with Samba, but we don't have space here to cover it all. Topics we have to omit include: sharing server-attached printers on your network, authenticating users using Microsoft's Active Directory services, setting up access control lists to maintain file ownership on both Windows and UNIX systems, and so on.

In the rest of this section, we'll cover just a few additional features Webmin can help you with.

Sharing home directories

On many systems, Samba creates home directory shares automatically. This allows users to access files stored in their home directories on your server over the network. If this is a feature you didn't intend to activate, you can disable it temporarily or delete the share configuration permanently. Here are the steps to make home directories unavailable:

1. Navigate to **Servers | Samba Windows File Sharing**.
2. Click **SharedFolder**.
3. Set **Available?** to **No**.
4. Click the **Save** button.

Checking who's connected and disconnecting sessions

If you would like to see who's connected to your server via Samba and disconnect them, perform the following steps:

1. Navigate to **Servers | Samba Windows File Sharing**.
2. Click the **View all connections** link.
3. Mark the process IDs associated with the sessions you would like to disconnect.
4. Click the **Disconnect Selected Users** button.

[Disconnecting a user whose files are open may bring programs on their Windows machine to a halt. Use caution when disconnecting users.]

Debugging Samba

If you run into problems with Samba, you should check for error messages in its log files. Samba's log messages are stored in /var/log/samba. You will find multiple files there, as the server keeps separate files for each connecting client. By default, Samba's logging is very quiet because logging every action would seriously slow the service down. If you're having problems, you may wish to temporarily increase the verbosity of Samba's logging; just make sure to set it back to defaults when you're done. Perform the following steps to change Samba's log verbosity level:

1. Navigate to **Servers | Samba Windows File Sharing | Miscellaneous Options**.
2. Set **Debug Level** to a higher value. Start with **1** and increase it further if you still don't find useful information in the log files.
3. Click the **Save** button.
4. On the **Samba Windows File Sharing** screen, click the **Restart Samba Servers** button. This will output information about how the server starts to log messages, which may contain useful diagnostic messages.

Mounting a Windows-shared folder

It's quite common for network attached storage volumes to use the CIFS protocol. Tools that allow setting up such sharing are built into popular operating systems such as Microsoft Windows and OS X. Many NAS devices also use this protocol, often running a version of the Samba package for Linux. Mounting CIFS shares in desktop environments is quite simple, but what if you want your server to have permanent access to a CIFS volume? Webmin can help you set up an automounting network filesystem that will connect to a remote CIFS server during system boot.

Getting ready

Before your system can access CIFS network volumes, you will need to install an additional package typically named cifs-utils. Refer to the *Installing software packages* recipe from *Chapter 1, Setting Up Your System*, for information about how to install packages using Webmin.

How to do it...

Follow these steps to mount a Windows shared folder in your filesystem:

1. Because we'll need to store the CIFS user credentials (username and password) in plain text, we need to start by creating a protected hidden file. Create a file on your server with the path `/root/.smbcredentials` and write the following lines in it, replacing `cifsusername` and `cifspassword` with the username and password of a user with access to the CIFS shared folder. Set the file's owner to `root` and permissions to `600`.

   ```
   username=cifsusername
   password=cifspassword
   ```

    You can use Webmin's file manager to create the file and edit its permissions. Check the *Managing files and directories on the server* recipe in this chapter.

2. Navigate to **System | Disk and Network Filesystems**.
3. Select **Common Internet Filesystem (cifs)** from the **Type** dropdown.
4. Click the **Add Mount** button.
5. Set **Mounted as** to a local path such as `/mnt/remoteshare`.
6. Set **Save mount?** to **Save and mount at boot**.
7. Set **Server Name** to the IP or fully qualified domain name of the remote CIFS server.
8. Set **Share Name** to the name of the remote share. If you created the share using the recipe in this chapter, the name would be `SharedFolder`.
9. Set **Credentials File** to `/root/.smbcredentials`.
10. Set **User files are owned by** to `root`.
11. Set **Group files are owned** by to `users`.

    You may specify another user or create a special pseudo user for use with Samba, as described in the *Setting up network-shared folders for Windows* recipe in this chapter.

12. Set **File permissions** to `0660`.

13. Set **Directory permissions** to `0770`.

14. Click the **Create** button.

Common Internet Filesystem Mount Details	
Mounted as	/mnt/remoteshare `...`
Save mount?	⦿ Save and mount at boot ◯ Save ◯ Don't save
Mount now?	⦿ Mount ◯ Don't mount
Server Name	192.168.1.50 Share Name SharedFolder

Mount Options	
Login Name	Login Password
Credentials File /root/.smbcredentials `...`	User files are owned by root `...`
Group files are owned by users `...`	File permissions ◯ Default ⦿ 0660
Directory permissions ◯ Default ⦿ 0770	Read-only? ◯ Yes ⦿ No
Allow users to mount this filesystem? ◯ Yes ⦿ No	
Client Name ⦿ Automatic ◯	
Server Address ⦿ Automatic ◯	
Workgroup ⦿ Automatic ◯	Code page ⦿ Default ◯
IO character set ⦿ Default ◯	

How it works...

The `/etc/fstab` directory contains information about all filesystems mounted by your system during boot. This includes both local disks and remote network volumes. When creating a permanent CIFS mount, Webmin creates an additional line in your file. This line will have the following format:

```
\\192.168.1.50\sharedfolder   /mnt/remoteshare     cifs
    credentials=/root/.smbcredentials,nounix,uid=0,
    gid=100,dir_mode=0770,file_mode=0660     0     0
```

The preceding line contains the following information:

▶ `192.168.1.50`: This is the IP or domain name of the CIFS server.

▶ `sharedfolder`: This is the name of the CIFS share.

▶ `/mnt/remoteshare`: This is the local file path to the directory where the share will be mounted.

- /root/.smbcredentials: This is the path to the file that stores the CIFS username and password.

- uid=0: This specifies that shared files are owned by the user root.

- gid=100: This specifies that shared files are owned by the users group, which will usually allow all of your system users to access them.

- file_mode=0660 and dir_mode=0770: These specify the permissions displayed on all shared files—read, write, and list—for all members of the users group.

There's more...

If you want to mount a CIFS share once and not make it a permanent fixture of your server's filesystem, you can simplify this recipe.

Follow the steps given in the *How to do it...* section in this recipe, but instead of creating a credentials file, put the username and password in the **Login Name** and **Login Password** fields. Also set **Save Mount** to **Don't save**.

This is equivalent to executing the following command:

```
$ sudo mount -t cifs //192.168.1.50/sharedfolder
  /mnt/remoteshare-o username=cifsusername,
  password=cifspassword,file_mode=0660,dir_mode=0770,
  nounix,uid=0,gid=100
```

Setting up an NFS-shared volume

Network File System (**NFS**) is a distributed filesystem protocol designed to allow systems to share file resources over the network. An NFS server can export part of its filesystem, and then a remote client system can mount the exported directories as part of its local filesystem. Webmin can assist you with exporting directories for sharing using NFS.

 NFS v3 preserves UNIX permissions and file ownership, but the job of checking who's who is left up to the client system. That means that if the NFS server has a user with a uid value of 500, then the same user should have the same uid number on the NFS client system. Otherwise, his files may be assigned to a different user or no user at all. This is an important security consideration when setting up NFS servers and clients. Make sure that both systems have the same user accounts.

Getting ready

The NFS server may come built into your system at installation. If it is, Webmin should recognize it and enable the NFS Exports module. If you find the module listed in the **Networking** section of the menu, the NFS server should already be installed; otherwise, we'll need to install it.

Depending on your system, the NFS server comes in a package named `nfs-kernel-server` or `nfs-utils`. Find the appropriate package in your repository and install it. Refer to the *Installing software packages* recipe in *Chapter 1, Setting Up Your System,* for more information.

Go to **System** | **Bootup and Shutdown** and verify that the `rpcbind` service is running on our system. If it isn't, select it and click the **Start Now and On Boot** button.

Running an NFS server on a system protected by firewall is a little tricky. Port numbers for various components of the NFS server that are listening are assigned dynamically and can change over time. You can coerce your system to assign static port numbers to the NFS-related services through editing configuration files. The location of these files and their syntax is specific to your system distribution and version. Do a web search for `nfs iptables` and the name of your OS to find instructions specific to your system.

If your system is running on a secure internal network protected by a firewall on another machine, you can also consider disabling the firewall on your NFS server.

How to do it...

In this recipe, we will export `/home/shared` and make it available to users of a remote system with the IP 192.168.1.60. We will use the simpler and more broadly supported NFS Version 3. Perform the following steps to set up an NFS shared volume:

1. Navigate to **Networking** | **NFS Exports**.
2. Click the **Add a new export** link.
3. Set **NFS Version** to **3**.

You may not see the version selection screen when setting up the first NFS export. Don't worry about that; Version 3 is the default.

4. Set **Directory to export** to `/home/shared`.

5. Set **Export** to **Host(s)** and specify the destination host IP or domain name, for example, `192.168.1.60`.

6. Set **Read-only?** to **No**.

7. Set **Trust remote users** to **Everyone except root** as shown in the following screenshot:

Module Index
Help..

Create Export

Export details

NFS Version	○ 4 ⊙ 3 (or lower)
NFSv4 Pseudofilesystem to export	/export `...`

Directory to export	/home/shared `...` in /home/shared	
Active?	⊙ Yes ○ No	
Export to.. (with or without Authentication)	○ Everyone ⊙ Host(s) 192.168.1.60	
	○ WebNFS clients ○ NIS Netgroup	
⊙ sys	○ IPv4 Network	Netmask
	○ IPv6 Address	/
	○ krb5 lipkey spkm-3	
Security level	⊙ None ○ Integrity ○ Privacy (including Integrity)	

Export security

Read-only?	○ Yes ⊙ No	Clients must be on secure port?	⊙ Yes ○ No
Disable subtree checking?	○ Yes ⊙ No	Hide the filesystem?	⊙ Yes ○ No
Immediately sync all writes?	○ Yes ○ No ⊙ Default		
Trust remote users	○ Everyone ⊙ Everyone except root ○ Nobody		
Treat untrusted users as	⊙ Default ○ `...`	Treat untrusted groups as	⊙ Default ○ `...`

NFSv2-specific options

Make symbolic links relative?	○ Yes ⊙ No	Deny access to directory?	○ Yes ⊙ No
Don't trust UIDs	⊙ None ○	Don't trust GIDs	⊙ None ○

Create

> The `root` user account is "squashed" by default when traversing NFS. This means that `root` from the client system appears as the user `nobody` on the server. You can change this behavior using the **Trust remote users: Everyone** option (which sets the `no_root_squash` flag on the export). This has serious security considerations and should only be done if absolutely necessary as you must trust all users with root access to all remote machines allowed to mount this share.

8. Click the **Create** button.

9. Back on the **NFS Exports** screen, click the **Apply Changes** button.

How it works...

NFS exports are listed in `/etc/exports`. When creating an export, Webmin adds a line to this file, which is read by the NFS server. For instance, the export we created would be represented by this simple entry:

```
/home/shared      192.168.1.60  (rw)
```

The first field in the line represents the directory that will be exported (`/home/shared`), followed by the IP or domain name of the machine, which will be able to access the export and options. In this simple case, the only option present is `rw`, which designates that the export can be mounted in read-write mode.

There's more...

If you want to check which exports are currently being served by your NFS server, you can execute the following command:

```
$ sudo exportfs
```

Granting access to multiple clients

If you would like to make the NFS export available to more than one machine, you can specify the hosts in terms of a wildcard. For instance, to make the export available to all servers in the `intra.mydomain.com` domain, you could set **Host(s)** to `*.intra.mydomain.com`.

If you would rather specify a subnet, you can use the **IPv4 Network** and **Netmask** fields instead. For instance, to make your export available to all machines with IPs in the 192.168.1.0-192.168.1.255 range, you would set **IPv4 Network** to `192.168.1.0` and **Netmask** to `24`.

See also

> ▶ Take a look at the *Mounting a remote NFS volume* recipe in this chapter for information about how you can make use of the exported folder on a client machine.

Mounting a remote NFS volume

If your server has access to a remote volume exported using NFS, Webmin can assist you with mounting the volume as part of your filesystem.

Getting ready

NFS client support may come installed by default on your system or have been installed together with NFS server software. Verify that the package named `nfs-utils` or `nfs-common` (depending on your system) is installed, or install it if needed. Refer to the *Inspecting installed software packages* and *Installing software packages* recipes in *Chapter 1*, *Setting Up Your System*, for more information.

How to do it...

In this recipe, we'll mount the `/home/shared` directory exported by a remote NFS server with the IP 192.168.1.50 in the local mount point `/mnt/remoteshare`. Perform the following steps to mount a remote NFS volume:

1. Navigate to **Networking | NFS Exports**.
2. Select **Network Filesystem (nfs)** from the **Type** dropdown.
3. Click the **Add mount** button.
4. Set **Mounted as** to `/mnt/remoteshare`.
5. Set **NFS Hostname** to `192.168.1.50`.
6. Set **NFS Directory** to `/home/shared`.

> At this stage, it's a good idea to click the ellipsis (...) button next to the **NFS Directory** field. A list of available exported directories should appear. If it does not, there may be a problem with the network connection or the NFS server is not exporting the directory to our client system properly.

7. Set **Wait until network interfaces are up?** to **Yes**.
8. Set **Retry mounts in background?** to **Yes**.
9. Set **Allow user interrupt?** to **Yes** as shown in the following screenshot:

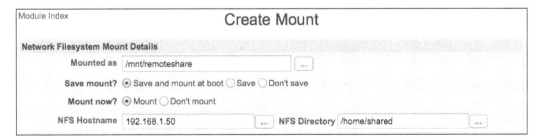

10. Click the **Create** button.

How it works...

During boot, your system mounts filesystems based on a description placed in `/etc/fstab`. When creating a permanent mount point, Webmin adds a line to this file corresponding to the NFS export.

This is the entry created by this recipe:

```
192.168.1.50:/home/shared       /mnt/remoteshare
   nfs       _netdev,intr,bg     0       0
```

The preceding entry contains the following fields:

- ▸ `192.168.1.50:/home/shared` specifies the address of the remote server and the path of the exported directory separated by a colon.
- ▸ `/mnt/remoteshare` specifies the local mount point location.
- ▸ `nfs` specifies that the entry represents an NFS export.
- ▸ `_netdev,intr,bg` field specifies mounting options, which we selected when creating the share. For instance, the `_netdev` option tells the system to wait for mounting until the network is available.
- ▸ The final two fields set to `0` specify that this filesystem should not be considered during backup or disk checking.

There's more...

You don't have to make an entry in `/etc/fstab` to mount an NFS volume temporarily. You can do this through Webmin; just set the **Save** option to **Don't save**. This is equivalent to issuing the following command:

```
$ sudo mount -t nfs -o intr,bg 192.168.1.50:/home/
  shared /mnt/remoteshare
```

Mounting NFS v4 exports

Webmin can also mount shares exported by NFS Version 4. In this version of NFS, the organization of exports is slightly different. Directories are not exported one by one, but rather as part of an entire pseudo filesystem. You mount this entire filesystem in your mount point, and the exported directories become subdirectories of the mount point.

The differences in creating an NFS v4 mount point using Webmin are twofold. You should select **Network Filesystem v4 (nfs4)** from the **Type** dropdown and set **NFS Directory** to / since the entire exported filesystem will be mounted in one location.

See also

▶ Take a look at the *Setting up an NFS-shared volume* recipe in this chapter for information about how you can set up NFS exports on your server.

Giving users access to your server via SFTP

Users may need to transfer files to and from your server over the Internet. You can enable this facility in a simple and secure way using **SSH File Transfer Protocol** (**SFTP**). Setting this up does not require installing any software other than the SSH server, which you are most likely running anyway, to control your server remotely. All users who have access to SSH may also use SFTP client programs (such as Filezilla) to access your server.

In this recipe, we will set up an account for a user who will be able to transfer files to your server but will not have shell access to your system.

Getting ready

If you haven't installed the SSH server on your system yet, follow the *Installing software packages* recipe in *Chapter 1, Setting Up Your System*, to install the `openssh-server` package.

After installation, follow the *Allowing access to a service through the firewall* recipe from *Chapter 3, Securing Your System*, to unblock TCP port 22.

How to do it...

In order to enable SFTP-only access to a user, we will have to set the user's shell to the `sftp-server` program. Let's begin by finding the location of this program on your system:

1. Navigate to **Servers | SSH Server | Edit Config Files**.
2. Make sure that the `sshd_config` (server configuration) file is selected from the dropdown and not the `ssh_config` file (default client configuration).
3. Find the line beginning with `Subsystem sftp`. On my Debian system, this line is as follows:

   ```
   Subsystem sftp /usr/lib/openssh/sftp-server
   ```

This means that the SFTP server binary is located at `/usr/lib/openssh/sftp-server`.

The next step is to add the path to the SFTP server binary to the list of available user shells listed in the `/etc/shells` file. You can do this by executing the following command as the user `root`:

```
echo '/usr/lib/openssh/sftp-server' >> /etc/shells
```

Follow these steps to grant users SFTP access to your server without granting them the ability to log in:

1. Navigate to **System | Users and Groups**.

2. Click the name of a user you would like to give SFTP access but not allow the ability to log in otherwise.

3. Change the users' **Shell** to `sftp-server`, which should be present in the dropdown list of available shells.

The user will now be able to access your server over SFTP. The user will not have the ability to log into your system's command-line shell.

> Users with shell set to `sftp-server` have access to your server's entire filesystem, in accordance with Unix permissions. You can grant users read and write permissions to other directories on your system if you want them to access files there.

To create additional SFTP-only users, follow the *Creating a system user account* recipe from *Chapter 2, User Management*, but make sure to set their **Shell** to `sftp-server`.

> When users connect to your server over SFTP, the first directory listing they will see is their home directory. Keep in mind that you can set a user's home directory to any place in the filesystem. You could also make life easier for your users by creating symbolic links in their home directories to locations on the system that they should be able to access most easily.

How it works...

The user's shell program is the first program started by the system for the user when they log in. If this shell is `sftp-server`, then the user can only interact with this program. This is what is needed for transferring files, but it won't allow the user to perform other actions on your system or start other programs.

The definitions of user accounts are stored in `/etc/passwd`. Webmin edits this file when we create accounts or change users' shell program settings.

See also

▶   For information about setting up a dedicated FTP service, take a look at the *Giving users access to your server via FTP* recipe in this chapter.

Giving users access to your server via FTP

The **File Transfer Protocol** (**FTP**) is one of the most popular data exchange protocols on the Internet. FTP servers allow your users to authenticate and upload files onto your machine. This type of access does not require granting users other privileges on your server and you may restrict access over FTP to a user's home directory.

 Please note that FTP is a very insecure protocol, because the username and password are exchanged without encryption unless you enable TLS. If your server is running in an untrusted network, consider running SFTP instead.

How to do it...

The first step toward allowing your users to access your system via FTP is to install an FTP server daemon. We'll be using the stable and feature-rich ProFTPd server, which Webmin supports well. Follow these steps to set up an FTP server:

1. Navigate to **Un-used Modules | ProFTPD Server**.

2. Click the link; this instructs Webmin to download and install the package automatically.

 At this stage, you may run into a problem if the ProFTPD package is not found in your system distribution's package repository. Most distributions include ProFTPD packages, but you may need to activate an additional repository.

For instance, if you're running a Linux distribution from the RedHat family (RHEL, CentOS, Fedora, and so on), you should add the **Extra Packages for Enterprise Linux** (**EPEL**) repository by executing a command as shown in the following:

```
$ sudo rpm -Uvh http://download.fedoraproject.
  org/pub/epel/6/x86_64/epel-release-6-8.noarch.rpm
```

On 32-bit (i386) systems, substitute `x86_64` with `i386`.

At the time of writing this book, the latest version of EPEL's index is 6.8; check what the latest version currently is at the EPEL site and modify the URL in the command if needed. More information can be found at `http://fedoraproject.org/wiki/EPEL`.

3. Refresh the page to update Webmin's interface.

4. Navigate to **System | Bootup and Shutdown**, check the box next to `proftpd`, and click the **Start Now and On Boot** button.

If the server doesn't start, run the following command to check your configuration:

```
$ sudo proftpd --configtest
```

You may see a warning such as this:

```
warning: unable to determine IP address of 'server-name'
```

This means that your server cannot determine its own IP address based on its hostname. The easiest way to fix this is to follow these steps:

1. Navigate to **Networking | Network Configuration | Host Addresses**.
2. Click the **Add a new host address** link.
3. Specify **IP Address** as `127.0.0.1` and **Hostnames** as `server-name`. Just substitute `server-name` with your server's hostname.
4. Click the **Create** button.

> This adds the following line to your `/etc/hosts` file:
> `127.0.0.1    server-name`

Opening FTP access in your firewall

If clients connect to your server from behind a firewall, you should use passive mode for establishing FTP connections. Follow these steps to tell ProFTPd which range of ports it should use for passive connections and then to open those ports along with port `21` on your firewall.

1. Navigate to **Servers | ProFTPD Server | Networking Options**.
2. Set **PASV port range** to a range within the IANA-recommended numbering for dynamic ports. For instance, between `60000` and `60099`. The size of this range determines how many concurrent clients can connect to your server in passive mode.
3. Click the **Save** button.
4. Back on the **ProFTPd Server** module page, click the **Apply Changes** button.
5. Follow the *Allowing access to a service through the firewall* recipe from *Chapter 3, Securing Your System*, and allow incoming TCP connections on port `21` and ports in the range set above `60000-60099` as shown in the following screenshot:

Action	Condition
☐ Accept	If state of connection is **ESTABLISHED,RELATED**
☐ Accept	If protocol is **TCP** and destination port is **21** and state of connection is **NEW**
☐ Accept	If protocol is **TCP** and destination port is **60000:60099** and state of connection is **NEW**

At this stage, your FTP server should be up and running. Try to connect to it from another computer using an FTP client. Try to log in as any regular user other then root.

If you're using SELinux, you may be unable to log into your FTP server and may find strange `Permission denied` error messages in ProFTPd's log. If this is the case, you'll need to set a SELinux flag, which allows FTP access. You can do this by executing one of the following commands:

To allow FTP access to user home directories only, use this:

```
$ sudo setsebool ftp_home_dir on
```

To allow FTP access to the entire filesystem, use this:

```
$ sudo setsebool allow_ftpd_full_access on
```

How it works...

Webmin is able to download and install the ProFTPd package using your system's package management system. The package comes with a startup script through which we started the server and set it to launch during system startup.

Passive and active FTP connections

File Transfer Protocol uses two simultaneous connections to exchange data between the server and client. One connection is used to send instructions (command channel) and the other to transfer files (data channel). The command channel is always opened by the client, which establishes a connection with your server on a port dedicated to FTP (usually, number 21). The data channel, however, can be opened in two different ways:

  ▶ **Active (non-passive)**: The server actively opens the data connection to the client. This is not a popular method, because client machines are often hidden behind multiple layers of firewalls and NATs, which makes the connection impossible.

  ▶ **Passive**: Here, the server sends the client a port number and then passively waits for the client to connect to that port. The number of the port is assigned dynamically from a range of ephemeral port numbers. The **Internet Assigned Numbers Authority** (**IANA**) suggests using numbers between 49152 and 65535 for dynamic ports.

Global configuration and virtual servers

The ProFTPd service can run multiple virtual servers with different configurations. Each virtual server runs on a different IP, so if your server is connected to the network or multiple networks using different interfaces, you can set up a different FTP server with a different configuration on each IP. The server-specific settings are accessible in Webmin via the **Virtual Servers** section. It will contain at least one configuration—**Default Server**. Settings in the **Global Configuration** section apply to all servers, but each virtual server may choose whether to use the default global value or override it. In most cases, your server will only run one virtual server. In such cases, there is no practical difference between storing settings in the **Global Configuration** or the **Default Server** sections. You should keep this in mind, however, because if you change a setting in **Global Configuration** and the change does not seem to have an effect, it may be overridden in the **Default Server** configuration.

There's more...

The ProFTPd server is very flexible. Here are some common options you may wish to set.

Restricting access to users' home directories

If you would like users to be able to access only files in their home directories using FTP, perform the following steps:

1. Navigate to **Servers | ProFTPD Server**.
2. Click **Default Server** in the **Virtual Servers** section.
3. Click **Files and Directories**.
4. In the **Limit users to directories** section, select **Home directory**.
5. Click the **Save** button.

Denying FTP access to some users

If you would like to deny some users access over FTP, perform the following steps:

1. Navigate to **Servers | ProFTPD Server | Denied FTP Users**.
2. You will see a list of system users who are denied access over FTP. Add the usernames of users you would like to prevent from accessing your server over FTP to the end of the list (one username per line).
3. Click the **Save** button.

FTP-only users

You may allow users to access your server over FTP, but prevent them from being able to log into your server otherwise, by performing the following steps:

1. Navigate to **System | Users and Groups**.

2. Click the username of the user you want to restrict from logging in.

3. Set user's **Shell** to `/usr/sbin/nologin`.

 The `nologin` binary may be placed under another path, such as `/sbin/nologin`, on your system.

4. Click the **Save** button.

See also

▸ You may enable file sharing on your server without installing an additional FTP server, relying on the SSH server instead. For more information, take a look at the *Giving users access to your server via SFTP* recipe in this chapter.

7
Backing Up Your System

In this chapter, we will cover the following topics:

- ▶ Backing up configuration files
- ▶ Restoring configuration files from backup
- ▶ Automatically backing up configuration files
- ▶ Creating a backup of a selected directory
- ▶ Creating a backup of an entire mount point
- ▶ Backing up to a remote host
- ▶ Setting up automatic backups
- ▶ Backing up databases

Introduction

Data stored on your server is usually more important and valuable than the server hardware on which it is stored. Keeping your server secure and your data safe is one of the top priorities of a system administrator. As much as we hope to avoid trouble such as hardware failures or malicious security breaches, we need to be prepared to fix the consequences of these problems. Making regular backups of your data is essential to recover from unforeseen disasters. You should also regularly test the backups you create to make sure they will actually allow you to recover data when you need it.

In this chapter, we will provide recipes that demonstrate how Webmin helps you keep a backup of the following things:

- ▶ Data files on your server, such as the source code of your applications and data entered and uploaded by users. See *Creating a backup of a selected directory*.
- ▶ Information stored in databases. See *Backing up databases*.
- ▶ Configuration settings. See *Backing up configuration files*.
- ▶ The entire server filesystem. See *Creating a backup of an entire mount point*.

Keep the following things in mind when designing your backup strategy:

- **Complete or incremental backups**: A complete backup of a server or directory stores every file from that location. A backup of this type may be quite large, even if it is compressed, and your server may need a long time to create it. An incremental backup, on the other hand, stores only the files that were changed since the previous backup. This consumes much less space and can be completed quickly. On the other hand, incremental backups are slightly harder to restore, because you must first restore your last complete backup and then add files from the incremental backups created since the complete backup was created.

- **Online or offline backups**: An online backup is readily accessible by your server or another computer, while an offline backup hand is stored on a tape or disconnected disk on a shelf. It cannot be accessed without the intervention of a human. Online backups are more convenient, but if a malicious attacker takes over your system, he/she can erase them. It's a good idea to keep offline copies of your data, as well.

- **Local or offsite backups**: Keeping your backups in the same building as your servers will not protect you in the case of a fire or other disaster. You may want to keep additional backups in another remote location.

A perfect backup strategy would store daily (and maybe even hourly) incremental backups and periodic (weekly or monthly) full backups in offline and offsite form. The number of backups you keep will determine how far back in time you can go to retrieve a lost or corrupted file.

[

Backups may contain sensitive data, such as passwords or other confidential information. Make sure to store backups securely, perhaps consider encrypting files stored offsite.
]

In this chapter, we'll demonstrate how to create backups, but it's up to you to make sure that the backup files are stored in a safe location and regularly tested.

Backing up configuration files

You spend a lot of time setting up your system and optimizing its settings for the best performance and features. Erasing a configuration file or even making changes that turn out not to be optimal can have dire consequences, especially in a production setting. Before making changes, you should make a backup of configuration files and keep it handy in case you need to revert to the previous configuration. Webmin has a facility to help you do just that.

Getting ready

In this recipe, we will create backup files with names containing the current date. We need to enable this feature. So, before starting the backup process, navigate to **Webmin | Backup Configuration Files | Module Config** and answer **Yes** to the question, **Do strftime substitution of backup destinations?**.

How to do it...

Perform the following steps to back up the configuration files:

1. Create a directory to store local backups in the root directory, for example, /backups.

Make sure that your backup directory is stored on a partition with enough disk space so you don't accidentally fill up your entire disk. Placing /backups on a separate partition or in /var/backups may be a good idea.

You should also protect the backup location from prying eyes. You can use permissions and ACLs to do this, as explained in the *Changing ACLs on a directory* section of the *Changing file ownership and permissions* recipe in *Chapter 6, Managing Files on Your System*.

2. Navigate to **Webmin | Backup Configuration Files**.
3. Select the **Backup now** tab.
4. From the **Modules to back up** list, select the module you're planning to work with, for instance, **Webmin Configuration**.

You can backup multiple modules, or even all of them, if you want a more complete backup.

5. Set **Backup destination** to **Local file** and specify the following for a filename:
    /backups/webmin-config-%Y%m%d%H%M.tgz.

6. Set **Include in backup** to **Server configuration files**:

Backup configuration now			
Modules to backup	ADSL Client **Apache Webserver** BIND DNS Server Bacula Backup System Bandwidth Monitoring **Bootup and Shutdown** CD Burner CVS Server Configuration Engine DHCP Server		
Backup destination	⦿ Local file	/backups/webmin-config-%Y%m%d%H%M.tgz	...
	○ FTP server		file on server
	Login as user michal		with password
	Server port ⦿ Default ○		
	○ SSH server		file on server
	Login as user		with password
	Server port ⦿ Default ○		
	○ Download in browser		
Include in backup	☐ Webmin module configuration files ☑ Server configuration files ☐ Other listed files ..		

7. Click the **Backup Now** button.

Webmin configuration files will be backed up in a file in the /backups directory. The name of the file will contain the date and time of the backup.

How it works...

Webmin knows which configuration files are used by the services it helps you configure. When you back up configuration files for a given module, Webmin creates a compressed TAR file with those files in the location you specify.

Since we activated strftime substitution, patterns preceded by a percent sign (%) are replaced by date components. For instance, %Y is replaced by the year number and %m by the month number. A full list of available tokens can be found by clicking the **Do strftime substitution of backup destinations?** link in the **Module Config** screen.

> Webmin only backs up the files that it is aware of. If you would like to perform a complete backup of all configuration files on your server, you should consider making a backup of the entire /etc directory. Take a look at the *Creating a backup of a selected directory* recipe in this chapter for more information.

There's more...

Webmin allows you to back up files to a remote server using the FTP or SFTP (SSH) protocol. The steps to do this are the same as listed in the preceding section, except for changing the **Backup destination** option to **FTP Server** or **SSH Server**. To transfer files to a remote server, you also need to specify the remote server's IP or domain name and a username and password on the remote server. You may also choose to download the backup to the computer from which you are connecting to Webmin by choosing the **Download in browser** destination option.

See also

▶   There are two other recipes in this chapter related to Webmin's backups of configuration settings files. Take a look at the *Restoring configuration files from backup* and *Automatically backing up configuration files* recipes of this chapter.

Restoring configuration files from backup

If you use Webmin to create backups of configuration files, you can use them later to restore system settings if you run into problems with the changes that you made since the backup.

How to do it...

To restore the configuration backups, follow these steps:

1.   Navigate to **Webmin | Backup Configuration Files**.

2.   Select the **Restore now** tab.

3.   From the **Modules to restore** list, select the module associated with the software whose configuration you would like to restore, for instance, **Webmin Configuration**.

4.   Set **Restore from** to **Local file**, click the ellipsis (**...**) button to bring up the file chooser, and select the backup file.

 You may also choose a file located on a remote FTP or SSH server, or upload a file from the computer you're using to connect to Webmin.

5.   Set **Apply configurations?** to **Yes**.

6.   Set **Just show what will be restored?** to **No**.

7.   Click the **Restore Now** button.

How it works...

Webmin keeps an index of files used by each module inside the backup archive. When you select one or more modules to restore, Webmin will replace their active configuration files with their backed up counterparts. If it's necessary, Webmin will restart the services that use the restored configuration files.

There's more...

It's a good idea to check which files would be restored from backup without actually making any changes before restoring the actual backup. To do this, follow the preceding section, but set the **Just show what will be restored?** option to **Yes**.

If you want, you can also inspect the content of the configuration files stored in the backup. After all, the backup is just a compressed TAR archive, so you can extract the files and view them. Take a look at the *Managing files and directories on the server* recipe in *Chapter 6, Managing Files on Your System*, to see how you can do this without leaving Webmin.

See also

> ▶ There are two other recipes in this chapter related to Webmin's backups of configuration settings files. Take a look at the *Backing up configuration files* and *Automatically backing up configuration files* recipes of this chapter.

Automatically backing up configuration files

Webmin allows you to set up a schedule it will follow to create backups of system configuration files automatically. You can use this option to keep a rolling archive of configuration changes made on your system.

Getting ready

In this recipe, we will create backup files with names containing the current date. We need to enable this feature, so before starting, navigate to **Webmin | Backup Configuration Files | Module Config** and answer **Yes** to the question, **Do strftime substitution of backup destinations?**.

How to do it...

Perform the following steps to automatically back up the configuration files:

1. Create a directory to store local backups in the root directory, for example, `/backups`.

> Make sure that your backup directory is stored on a partition with enough disk space so you don't accidentally fill up your entire disk. Placing `/backups` on a separate partition or in `/var/backups` may be a good idea.
>
> You should also protect the backup location from prying eyes. You can use permissions and ACLs to do this, as explained in the *Changing ACLs on a directory* section of the *Changing file ownership and permissions* recipe in *Chapter 6, Managing Files on Your System*.

2. Navigate to **Webmin | Backup Configuration Files**.
3. Select the **Scheduled backups** tab.
4. Click the **Add a new scheduled backup** link.
5. Select all modules in the **Modules to backup** list.
6. Set **Backup destination** to **Local file** and specify the following for a filename: `/backups/system-config-%Y%m%d%H%M.tgz`.
7. Set **Include in backup** to **Server configuration files**.
8. Open the **Backup schedule** section.
9. Provide your e-mail address in the **Email result to address** field.
10. Set **When to send email** to **Always**.

> After you receive a few e-mails to confirm that backups are working as expected, you can come back and switch this option to **Only when an error occurs**.

11. Set **Scheduled backup enabled?** to **Yes**, select **Simple schedule**, and choose **Daily (at midnight)** from the dropdown.
12. Click the **Create** button.

System configuration files will be backed up every day at midnight to a file in the `/backups` directory. The name of the file will contain the date and time of the backup.

How it works...

Webmin creates a **cron** job that runs at every midnight. The task creates a compressed TAR archive containing all the configuration files that Webmin is aware of. If an error occurs while creating the backup archive, an e-mail will be sent to the provided address.

See also

▸ Take a look at the *Restoring configuration files from backup* recipe of this chapter for information about getting your settings back in case of a problem.

Creating a backup of a selected directory

Webmin allows you to easily back up the contents of a directory to a TAR (tape archive) file. Backup tasks are saved, so you can perform the backup again with a single click in the future.

 The TAR file format preserves information about file ownership and permissions set on each file. It does not, however, store the extended attributes of the files. If you're using extended attributes and an ext filesystem, you should use the dump command instead. Take a look at the *Creating a backup of an entire mount point* recipe of this chapter for more information about making backups with the dump command.

Getting ready

In this recipe, we will create backup files with names containing the current date. We need to enable this feature. So, before starting, navigate to **System | Filesystem Backup | Module Config** and answer **Yes** to the question, **Do strftime substitution of backup destinations?**.

How to do it...

1. Create a directory to store backups in the root directory, for example, /backups.
2. Navigate to **System | Filesystem Backup**.
3. Enter the path of the directory you would like to back up, for example, /var/www in the text field.
4. Select the **In TAR format** option.
5. Click the **Add a new backup of directory** button.
6. Set **Backup to** to **File or tape device** and enter the destination backup filename in the text field, for example, /backups/www-%Y%m%d%H%M.tgz.

7. Open the **Backup Options** section.

8. Set **Compress archive?** to **Yes, with gzip**.

9. Click the **Create and Backup Now** button.

A backup of the directory will be created in a compressed TAR archive at the specified destination. The filename will include the date and time of creation.

How it works...

Webmin creates a Gzip compressed TAR archive of the selected directory in the specified backup location. This is roughly equivalent to running the following command at the command line:

```
$ tar -czf /backups/backup-destination.tgz /backup/source/directory
```

Before creating the backup, Webmin also executes the sync command that flushes the filesystem buffers, committing unwritten changes to the disk.

There's more...

When the time comes to restore files from a backup, you have a number of options. You can restore the files to a separate directory and then move them to the original location. You can also restore files from the archive directly to their original locations.

Restoring files from a backup archive

The following steps extract files to a temporary location from which you'll have to move them to their final locations:

1. Create a temporary directory (/tmp/restore) in which we'll store restored files before putting them in their original places.

2. Navigate to **System | Filesystem Backup**.

3. If you are presented with the option of filesystem type to restore, select **TAR**.

4. Click the **Restore backup of filesystem** button.

5. Set **Restore from file or device** to **File or tape device** and use the file chooser (the **...** button) to locate the backup archive you would like to restore.

6. Set **Restore to directory** to /tmp/restore.

7. Set **Only show files in backup?** to **No**.

8. If your backup archive was compressed with Gzip, set **Uncompress archive?** to **Yes, with gzip**.

9. Click the **Restore Backup Now** button.

10. Move the files you want to restore from the /tmp/restore directory to their original locations.

11. Delete the /tmp/restore directory.

 To place files in their original locations automatically, use the root directory (/) as **Restore to directory**. Note that this option will place files from the backup back in place, but will not delete files created since the backup was created. If you would like to restore only those files that were deleted since backing up, use the **Don't overwrite files?** option.

See also

▸ Take a look at the *Creating a backup of an entire mount point, Backing up to a remote host,* and *Setting up automatic backups* recipes of this chapter for more information about backing up files on your system.

Creating a backup of an entire mount point

Webmin allows you to set up backup tasks that use the UNIX dump command to archive the entire ext filesystem's mount points. This strategy has a number of advantages over creating archives using TAR. Firstly, all information contained in the filesystem is preserved, including extended file attributes, ACLs, special files, and so on.

Secondly, dump allows you to create incremental archives containing only the files changed since the previous backup. The dump command uses the concept of levels to distinguish between full and partial backups. A level 0 backup will archive all files (full backup), while a level 1 will only archive files changed since the last level 0 backup. A level 2 backup will archive all files changed since the last level 1 backup, and so on. There are 10 levels to choose from, and you don't need to use consecutive level numbers. One possible dump strategy is to perform a level 0 backup every month, a level 3 backup every week, and a level 6 backup every day. This means that the daily backups will be relatively small and fast, as they keep track only of changes made during the week.

If you use an incremental backup strategy with dump, you'll need to restore backups from archives of each level. For example, if you followed the 0-3-6 strategy described in the previous paragraph, you would start by restoring files from the most recent level 0, then the most recent level 3, and finally, the most recent level 6 archive.

The dump command was designed to write backup archives to magnetic tape drives. Webmin will be able to assist you in writing files to a tape device; just specify the device name instead of a destination filename when creating a backup task.

Getting ready

Before starting, install the dump package on your system, or check that it is installed. Refer to the *Installing software packages* recipe from *Chapter 1, Setting Up Your System*, for more information.

You should also prepare a backup destination that is located on another filesystem, other than the one you're planning to back up. This may be an external drive, a network filesystem, or a magnetic tape device. In this recipe, I will assume you're backing up to an external disk mounted as /media/backups.

How to do it...

1. Navigate to **System | Filesystem Backup**.

2. In the text field, enter the mount point that you would like to back up, for example, /.

3. Click the **Add a new backup of directory** button.

4. Set **Backup to** to **File or tape device** and enter the destination backup filename in the text field, for example, /media/backups/root-fs-level0-%Y%m%d%H%M.ext4dump.

 You don't need the file extension, but you may find it useful in the future to quickly check what type of filesystem is contained in a backup archive. Change ext4 to ext3 or ext2, depending on your system.

5. Open the **Backup Options** section.

6. Set **Update /etc/dumpdates file?** to **Yes**.

7. Set **Dump level** to **0 (full backup)**.

8. Set **Compress data?** to **Yes, with level** and enter 2.

9.   Click the **Create and Backup Now** button:

Module Index
Help..
Add New Backup

EXT4 filesystem backup details

Backup format	EXT4 filesystem dump
Directory to backup	/ [...]
Backup to	⦿ File or tape device [ia/backups/root-fs-level0-%Y%m%d%H%M.ext4dump] [...]
	○ Host [ ] as user [ ] in file or device
	[ ]
Remote backup command	○ Default (RSH) ⦿ SSH ○ FTP
Password for SSH/FTP login	[ ]

Backup options

Update /etc/dumpdates file?	⦿ Yes ○ No	Split across multiple files?	○ Yes ⦿ No
Dump level	[0 (Full backup) ÷]	Backup label	[ ]
Tape size	⦿ Work out automatically ○ kB		
Dump record block size	⦿ Default ○ kB	Always exclude marked files?	○ Yes ⦿ No
Compress data?	○ No ⦿ Yes, with level [2]		
Remount with noatime option during backup?	○ Yes ⦿ No		
Attempt test restore after backup to verify?	○ Yes ⦿ No		
Extra command-line parameters	[ ]		
Command to run before backup	[ ]	☑ Halt if command fails	
Command to run after backup	[ ]	☑ Report failure If command fails	

Backup schedule

[Create]   [Create and Backup Now]

🔙 Return to backups list

A backup of the entire filesystem's mount point will be created in a compressed `dump` archive at the specified destination. The filename will include the date and time of creation.

How it works...

Webmin uses the `dump` command to create a backup archive containing all the files from the filesystem mounted in the specified source directory. All the metadata contained in the filesystem is also stored in the archive. The backup is compressed using the `bzip` algorithm to reduce the size of the archive.

There's more...

In order to create an incremental backup that will be completed more quickly and use less disk space, create a `dump` of a level other than 0.

Creating an incremental backup archive

A `dump` archive of another level will contain only the files that were modified since the most recent dump of a lower level was performed. Follow the same steps that were given in the preceding section to create an incremental backup, but change the **Dump level** parameter to a different value and make sure that the filename (or tape label) reflects that this archive contains a backup of this level. Remember that you will need the most recent archives of all levels, down to level 0, to restore all backed up files.

Restoring data from a backup archive

To restore a backup from a `dump` archive, follow these steps:

1. Navigate to **System | Filesystem Backup**.

2. If you are presented with the option of the type of filesystem to restore, select the type of filesystem you backed up, for example, **EXT4**.

3. Click the **Restore backup of filesystem** button.

4. Set **Restore from file or device** to **File or tape device** and use the file chooser (the **...** button) to locate the backup archive you would like to restore.

5. Set **Restore to directory** to the location of the mount point which was backed up, for example, / for the root mount point, `/home/`, and so on.

 You do not have to enter the original path as the restore destination. You can enter another path to extract the backup to a different location.

6. Set **Files to restore** to **Everything in backup**.

7. Set **Only show files in backup?** to **No**.

8. Click the **Restore Backup Now** button.

 You can check what files are contained in the backup archive by choosing the **Only show files in backup?** option.

If you would like to restore only a few files or directories, set **Files to restore** to **Listed files** and enter a list of pathnames separated by spaces.

See also

▸ Take a look at the *Backing up to a remote host* and *Setting up automatic backups* recipes of this chapter for more information about backing up files on your system.

Backing up to a remote host

Storing backup archives locally on the same machine will not protect you from hardware failure or malicious attack. When the machine goes down, backups will go down with it. For this reason, backups should be stored remotely on another server.

The easiest way to back up to a remote host is to use a network file sharing protocol such as NFS or CIFS. You start by creating a network volume on the remote server and then mount the volume on your server. Now, you can back up to the files on the remote system just as easily as if they were stored locally. Take a look at *Chapter 6, Managing Files on Your System*, for instructions on setting up network file sharing using NFS or CIFS.

If you have only SSH access to the remote host or want to back up to a remote magnetic tape device, you can follow the steps outlined in this recipe. We'll demonstrate how Webmin helps you set up either `tar` or `dump` to create remote backups over SSH.

Getting ready

The `root` user of our server will need to access the remote server over SSH without entering a password. Instead of a password, SSH will use a key; so, we'll need to instruct the remote server to accept it.

Let's start by locating the public RSA key of our server's `root` user. The key is stored in a file named `/root/.ssh/id_rsa.pub` by default.

If this file does not exist, you may need to create a SSH public and private key pair for the `root` user of your server. This can be done by entering the following command at the terminal, but by substituting `root@my_server` with the e-mail of your server's root user:

```
# ssh-keygen -P "" -f "/root/.ssh/id_rsa"
  -t rsa -C "root@my_server"
```

The next step is to instruct the remote server to accept SSH connections using this key. Let's say that we are going to log in as a user called `backups` on the remote server. We would need to append the content of the `/root/.ssh/id_rsa.pub` file from our local server to the end of the `/home/backups/.ssh/authorized_keys` file in the home directory of the user on the remote server.

Connections made using any of the keys placed in a file named ~/.ssh/
authorized_keys in a users' home directory are treated as legitimate,
authorized connections.

When this is done, the root user of our server should be able to log in over SSH to the remote
server as the user, backups, without providing a password.

The final step is to make sure that the rmt command is installed on the remote host while
also noting the path to the rmt binary. You can check for this by running the command,
which rmt as root. If the command is not found, install the rmt or tar package on the
remote host.

How to do it...

You can convert any filesystem backup task created in Webmin into a remote backup. Start
by creating a backup task as described in the *Creating a backup of a selected directory* or
Creating a backup of an entire mount point recipes of this chapter. Perform the following
steps to back up to a remote host:

1. Navigate to **System | Filesystem Backup**.
2. Click a link in the **Directory to backup** column for the backup that you would like
   to modify.
3. Switch the **Backup to** option to **Host** and enter the IP address or domain name of the
   remote host, followed by the name of the user and the path to the backup file on the
   remote server.
4. Set **Remote backup command** to **SSH**:

5. Open the **Backup options** section.
6. If you're modifying a TAR backup job, set the **Path to rmt on remote system** to the
   path where the rmt binary is located on the remote server.
7. Click the **Save and Backup Now** button.

The backup job will run and an archive containing the backup will be created in the location
specified on the remote server.

How it works...

Modern versions of both the `tar` and `dump` commands are able to use the SSH protocol to transfer backup archives securely over the Internet to a remote destination backup server. Webmin assists you by setting the slightly complex set of options needed to run `tar` or `dump` over SSH.

Setting up automatic backups

Backups should be performed on a regular schedule. You can use cron to automate this process and run backup tasks at specified times. Webmin's backup facility makes this very simple.

How to do it...

You can convert any filesystem backup task created in Webmin into an automatic backup. Start by creating a backup task as described in *Creating a backup of a selected directory* or *Creating a backup of an entire mount point* recipes of this chapter. Perform the following steps to set up automatic backups:

1. Navigate to **System | Filesystem Backup**.
2. Click a link in the **Directory to backup** column for the backup you would like to modify.
3. Open the **Backup schedule** section.
4. Set **Scheduled backup enabled?** to **Enabled, at times chosen below**.

> If you have a series of backups that you would like to run together, Webmin allows you to schedule a backup to run after another backup completes.

5. Select **Simple schedule** and **Weekly (on Sunday)**.

> Choose a more complex schedule—if you require one—by marking the minutes, hours, and days of the month at which the job is to be performed.

6. Set **Email scheduled output** to your e-mail address.
7. Click the **Save** button.

How it works...

Webmin adds an entry, which starts the backup job to the cron table of your system's `root` user. Whenever cron is running during the scheduled time, the backup job will be started. When the backup task is completed, you should receive a message with information about the success or failure of the job.

Backing up databases

Webmin can help you set up a schedule to perform automatic backups of all databases hosted on your system. Webmin will dump the databases as SQL files into a directory on your local filesystem or locally mounted remote network volume.

> You can make backups of databases to a local directory and back that directory up to a remote server. You can also instruct Webmin to run a command that will remove old local backups after transferring them to a remote location.

How to do it...

1. Depending on the database system you're using, click either the **MySQL Database Server** or **PostgreSQL Database Server** link in the **Servers** section of Webmin's main menu.

2. Click the **Backup Databases** button.

3. In the **Backup to directory** field, enter a directory where the database backups will be created, for instance, `/backups/databases`.

4. Set **Create destination directory?** to **Yes**. Webmin will create a directory with the appropriate owner and permissions for the database system to write output there.

5. In the **Backup schedule** section, set **Scheduled backup enabled?** to **Yes, at times chosen below**.

6. Enter your e-mail address in the **Send backup status email to** field.

7. Set **Send email for** to **All backups**.

> After you receive a few e-mails to confirm that backups are working as expected, you can come back and switch this option to **Only when an error occurs**.

8. Choose **Simple schedule** and select **Daily (at midnight)**.

 Choose a more complex schedule—if you require one—by marking the minutes, hours, and days of the month at which the job is to be performed.

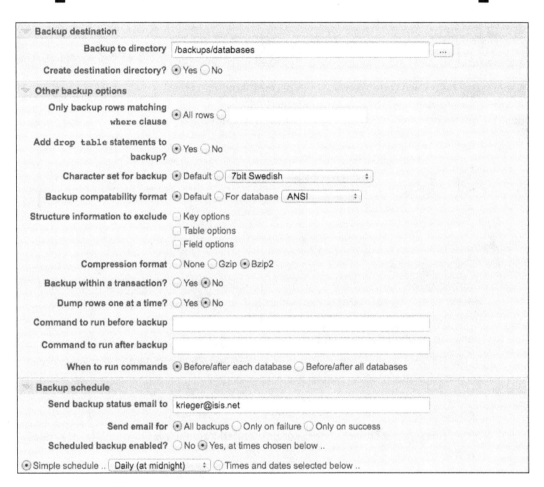

9. Click the **Save** button.

 You can click the **Backup Now** button to save the databases to SQL files immediately.

How it works...

Webmin accesses your database system and creates an SQL dump file for each database on your server. The database files are stored on the disk in the specified directory. When you set up a schedule for automatic backups, Webmin adds a job to the `root` user's cron table to create the backups at specified times. When a backup task is completed, Webmin sends an e-mail to the address specified, but we set it to only send e-mails in the event of problems to avoid spamming you unnecessarily.

See also

▸ Take a look at *Chapter 9, Running a MySQL Database Server,* and *Chapter 10, Running a PostgreSQL Database Server,* for more information about running a database server with the assistance of Webmin.

8
Running an Apache Web Server

In this chapter, we will cover the following points:

- ▸ Installing Apache on your system
- ▸ Restarting Apache
- ▸ Enabling Apache modules
- ▸ Creating a static HTML site
- ▸ Creating a virtual host
- ▸ Setting options for directories, files, and locations
- ▸ Creating a password-protected website
- ▸ Displaying a listing of files in a directory
- ▸ Redirecting incoming requests
- ▸ Setting up encrypted websites with SSL
- ▸ Logging incoming requests and errors
- ▸ Analyzing logfiles using Webalizer

Introduction

For most people, the Web is the Internet. Since it gained popularity in the 1990s, the World Wide Web has become a part of the everyday life of nearly every person on this planet. Websites provide us with information; social media allow us to communicate with other people; and online retail allows us to shop all over the world. The humble **Hypertext Transfer Protocol** (**HTTP**) makes all these killer features of the Internet possible.

Modern web browsers are capable of much more than just displaying hypertext. Thanks to the inclusion of the JavaScript runtime, the web has become the most widespread computing platform available. Programmers who want to reach the broadest number of users don't have to dedicate resources to creating a version of their application for every operating system. Instead they can create a web application, which can run on every device with a capable browser.

This arrangement is also a boon for system administrators, who can choose to implement many services in the form of web applications and not worry about supporting software installed locally on many client computers. Come upgrade time, it's much more efficient to update one server than each client system.

There are many web servers to choose from but Apache is by far the most popular solution, and Webmin supports it very well. Another open source web server, which is currently gaining popularity, is Nginx, but Webmin's support for it is currently very limited.

In this chapter, we will cover topics related to setting up Apache, configuring it to serve static websites, and analyzing logfiles. In *Chapter 11, Running Web Applications*, we'll cover topics related to running dynamic sites and web applications.

Installing Apache on your system

Some operating systems come bundled with the Apache web server as a matter of course. Others provide packages in their repositories, which allow you to quickly install Apache with a working default configuration.

Getting ready

Start by checking whether Apache is already installed on your system. If it is, Webmin should recognize it and place the **Apache Webserver** module in the **Servers** section of its menu.

How to do it...

Follow these steps to set up Apache on your system:

1. Follow steps described in the recipe *Installing software packages* in *Chapter 1, Setting Up Your System*, to find and install the Apache web server package. You should use the Apache 2 package if available.

 Depending on your system, the Apache version 2 package may be named `apache2` or simply `httpd`.

2. If you're using the `iptables` firewall, follow steps described in the recipe *Allowing access to a service through the firewall* in *Chapter 3, Securing Your System*, to allow incoming connections on port `80` and, if you plan to use HTTPS, on port `443`.

☐ Accept   If protocol is **TCP** and state of connection is **NEW** and destination ports are **80,443** ↓↑   ↧↥

3. Navigate to **Servers | Apache Webserver**, and click the **Start Apache** link to start the web server if it wasn't started automatically during installation.

4. To verify that Apache is working correctly, use your browser to visit the URL `http://your.server`, where `your.server` is either the domain name or the IP address of the machine you installed Apache on.

The Apache test page should greet you. It may simply state **It works!** or provide more information about running Apache on your operating system.

How it works...

Your operating system's package maintainers provide a working default configuration of Apache for your system. Installing the package and starting the HTTP server daemon should be sufficient to get a functional starting point for further customization.

HTTP servers listen on ports 80 and 443 by default. When you point your browser at a web server it will try to connect to port 80 when making a standard `http://` request or to port 443 when making a secure `https://` request. You should make sure those connections to your server on these ports are not dropped by your system firewall.

Apache can be configured to listen for connections on other ports, but the port number will then have to be entered in the URL field for each connection. This would be similar to connecting to Webmin, which runs an HTTP server on a non-standard port 10000.

There's more...

We don't want to have to start Apache manually every time our server is restarted, so we should activate an `init` script included in the software package to start the service automatically. We should also monitor the server and allow it to alert us if the HTTP service becomes unavailable.

Setting Apache to start at system boot time

Follow these steps to start Apache at system boot time:

1. Navigate to **System | Bootup and Shutdown**.
2. Select the checkbox next to the init script for the Apache web server (it will be named `apache2`, `httpd`, or similarly).
3. Click the **Start On Boot** button.

Monitoring that Apache is up and running

If the HTTP server crashes users will be unable to connect to your website or use your web application. If this happens, you should be notified as soon as possible so that you can take appropriate action to restart and fix your server.

Chapter 5, Monitoring Your System, covers topics related to monitoring the status of your server in detail. Take a look in particular at the recipes *Receiving an e-mail if a service stops running* and *Automatically restarting a service that goes down*. It's also a good idea to monitor your server from a second machine so that you will be notified of trouble even if the entire server becomes unavailable. Take a look at the recipe *Monitoring a remote server* for more information.

See also

▶   Apache has a modular architecture, and installing and activating additional components can extend its functionality. Take a look at the recipe *Enabling Apache modules* in this chapter for more information.

Restarting Apache

Whenever you make changes to the configuration of the Apache web server, associated runtime environments (such as PHP), or web applications served by Apache through additional modules (such as `mod_wsgi`), you will need to restart the server daemon processes.

How to do it...

Restarting Apache using Webmin is very simple:

1. Navigate to **Servers | Apache Webserver**
2. Click the **Apply Changes** link to restart the server.

How it works...

Clicking on **Apply changes** in Webmin's Apache web server module causes Apache to restart gracefully. This causes Apache to finish processing all requests but to stop accepting new connections. When Apache finishes sending the last response, it restarts and resumes accepting connections. From the perspective of a user, this will cause some requests to take longer to complete, but otherwise the server restart should be transparent. After the restart, Apache will work in accordance with the new configuration files.

You can also restart Apache in a similar fashion using the following command:

```
$ sudo apachectl graceful
```

There's more...

Making Apache configuration changes through Webmin allows you to not worry about making syntax errors. Sometimes, however, you will need to make custom configuration changes manually. When you do, you should check configuration syntax before restarting the server because a syntax error will prevent Apache from coming back up after a restart.

Verifying Apache configuration syntax

To check whether your configuration files contain no error, which would prevent Apache from starting, issue the following command:

```
$ sudo apachectl configtest
```

If everything is fine, the command will return the message `Syntax OK`.

Enabling Apache modules

The Apache HTTP server employs a modular architecture. Additional functionality can be added to the server by including additional modules. While these modules can be compiled into the server itself, on most systems they are installed separately as shared libraries. Apache's configuration files decide which modules are loaded when the server starts.

Webmin provides a simple form to enable and disable Apache modules. In this recipe, we will activate the mod_rewrite module.

How to do it...

Follow these steps to enable an Apache module:

1. Navigate to **Servers | Apache Webserver | Global configuration | Configure Apache Modules**.
2. Mark the checkbox for the rewrite module.
3. Click the **Enable Selected Modules** button.

How it works...

Webmin adds a line to Apache's configuration, which loads the selected module. In Apache Version 1, the directive for loading modules is AddModule, while in Version 2 it is LoadModule.

On some systems Apache2 doesn't actually store the LoadModule lines in the main configuration file (/etc/apache2/httpd.conf) but instead stores a separate file for each module in the /etc/apache2/mods-available/ directory. The modules are activated by making symbolic links to their activation files in the /etc/apache2/mods-enabled directory, from which all files are included in the configuration during server start. When using this form of configuration, special scripts are provided which take care of creating or deleting these symbolic links as needed. In effect, we can enable the rewrite module by issuing the following command and restarting Apache:

```
$ sudo a2enmod rewrite
```

The module can be disabled by using this command:

```
$ sudo a2dismod rewrite
```

There's more...

Apache HTTP server packages include most of the more commonly used modules, but additional modules can be installed as software packages or compiled from sources.

Installing additional modules from software packages

If you want to include an additional Apache module, which did not come bundled with the server, search for it in your system packages repositories. The name of the package with an Apache module may differ from distribution to distribution. For instance, if you wanted to install the `mod_wsgi` module, you could find it in a package named `libapache2-mod-wsgi`, `apache2-mod_wsgi` or simply `mod_wsgi` depending on your system. Follow the steps described in the recipe *Installing software packages* in *Chapter 1, Setting Up Your System*, to install the package.

Creating a static HTML site

The simplest task that an Apache server can perform is to serve a static website. When a browser sends an HTTP request to such a site, Apache processes the incoming URL, maps its path to a file on disk, and returns the contents of that file to the browser. If the file contains HTML code, a web page is rendered in the browser.

A single Apache instance can serve multiple websites, but for this recipe, we will configure only a single website as Apache's default site. If this is your only configuration, it will be used regardless of what IP address or domain name is associated with the incoming request.

In this recipe, we will configure Apache as a single-site server. It will respond to incoming requests with static files from the directory `/var/www/default`.

If you want to serve different websites under different domain names, you will have to create virtual host configurations for each domain. This topic is covered in the recipe *Creating a virtual host*.

How to do it...

We will instruct Apache to listen for all incoming requests on port 80 in order to create a single-site server as follows:

1. Navigate to **Servers | Apache Webserver**. In the **Global configuration tab**, select **Networking and Addresses**.
2. Set **Listen on addresses and ports** to **All** addresses on **Port** 80.

3. Clear the **Addresses for name virtual servers** field.

Networking and Addresses			
Listen on addresses and ports	**Address**		**Port**
	○ None ⦿ All ○		80
	⦿ None ○ All ○		
Addresses for name virtual servers	☐ Include all addresses		

We can now set the server's root document directory, from which the files will be served.

1. Create a directory which will contain the HTML files of the static site: `/var/www/default`.

2. Create a basic HTML page by creating a file named `/var/www/default/index.html` with the following content:

```
<!DOCTYPE html>
<html>
  <body>
    <h1>Hello World!</h1>
  </body>
</html>
```

3. Navigate to the configuration section of the default Apache server: **Servers | Apache Webserver | Existing virtual hosts**.

4. Click the icon for the default virtual host. In most cases, this configuration will be called **Default Server**, but if your installation came with a **Virtual Server** configuration set to handle any address and automatically adjust to all server names as shown in the following screenshot, use this configuration instead:

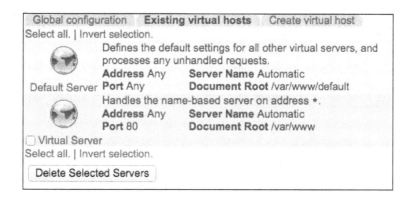

5. Click **Document Options**, and set **Document root directory** to /var/www/default.

6. Click the **Save** button.

7. Click the **Apply Changes** link.

8. Point your browser to your server's IP address or domain name: http://your. server. You should be greeted by the words **Hello World!** from the index.html file we just created.

You can now upload your entire static site to the /var/www/default directory and host it on your server.

How it works...

The Apache configuration is divided into three main sections: global settings, default server settings, and settings for virtual hosts. Virtual host settings are used if a request comes in with a host name or IP address that matches the name or address of a configured virtual web server. If no matching virtual host configuration is found, the request is passed on to the default host.

In our configuration, we specified no virtual hosts, so the default host will handle every incoming request. We configured the default host to serve files from the /var/www/default directory, which is equivalent to setting the DocumentRoot directive in the main Apache configuration file.

See also

▸ Apache is a very feature-rich web server, so there are many options to set, and Webmin can assist you with many of them. Browse through all the other recipes in this chapter for ways to customize your server.

Creating a virtual host

An Apache server can host multiple websites at the same time. Each website can be hosted on a separate IP address if your server has multiple network interfaces, but more commonly all websites share the same IP address and are distinguished by the domain name associated with the site.

> The ability of a single web server to host multiple websites in different domains from the same IP address is an aspect of the HTTP protocol. When you type in the URL `http://example.com` into your address bar, the browser looks up the IP address of the server associated with the `example.com` domain and opens a connection to port 80 of a server at that IP. The name of the web host (`example.com`) is passed as the `Host:` header of the request.

A single Apache instance can support multiple configurations. The server checks the IP and `Host:` header of every incoming request and decides which configuration to use based on this information. If you have a special configuration (virtual host) associated with `example.com`, Apache will use it for all arriving requests addressed to `http://example.com`. If you don't have a configuration for that address, the default server configuration will be used.

Getting ready

In this recipe, we will create a virtual server configuration for the domain `example.com`.

You can configure a domain to point at your server by setting up a DNS entry with your domain provider. If your domain isn't pointed at your server yet, you can simulate this during tests by making an entry in the `/etc/hosts` file of the client computer from which you will be connecting to test your server.

> If you're using a Windows machine for testing, you will have to find the `hosts` file in the directory `%SystemRoot%\system32\drivers\etc`.
> Wikipedia provides the locations of `hosts` file on other systems:
> `http://en.wikipedia.org/wiki/`
> `Hosts_%28file%29#Location_in_the_file_system`.

The `hosts` file entry contains the IP address of your server and the host name you would like to point to that IP, separated by whitespace, for instance:

```
198.51.100.1     example.com
```

How to do it...

Perform the following steps to create a virtual host:

1. Create a directory that will contain the HTML files of the static site `/var/www/example.com`.

2. Create a basic HTML page by creating a file named `/var/www/example.com/index.html` with the following content:

```
<!DOCTYPE html>
<html>
  <body>
    <h1>Welcome to Example.com</h1>
  </body>
</html>
```

3. Navigate to **Servers | Apache Webserver**.

4. Select the **Create virtual host** tab.

5. Set **Document Root** to `/var/www/example.com`.

6. Set **Server Name** to `example.com`.

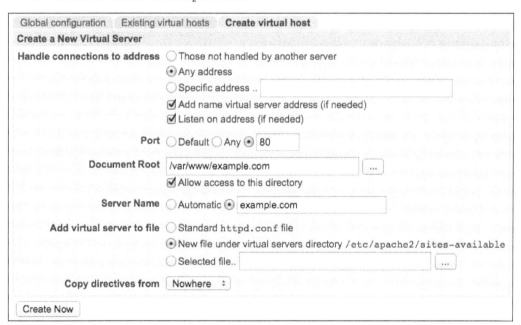

7. Click the **Create Now** button.

8. Click the **Apply Changes** link.

You should now be able to use your browser to visit a new site at the URL `http://example.com`.

How it works...

Webmin creates a virtual server by adding the following section to your Apache configuration:

```
<VirtualHost *:80>
ServerName example.com
DocumentRoot "/var/www/example.com"
</VirtualHost>
```

The preceding directive specifies that the server should listen to connections on port `80`, and if it encounters any requests directed at `Host: example.com`, it should use this configuration to serve them. The only other line in this `VirtualHost` section specifies which directory HTML files should be served from. Further options for this host will be added to this `VirtualHost` section to further customize the configuration of the virtual server.

There's more...

An Apache virtual host is highly customizable. You can find the configuration screen of the newly created virtual server by navigating to **Servers | Apache Webserver | Existing virtual hosts** and clicking the icon next to the server with **Server Name example.com**.

Creating an IP-based virtual host

Apache can also create separate virtual hosts at different IP addresses if your machine is equipped with multiple network interfaces. The procedure is very similar to the steps described previously, but instead of specifying **Server Name**, you should set **Handle connections to address** to **Specific address** and provide the IP for the virtual host:

Global configuration	Existing virtual hosts	**Create virtual host**
Create a New Virtual Server		

Handle connections to address	○ Those not handled by another server
	○ Any address
	● Specific address .. `198.51.100.1`
	☑ Add name virtual server address (if needed)
	☑ Listen on address (if needed)
Port	○ Default ○ Any ● `80`
Document Root	`/var/www/example.com` `...`
	☑ Allow access to this directory
Server Name	● Automatic ○

See also

▸ You can create a virtual host, which will use the encrypted HTTPS protocol instead of standard HTTP. Take a look at the recipe *Setting Up encrypted websites with SSL,* for details.

Setting options for directories, files, and locations

Apache allows you to customize settings at the level of a directory or file. This means that requests matching a specific path on your server are treated differently from requests for other parts of the site.

Per-directory options can be set as part of Apache's configuration files using the `<Directory>` directive. Options set this way will apply to the chosen directory and all of its subdirectories. The `<Directory>` options set on a subdirectory will override the settings of a higher-level directory.

Local settings can also be specified by placing them in a special file (called `.htaccess` by default) placed in a directory. The `AllowOverride` option must be set on the directory for `.htaccess` files to have an effect.

In this recipe, we will create a directory-specific configuration, which allows the usage of `.htaccess` files in that directory and its subdirectories.

Getting ready

We will set specific options on the directory `/var/www/default` inside of the **Default Server** configuration. Before you begin, note the full path to the directory you would like to set configuration directives for, and identify which virtual host serves files from that directory (if other then the default virtual server).

How to do it...

Perform the following steps to set options for directories, files and locations:

1. Navigate to **Servers | Apache Webserver | Existing virtual hosts**.

2. Select the virtual host you want to customize, for instance, **Default Server**.

3. In the **Create Per-Directory, Files or Location Options** section, set **Type** to **Directory**.

4. Select **Exact match** and set **Path** as `/var/www/default`.

 You may also enter a wildcard path such as `/var/www/default/site*`. Options set this way will apply to all directories that match.

If you require even more flexibility, you can select the **Match regexp** option and specify the path using a regular expression.

5. Click the **Create** button.

6. You will be brought to the **Virtual Server Options** screen, which will have a new entry in the **Per-Directory Options** section. Click the icon labeled **Directory /var/www/default**.

7. In the directory configuration screen, click the icon labeled **Document Options**.

8. In the **Options file can override** section, select **Selected below...** and check all the boxes.

Module Index   **Document Options**   Apply Changes
Stop Apache

For Directory `/var/www/default` on default server

Document Options for Directory `/var/www/default`

Directory options ⦿ Default ◯ Selected below..

Option	Set for directory	Merge with parent
Execute CGI programs	◯ Yes ⦿ No	◯ Enable ◯ Disable
Follow symbolic links	◯ Yes ⦿ No	◯ Enable ◯ Disable
Server-side includes and execs	◯ Yes ⦿ No	◯ Enable ◯ Disable
Server-side includes	◯ Yes ⦿ No	◯ Enable ◯ Disable
Generate directory indexes	◯ Yes ⦿ No	◯ Enable ◯ Disable
Generate Multiviews	◯ Yes ⦿ No	◯ Enable ◯ Disable
Follow symbolic links if owners match	◯ Yes ⦿ No	◯ Enable ◯ Disable

Options file can override.. ◯ Default ⦿ Selected below...   **Generate MD5 digests**

☑ Authentication options
☑ MIME types and encodings
☑ Indexing and index files   ◯ Yes ◯ No ⦿ Default
☑ Hostname access control
☑ Directory options

Generate ETag header from ⦿ Default ◯ Selected attributes : ☐ INode number ☐ Last modified time ☐ File size

Error message footer [Default ⬍]

[Save]

9. Click the **Save** button.
10. Click the **Apply Changes** link.

How it works...

When we choose to set per-directory options, Webmin creates a `<Directory>` directive for us and fills it with the selected options. In the example we presented, we chose to allow all settings to be overridden by local `.htaccess` files. This created the following configuration section:

```
<Directory "/var/www/default">
AllowOverride All
</Directory>
```

If we chose to edit the Default Server, the `<Directory>` directive will be created in the main Apache settings file. These settings will always apply to the directory regardless of which virtual host is used to access it. If you wanted to create per-directory settings, which apply only to a selected virtual server, you would choose that server in the **Existing virtual hosts** tab. Settings created in this way would be saved within the particular `<VirtualHost>` section.

There's more...

Webmin allows you to set most local options available to your version of Apache through the **Per-Directory Options** user interface. Browse around to familiarize yourself with this section, and you will be able to tweak settings quickly when needed.

Apache allows you to set local options by matching the filesystem path of a directory, but you can also match names of requested files or URL addresses.

Setting options on files with names matching a pattern

Apache allows you to set specific options on files with names matching a particular pattern. For instance, it's a bad idea to allow external users to read the contents of .htaccess and other local Apache configuration files. You can prevent access to all of these files (collectively matching the regular expression ^\.ht) by following these steps:

1. Navigate to **Servers | Apache Webserver | Existing virtual hosts**.
2. Select the **Default Server** option.
3. In the **Create Per-Directory, Files or Location Options** section, set **Type** to **Files**.
4. Select **Match regexp**, and set **Path** to the regular expression ^\.ht.
5. Click the **Create** button.
6. Click the icon labeled **Files regexp ^\.ht**.
7. Click the icon labeled **Access Control**.
8. In the **Restrict access** section, set the only action to **Deny All Requests**.

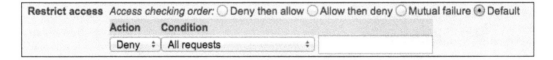

9. Click the **Save** button.
10. Click the **Apply Changes** link.

Setting options for specific URLs

You may wish to apply custom settings to specific URLs, which don't necessarily match a particular underlying filesystem path or filename. Apache's <Location> directive can be used in such cases, and Webmin will assist you in its configuration.

Let's use as an example the dynamically generated /server-status page that gives you an overview of your server if the mod_status module is enabled. There is no path on your disk called server-status, but you may still control requests to this URL by creating a location-based configuration.

You would want the server information to be available only to a limited group of users. Let's limit access to this URL to requests coming from the localhost IP of `127.0.0.1`:

1. Navigate to **Servers | Apache Webserver | Existing virtual hosts**.
2. Select the **Default Server** option.
3. In the **Create Per-Directory, Files or Location Options** section, set **Type** to **Location**.
4. Select **Exact match**, and set **Path** to `/server-status`.
5. Click the **Create** button.
6. Click the icon labeled **Location /server-status**.
7. Click the icon labeled **Access Control**.
8. In the **Restrict access** section, set **Access checking order** to **Allow then deny**.
9. Set the only action to **Allow Request from IP..**, and specify `127.0.0.1`.
10. Click the **Save** button, and enter **Access Control** again.

 Webmin always provides one empty entry in the list. When you enter the section again, you will be able to add a second access restriction.

11. In the **Restrict access** section, add a second action to **Deny All Requests**.

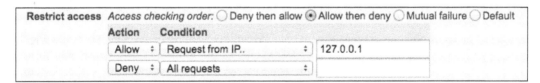

Restrict access	Access checking order:	⭘ Deny then allow	◉ Allow then deny	⭘ Mutual failure	⭘ Default
	Action	**Condition**			
	Allow ⬍	Request from IP..	⬍	127.0.0.1	
	Deny ⬍	All requests	⬍		

12. Click the **Save** button.
13. Click the **Apply Changes** link.

Changing matching path or pattern

If you have already created a set of local settings, but need to change the path they are applied to, follow these steps:

1. Navigate to **Servers | Apache Webserver | Existing virtual hosts**.
2. Click the icon for the virtual host you want to customize.
3. In the **Per-Directory Options**, click the icon of the local settings you want to relocate.
4. Modify the matching pattern in the **Options apply to** section.

Setting options using an .htaccess file

Using the `.htaccess` files is a convenient way to allow users without administrative privileges on your server to customize local settings of the Apache server at the level of a directory. As long as the user has the ability to modify the settings file, they can tweak the server without the need for support from an administrator. Changes in settings done through the `.htaccess` file do not require the server to be restarted.

 You should be aware that using the `.htaccess` files causes a reduction in Apache's performance as the server has to look for the settings file in the requested directory (and potentially also the `.htaccess` files in higher-level directories) during every request.

The following are the steps to create the `.htaccess` options file:

1. Navigate to **Servers | Apache Webserver | Global configuration | Per-Directory Options Files**.

2. Enter the path to the directory that you would like to write an `.htaccess` file for, for example, `/var/www/example.com`, and click the **Create Options File** button.

You will arrive at a screen that allows you to modify local settings through the `.htaccess` file.

Creating a password-protected website

The HTTP protocol provides a basic functionality for authenticating users. When a request is sent to a protected site, or a protected area within a site, the browser presents the user with a prompt for name and password. If the provided values match an authorized user, access to the site is granted.

 The basic HTTP authentication method is simple to set up on Apache, especially with assistance from Webmin. The main drawback to this functionality is that it isn't very secure or customizable. If you plan to use this form of authentication on the open Internet, make sure you use it in combination with the encrypted HTTPS protocol.

Getting ready

Before starting, make sure that the module `auth_basic` is enabled in your Apache configuration. Take a look at the recipe *Enabling Apache modules* for more information.

How to do it...

Perform the following steps to create a password-protected website

1. Navigate to **Servers | Apache Webserver | Existing virtual hosts**.
2. Select the virtual server you would like to protect with a password.
3. If you already have a settings section for the directory you would like to protect with a password, you can skip to step 7.
4. In the **Create Per-Directory, Files or Location Options** section, set **Type** to **Directory**.
5. Select **Exact match**, and set **Path** to the root document of your site, for instance, `/var/www/example.com`.

 You can protect a subsection of your site with a password by creating the per-directory settings for a subdirectory.

6. Click the **Create** button.
7. In the **Per-Directory Options** section, click the link to the directory configuration section.
8. Click the icon labeled **Access Control**.
9. In the **Authentication realm name** section, specify a description, which will be shown to the user when prompting for a password, for example, `Please enter your ISIS password`.
10. Set **Authentication type** to **Basic**.
11. Set **Restrict access by login** to **All valid users**.
12. Set **Basic login user file types** to **Text file**.
13. Set **User text file** to `/etc/apache2/htpasswd` or `/etc/httpd/htpasswd` depending on where your Apache configuration directory is located.

The passwords file should never be accessible through the web server. You should save it in a location outside of the document root. If you need to keep it within the document root directory, restrict access to it by following the steps described in the *Setting options on files with names matching a pattern* section of the *Setting options for directories, files, and locations* recipe.

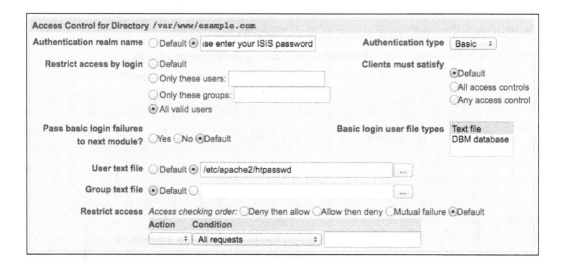

14. Click the **Save** button, and restart Apache by clicking on the **Apply Changes** link.

Creating a user account

Perform the following steps to create a user account:

1. Enter **Access Control** for the directory once again.

2. Click the new link labeled **Edit users** in the **User text file** line.

3. Click the **Add a new user** link.

4. Specify a username and a password in plain text.

5. Click the **Save** button.

How it works...

Webmin creates a password-protected site by creating a `<Directory>` directive in your Apache configuration with the appropriate instructions for the `auth_basic` module. For example, the instructions outlined earlier would add the following section to your Apache configuration:

```
<Directory "/var/www/example.com">
AuthName "Please enter your ISIS password"
AuthType Basic
require valid-user
AuthBasicProvider file
AuthUserFile /etc/apache2/htpasswd
</Directory>
```

Webmin also helps you to create valid username and password pairs, which will be treated as valid users. This information is stored in the file specified by the `AuthUserFile` directive.

There's more...

Apache passwords are kept separate from your system's user account information. If you would like these accounts to be kept synchronized, Webmin can help you substantially by performing the task for you.

Keeping Apache and system accounts synchronized

Perform the following steps to keep Apache and system accounts synchronized:

1. Navigate to **Servers | Apache Webserver | Existing virtual hosts**.
2. Select the virtual server, which is protected with a password.
3. In the **Per-Directory Options** section, click the link to the password-protected directory configuration section.
4. Click the icon labeled **Access Control**.
5. Click the new link labeled **Edit users** in the **User text file** line.
6. Mark the checkboxes labeled **Add a user when a Unix user is added, Change the user when a Unix user is changed**, and **Delete the user when a Unix user is deleted**.
7. Click the **Save** button.

See also

▶ If you want to use HTTP Basic authentication on the Internet, make sure to combine it with SSL encryption of the connection. Take a look at the *Setting Up encrypted websites with SSL* recipe for details.

▶ Also make sure that the `htpasswd` file is not accessible via the web server. Refer to the *Setting options for directories, files, and locations* recipe for ways to prevent access to its location.

Displaying a listing of files in a directory

A web server makes a great repository for downloadable files. This system of file distribution has for the most part replaced anonymous FTP as it offers a more seamless experience for users. If you would like to give users access to a directory of files with an automatically generated index, Apache is the right tool for the job.

 In most cases, listing files in directories of a website is unnecessary, and in some cases it may even expose sensitive information to potential attackers. Use directory listings only where it makes sense.

Getting ready

In this recipe, we will expose a listing of the directory `/var/www/example.com/downloads`, which is served by the virtual host named `example.com` from the URL `http://example.com/downloads`. Note the file path, virtual host name, and URL of your case and substitute appropriately.

How to do it...

Perform the following steps to display a listing of files in a directory:

1. Create the directory `/var/www/example.com/downloads`, and place some files for download in it.
2. Navigate to **Servers | Apache Webserver | Existing virtual hosts**.
3. Select the virtual host, which will be serving files, for example, **Server Name example.com**.
4. In the **Create Per-Directory, Files or Location Options** section, set **Type** to **Directory**.
5. Select **Exact match**, and set **Path** to the root document of your site, for instance, `/var/www/example.com/downloads`.

6. Click the **Create** button.

7. In the **Per-Directory Options** section, click the link labeled **Directory /var/ www/example.com/downloads**.

8. Click the link labeled **Document Options**.

9. Set **Directory options** to **Selected below**.

10. Set **Generate directory indexes** to **Yes**.

11. Click the **Save** button.

12. Click the button labeled **Directory Indexing**.

13. Set **Directory index options** to **Selected below**.

14. Mark the checkbox labeled **Display fancy directory indexes**.

15. Set your preferences for how the directory listing should be displayed using this form.

16. Click the **Save** button.

17. Click the **Apply Changes** link.

You should now be able to see a listing of files under the URL `http://example.com/ downloads`.

How it works...

Webmin creates a directory-listing configuration by making a `<Directory>` directive in your Apache configuration. For example, the steps outlined would add the following section to the virtual host configuration:

```
<Directory "/var/www/example.com/downloads">
Options Indexes
IndexOptions FancyIndexing
</Directory>
```

There's more...

By default, Apache's directory listings pages include a header containing the directory path and a footer containing information about the server and Apache. You can customize the content of the header and footer by placing files named `HEADER.html` and `README.html` inside the directory. Any HTML code placed in those files will be displayed on the file listing page. If you want to prevent Apache from listing these files, go to the **Directory Indexing** options screen, and type their names in the **Files to ignore in directory index** field (one filename per line).

▶ For more information about Apache directory indexing options, take a look at this manual page:
`http://httpd.apache.org/docs/current/mod/mod_autoindex.html`.

Redirecting incoming requests

You can use Apache's HTTP redirects to forward an incoming request to another address. This can be useful if the address of your webpage changes or you would like to create a memorable URL address, which will redirect to a longer address of a specific page.

Let's say that we used to host a number of articles at `http://oldsite.com/articles/`, and we decided to move our site to another domain, and the same articles will now be hosted at `http://example.com/info/`.

We can configure Apache at our old site to redirect all incoming requests to the new domain.

Getting ready

Before starting, make sure that the module `alias` is enabled in your Apache configuration. Take a look at the recipe *Enabling Apache modules* for more information.

How to do it...

On your old server, follow these steps to create a redirect to your new domain:

1. Navigate to **Servers | Apache Webserver | Existing virtual hosts**.
2. Select the virtual host, which will perform the redirect, for example, **Default Server**.
3. Click the icon labeled **Aliases and Redirects**.
4. Fill out the **Regexp URL redirects** form with the following data:
    - **From:** `/articles/(.*)`
    - **Status:** `301`
    - **To:** `http://example.com/info/$1`

The regular expression group marked by (.*) in the **From** field captures any string which comes after /articles/ and the content of the captured group is placed in the $1 placeholder of the **To** field.

An HTTP redirection status 301 means that the resource was moved permanently. If the redirection is temporary, status 302 is commonly used.

5. Click the **Save** button.
6. Click the **Apply Changes** link.

How it works...

Webmin creates the redirect by adding a RedirectMatch directive in your virtual host's configuration file. Steps in the preceding example would create the following instruction:

```
RedirectMatch 301 /articles/(.*) "http://example.com/info/$1"
```

If we weren't using regular expressions, a simpler Redirect directive would suffice, for example:

```
Redirect 301 /articles/ "http://example.com/info/"
```

There's more...

An Apache module called mod_alias provides the Redirect directives. These directives allow you to create simple forwarding between addresses. Another module called mod_rewrite provides a much more sophisticated mechanism of redirecting incoming requests based on every part of the URL, filesystem tests, server and environment variables, HTTP headers, time stamps, and so on. Unfortunately, the syntax for mod_rewrite directives can be quite unique and complex, so editing its configuration by hand remains your best option.

More information can be found on the Apache website: http://httpd.apache.org/docs/current/rewrite/.

Creating a filesystem alias

If you want to serve files from a directory outside of your server's document root or you want to serve files from one directory in a number of locations, you can use local aliases instead of redirects. A redirect forwards the user to a different URL, while an alias is transparent to the user and it serves different content from the same URL.

For example, we can store site images in the directory /var/www/resources/images but use an alias to serve them from the URL /images/. The end user will see no difference between files served directly or through an alias.

Follow these steps to serve files located in `/var/www/resources/images` from URLs starting with `/images/`:

1. Navigate to **Servers | Apache Webserver | Existing virtual hosts**.
2. Select the virtual host, which will perform the redirect, for example, **Default Server**.
3. Click the icon labeled **Aliases and Redirects**.
4. Fill out the **Document directory aliases** form with the following data:

   - **From**: `/images/`
   - **To**: `/var/www/resources/images`

> Before you can serve files from another filesystem location, you may need to create a directory-specific Apache configuration, which will allow the server to make these files publicly available. Take a look at the recipe *Setting options for directories, files, and locations* for more information.

Setting up encrypted websites with SSL

The HTTP protocol is transmitted over the Internet as plain text. This means that the communication can be intercepted and read by people other than the end user of the website and server administrator. In most cases, the exchanged information is public, and this security vulnerability is acceptable. In other cases, where passwords or other secret information is exchanged, simple HTTP should not be used. Thankfully, securing web communications is not very difficult thanks to the HTTPS protocol, which adds a layer of encryption.

> SSL encryption that is used by HTTPS is added before the actual HTTP conversation is initiated. This means that name-based virtual servers, which are specified in HTTP headers, cannot be used with HTTPS. In practice, this means that each SSL-protected website has to be served from a dedicated IP address.
>
> If you only plan to create a single HTTPS website on your server, you're fine. However, if you plan to create more secure websites, you will need to add a separate network interface with its own IP addresses to your server for each site.
>
> If your server has only one IP address, and you must serve multiple HTTPS sites, you have the option of using a technology called **Server Name Indication (SNI)**. For more information take a look at this Wikipedia page: `http://en.wikipedia.org/wiki/Server_Name_Indication`.

Getting ready

Before starting, make sure that the module `ssl` is enabled in your Apache configuration. Take a look at the recipe *Enabling Apache modules* for more information.

The next step will be obtaining a key and certificate, which will be used to sign and encrypt HTTPS communication. You have a choice of creating your own self-signed certificate or purchasing a signed certificate from a commercial certificate authority. You can generate a self-signed certificate quickly and for free, but visiting browsers will complain to users that your site cannot be fully trusted because an external authority did not certify the certificate used to encrypt communication. A third party could also potentially spoof a self-signed certificate, so it does not guarantee that someone else isn't pretending to be you.

A commercial certificate will be slightly harder to obtain and will cost a few dollars per year, but your users will be able to trust that they are connecting to your site and will see no warnings and a pleasing colorful padlock in the browser's address bar.

The process of creating an SSL certificate requires the `openssl` package to be installed on your system. Take a look at the recipe *Installing software packages* from *Chapter 1, Setting Up Your System*, if you need to install it. Keys and certificates don't have to be generated on the server; you can generate them on any machine that has the `openssl` command available.

Generating a private key

SSL is built around asymmetric cryptography, which uses two keys: one of which is public, and the other secret (or private). The public key is used to encrypt messages or verify their signature, while the private key is used to decrypt messages and create signatures. The private key should be known only to its owner and kept in a protected file.

Use this command to generate a strong RSA private key, and save it to the file `key.pem`:

```
$ openssl genrsa -out key.pem 2048
```

A person with your private key can pretend to be you even if you pay for a signed certificate. Change permissions on the key file so that only the root user can read it, and make sure it doesn't fall into the wrong hands. Use the following command to change permissions:

```
$ chmod 400 key.pem
```

Making a self-signed certificate

You can create a self-signed certificate using the next command. The certificate will be saved to the file `cert.pem`, it will be signed by your private key (from `key.pem`) and will be set to expire in 365 days:

```
$ openssl req -new -key key.pem -x509 -nodes -days 365 -out cert.pem
```

When generating a certificate, you will be asked a series of questions, including country name, state or province, locality, organization, organization unit, and e-mail address. If you want to leave any of these fields blank, enter a single dot (.), and press *Enter*. You will also be asked to provide a **Common Name** for the certificate, which in this case will be the full domain name of your site (for example, www.example.com). Remember that the common name in a certificate must match your domain exactly, so a certificate generated for www.example.com will not work on example.com and vice versa.

 If you need a certificate, which will work on multiple domains, you can prepare a **wildcard** certificate, or one with multiple domains specified in the **Subject Alt Name** field.

Obtaining a commercially signed certificate

In order to obtain a commercially signed certificate, you will need to generate a **certificate signing request** (**CSR**) file signed with your private key. You send this file to a commercial certificate authority that will verify your identity, process your payment, and then send you back a signed certificate.

You can use this command to generate a CSR file (csr.pem) based on your private key (key.pem):

```
$ openssl req -new -key key.pem -out csr.pem
```

You will be asked the same series of questions as when making a self-signed certificate. Make sure you specify this information precisely; any discrepancy between this data and information provided to the certificate authority can throw the certification process off course.

Inspecting certificate data

Once you have a certificate (cert.pem), you can display information contained within by issuing the following command:

```
$ openssl x509 -noout -text -in cert.pem
```

How to do it...

Follow these steps to set up an SSL-protected HTTPS website run by Apache:

1. Prepare the following:
   - ❏ A private key file (key.pem)
   - ❏ A certificate file (cert.pem)
   - ❏ An IP address that will be used with SSL (for example, 198.51.100.1)

❑ A domain name which is specified as the common name in the certificate (for example, `www.example.com`)

❑ A path to directory containing website files (for example, `/var/www/www.example.com`)

❑ A path to the Apache configuration directory on your system (for example, `/etc/apache2`)

2. Copy the `key.pem` and `cert.pem` files to the Apache configuration directory.

 Under no circumstances should these files ever find their way to a publicly available document directory. Keep them in a secure location available only to the root user.

3. Make sure that permission flags on `key.pem` are set restrictively as follows:

```
$ sudo chmod 400 key.pem
```

4. Navigate to **Servers | Apache Webserver | Create virtual host**, and prepare a virtual server with the following settings. Refer to the recipe *Create a virtual host* for more information:

❑ Handle connections to specific address: `198.51.100.1`

❑ **Port**: `443`

❑ **Document Root**: `/var/www/www.example.com`

❑ **Server Name**: `www.example.com`

Create a New Virtual Server

Handle connections to address
- ○ Those not handled by another server
- ○ Any address
- ⦿ Specific address .. `198.51.100.1`
- ☑ Add name virtual server address (if needed)
- ☑ Listen on address (if needed)

Port ○ Default ○ Any ⦿ `443`

Document Root `/var/www/www.example.com` `...`
☑ Allow access to this directory

Server Name ○ Automatic ⦿ `www.example.com`

Add virtual server to file
- ○ Standard `httpd.conf` file
- ⦿ New file under virtual servers directory `/etc/apache2/sites-available`
- ○ Selected file.. `...`

Copy directives from `Nowhere ⇕`

5. Navigate to the options screen of the newly created virtual server, and click the **SSL Options** icon.

6. Set **Enable SSL?** to **Yes**.

7. Set **Certificate/private key file** to `/etc/apache2/cert.pem`.

8. Set **Private key file** to `/etc/apache2/key.pem`.

9. Click the **Save** button.

10. Click the **Apply Changes** link.

You can now use your browser to connect to the HTTPS address of your site `https://www.example.com`.

How it works...

Webmin activates SSL by adding the following instructions to the configuration of an Apache virtual host:

```
SSLEngine on
SSLCertificateFile /etc/apache2/cert.pem
SSLCertificateKeyFile /etc/apache2/key.pem
```

This basic configuration enables communication with the server using the HTTPS protocol. When a browser makes an HTTPS connection, the request is sent to the server's port 443. Before the HTTP dialog begins, an SSL handshake is performed, and all subsequent communication is encrypted.

There's more...

If you prepare a virtual server that listens for HTTPS requests on port 443, clients will not be able to connect to it using standard HTTP requests to port 80. You may want to prepare a second virtual host for the same domain that will redirect all incoming traffic to URLs beginning with `https://`. Take a look at the recipe *Redirecting incoming requests* for more information.

Logging incoming requests and errors

A server hosting a website on the Internet gets a lot of attention. It's visited by users, scanned by indexing search bots, and looked over by would-be attackers trying to see if it could be broken into. Your web server should record information about all this traffic, and you should look through it regularly to ascertain that everything is working correctly.

By default, Apache keeps two types of logfiles: an access log, which contains information about each incoming request and an error log with information about encountered problems. You can configure Apache to keep a single pair of logfiles, but in most cases it's more useful to keep a separate access and error log for each virtual server.

Getting ready

Apache's logging facility is highly customizable, and you can set your server to output log entries in many different ways. A few of the formats have become recognized as standard, and currently, the recommended logging standard is nicknamed *combined log format*. It logs many pieces of information, among which are:

- Remote IP or hostname (`%h`)
- Remote user if the request was authenticated (`%u`)
- The time (`%t`)
- The first line of a request, which contains the HTTP method used and the requested path (`%r`)
- The HTTP response status: 200 for OK, 404 for not found, and so on (`%>s`)
- Response size in bytes (`%O`)
- The page which initiated this request (`%{Referer}i`)
- User-agent string identifying the requesting browser type and version (`%{User-Agent}i`)

All these fields form the combined log format denoted as:

```
%h %l %u %t "%r" %>s %O "%{Referer}i" "%{User-Agent}i"
```

You should make sure that the format nicknamed combined is available in your server's configuration. Here's how you can add it in case it isn't:

1. Navigate to the configuration section of the default Apache server at **Servers | Apache Webserver | Existing virtual hosts | Default Server**.

2. Click **Log Files**.

3. Make sure that the list contains a log format named `combined`. If this format is missing, add an entry with the nickname `combined` and the following format string:

    ```
    %h %l %u %t "%r" %>s %O "%{Referer}i" "%{User-Agent}i"
    ```

4. Set the **Default log** format to `combined`.

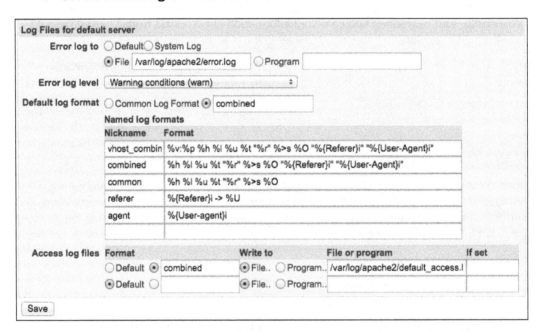

5. Click the **Save** button.
6. Click the **Apply Changes** link.

You can find more information about Apache log formats in its documentation:

```
http://httpd.apache.org/docs/current/mod/mod_log_config.html
```

How to do it...

In this recipe, we will set logging for the virtual host serving the domain `example.com`. We'll direct Apache to save access log entries in `/var/log/apache2/example.com-access.log` and errors in `/var/log/apache2/example.com-error.log`. If your system uses the `/var/log/httpd` or another directory for Apache logs, modify the path accordingly. Perform the following steps for logging incoming requests and errors:

1. Navigate to **Servers | Apache Webserver | Existing virtual hosts**.
2. Click the icon of the host you want to set logging options for.
3. Click **Log Files**.
4. Set the **Error log to** to **File**, and enter the logfile path: `/var/log/apache2/example.com-error.log`.
5. Set **Error log level** to **Warning conditions (warn)**.
6. Set **Default log format** to `combined`.
7. Under **Access log files** set **Format** to **default** and **Write to File with path** `/var/log/apache2/example.com-access.log`.

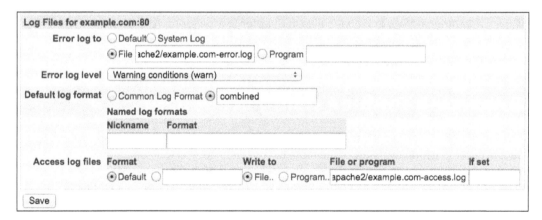

8. Click the **Save** button.
9. Click the **Apply Changes** link.

How it works...

Webmin configures logging for a virtual server by adding the following directives to its
`<VirtualHost>` section:

```
ErrorLog /var/log/apache2/example.com-error.log
LogLevel warn
LogFormat "combined"
TransferLog /var/log/apache2/example.com-access.log
```

These instructions tell Apache where to save this host's access and error logs, what format
should be used for access logs (`LogFormat`), and how detailed the error reporting should
be (`LogLevel`).

See also

> ▶ Apache logfiles grow quickly on highly trafficked sites. Check out the recipe
> *Configuring logfile rotation* from *Chapter 5, Monitoring Your System*, for information
> about setting up `logrotate` to deal with growing logfiles.

> ▶ Webmin can display collected logfiles messages for you; take a look at the recipe
> *Add other logfiles to Webmin* also in *Chapter 5, Monitoring Your System*.

> ▶ A program called Webalizer can help you make sense of your Apache logfiles. Check
> out the recipe *Analyzing logfiles using Webalizer* in this chapter for more information.

Analyzing logfiles using Webalizer

Web server logfiles contain a lot of useful information, but they are too long and verbose to
read. In order to get an overview of the state of your website, you will need a tool to analyze
the contents of its access logfiles. One such tool is called **Webalizer**; it's easy to install and
integrates well with Webmin. Webalizer parses your logfiles and generates a graphical report
in HTML turning your logfiles into clear graphs and tables.

Getting ready

Follow the steps described in the recipe *installing software packages* in *Chapter 1, Setting Up
Your System*, to install the `webalizer` package on your system.

How to do it...

Make a note of the location of the Apache access logfile you want to analyze. In this recipe, we will prepare a Webalizer report for the website hosted at example.com with an access logfile stored in /var/log/apache2/example.com-access.log. Perform the following steps to analyze logfiles using Webalizer:

1. Make a directory to store the Webalizer reports for this website. A good location could be /var/stats/example.com for instance.

2. Navigate to **Servers | Webalizer Logfile Analysis**.

3. Click the **Add a new log file for analysis** link.

4. Set **Base logfile path** to /var/log/apache2/example.com-access.log.

 Even if you rotate logs with logrotate, Webalizer will pick up the entire family of logfiles, including compressed backup log archives.

5. Set **Write report to directory** to the report directory you created /var/stats/example.com.

6. Set **Run webalizer as user** to root.

7. Set **Always re-process log files?** to **No**.

8. Set **Clear log file(s) after scheduled report?** to **No**.

9. Set **Report options** to **Use global options**.

10. Set **Scheduled report generation** to **Enabled, at times chosen below**.

11. Use a **Simple schedule** set to **Daily (at midnight)**.

12. Click the **Create** button.

A new Webalizer analysis entry will appear in the list. If you don't want to wait until the next day, you can generate a report immediately:

1. Click the newly created log analysis entry.

2. Click the **Generate Report** button and then the **View completed report** link on the following screen.

From now on, you can always come to the **Servers | Webalizer Logfile Analysis** and click the link at the right-hand side of the screen to view a Webalizer report updated daily.

How it works...

Webmin creates a cron job, which executes the `webalizer` binary every night at midnight. Webalizer parses the specified logfile and generates a graphical report in the form of an HTML page. When you decide to view the report, Webmin displays the Webalizer-generated HTML page in your browser.

There's more...

You can customize certain aspects of the way Webalizer generates reports. You can edit the settings globally by going to the **Servers | Webalizer Logfile Analysis** page and clicking the **Edit Global Options** button.

You can also set custom settings for a report by following these steps:

1. Navigate to **Servers | Webalizer Logfile Analysis**.
2. Click the name of the logfile for which you would like to customize the report.
3. Set **Report options** to **Custom options**.
4. Click the **Save** button.
5. Back on the screen listing Webalizer reports click the name of the logfile again.
6. Click the new **Edit Options** button at the bottom of the screen.
7. Customize report settings, and click the **Save** button.

9
Running a MySQL Database Server

In this chapter, we will cover the following topics:

- ▸ Installing the MySQL database server
- ▸ Allowing access to MySQL over the network
- ▸ Accessing your MySQL server over an SSH tunnel
- ▸ Creating a new database
- ▸ Creating users and granting permissions to databases
- ▸ Creating a backup of your database
- ▸ Executing custom SQL commands
- ▸ Restoring database from the backup
- ▸ Editing the structure of your database
- ▸ Editing records in a database
- ▸ Checking who is using your database server
- ▸ Installing phpMyAdmin

Introduction

MySQL is a powerful open source database management system. MySQL servers are easy to set up and scale quite well. This database system powers some of the world's largest websites including Facebook, Twitter, and Wikipedia.

MySQL employs a distributed client-server architecture. A single server can provide database services to multiple client programs simultaneously. Clients running on the same machine as the server usually connect using a Unix socket. Clients can also run on separate machines and connect to the database server over the network. MySQL uses TCP connections, and the server's default listening port is 3306.

 Unix domain sockets are channels used for inter-process communication. Different programs running on the same machine can read and write information to a socket, enabling communication between the programs. Unix sockets are represented as nodes of the filesystem, so you can find a socket by listing the contents of a directory in which it was created.

The permissions system of MySQL is very granular. Each client can have access limited to a subset of databases and be allowed to execute a different set of SQL commands on each database.

The database server maintains a list of client accounts, which are separate from the system user accounts. Each client account is defined not only by a username and password, but also by the host from which the user is connecting. Thanks to this solution, complex permission definitions are possible. For instance, the same username and password may be used locally to perform administrative tasks, but allowed only to view the server state remotely.

The default MySQL installation creates an administrative superuser called `root` as well as an anonymous account, which makes it possible to connect to the database server without authentication. It's important to equip the `root` account with a strong password and disable anonymous accounts on a production system.

 In addition to a username and password, MySQL may require the client to provide a certificate for increased security.

Webmin's support for MySQL is excellent and allows you to perform most tasks related to the running of the database server. In this chapter, we will demonstrate how Webmin can help you install MySQL, set up access to the server over a network, manage user accounts, create databases, and edit the structure and data of databases. We'll also demonstrate how to automatically backup databases and restore backup files. If you find that you need an even more advanced web-based management tool, we will demonstrate how to set up phpMyAdmin on your server.

Installing the MySQL database server

Practically all operating systems that come with a package management solution for open source software make MySQL packages available for installation. In this recipe, we will install MySQL from a package and set it up on your system. The server package automatically installs MySQL's command-line client package as well.

How to do it...

Follow these steps to set up MySQL on your server:

1. Follow the steps described in the _Installing software packages_ recipe in _Chapter 1,
   Setting Up Your System_, to find and install the MySQL database server package.

> Most distributions make multiple versions of MySQL available in their
> package repositories. On some systems, you will find a meta-package
> called `mysql-server` that installs the latest version. On other systems,
> you will find packages with version numbers in the name, for instance
> `mysql-server-5.5` or `mysql55-server` for version 5.5.x. Pick the
> package with the latest version unless you have reasons to stick to an
> older one.

2. Navigate to **System | Bootup and Shutdown**.
3. Select the checkbox next to the init script for the MySQL database server (it will be
   named `mysql`, `mysqld`, `mysql-server`, or similarly).
4. Click the **Start Now and On Boot** button.
5. Click the **Refresh Modules** link at the bottom of Webmin's main menu and reload the
   browser to update the menu.
6. Navigate to **Servers | MySQL Database Server**.

Webmin should be able to connect to your MySQL server. You will see a list of databases that,
at this stage, should include default databases such as `information_schema` and `mysql`.

> If you see **Warning: The Perl modules DBI and DBD::mysql are not installed
> on your system**, click the link and follow Webmin's instructions to install the
> missing Perl modules.

The default MySQL setup is fine for a development or testing server. However, if you plan to
use the database in production or on a shared server, please continue reading the _There's
more_ section of this recipe.

How it works...

Webmin helps you find and install the `mysql-server` package from your distribution's
repositories. The package contains an init script, which we enabled in order to start the
database server whenever your machine boots.

The default MySQL installation contains a number of convenient features, such as anonymous
user accounts or the ability to log in as root without providing a password. These default
options make it easier to get started with MySQL. However, they should never be used in
production because they constitute a major security risk.

There's more...

Perform the following steps to make MySQL more secure for use in a production setting.

Making MySQL ready for production use

Follow these steps to provide basic security for your MySQL server:

1. Connect to your server using a terminal emulator, for instance over SSH.

 You may also use Webmin's **Text Login** module.

2. Type in the following command: `mysql_secure_installation`.
3. Answer yes to all questions by pressing *Y* and then *Enter*, unless you know that you want settings other then the recommended ones.

The `mysql_secure_installation` script performs the following tasks:

- Sets a password for the database `root` user
- Removes anonymous access to the database; MySQL will only allow authorized users access from now on
- Disallows remote login by the `root` user, because this user should normally only access the database from the same computer
- Removes the `test` database.

See also

- If you want to allow other computers access to your databases, take a look at the *Allowing access to MySQL over the network* recipe of this chapter.

Allowing access to MySQL over the network

Programs that access MySQL databases, which are called clients, may be running on the same machine as the server. In this case, the client and server will communicate most efficiently using a Unix domain socket, which is a channel of inter-process communication accessed through the filesystem like a file or directory. Access to a socket is controlled by the filesystem's permissions.

Other client programs may be able to communicate only over TCP network sockets. These clients may connect to the local server using the loopback interface and IP address of 127.0.0.1. In this case, the MySQL server must be compiled with networking support and configured to listen for connections on the loopback interface.

However, if the client program is located on a machine other than the server, then communication between them must take place over the network using the TCP protocol. In order to make this communication possible, you will need to open an exception in your firewall and instruct MySQL to listen for incoming network connections on a physical network interface.

 You may also tunnel MySQL traffic over SSH, which may be a more secure solution. Take a look at the *Accessing your database server remotely over an SSH tunnel* recipe for more information.

Getting ready

If you plan to make your database server available over the network, you should definitely take measures to secure it. Take a look at the *Making MySQL ready for production use* section of the *Installing the MySQL database server* recipe in this chapter for more information.

Before starting, follow steps described in the *Allowing access to a service through the firewall* recipe in *Chapter 3, Securing your system*, to allow incoming TCP traffic to port `3306` through your firewall as shown in the following screenshot:

 Accept   If protocol is **TCP** and destination port is **3306** and state of connection is **NEW**

How to do it...

Steps in this recipe will be divided into the following four sections:

- First, we'll instruct MySQL to listen for incoming network connections on the standard MySQL port (`3306`)
- Then, we'll create a database user named `dbuser`
- We will grant access to a database named `testdb`
- Finally, we will test the setup by connecting to our server from a secondary client machine

Instructing MySQL server to listen for network connections

For MySQL to accept incoming network connections, perform the following steps:

1. Navigate to **Servers | MySQL Database Server | MySQL Server Configuration**.
2. Set **MySQL server listening address** to **Any**.
3. Click the **Save and Restart MySQL** button.

Creating a new user

In order to create a new user, perform the following steps:

1. Navigate to **Servers | MySQL Database Server | User Permissions**.
2. Click the **Create new user** link.
3. Set **Username** to dbuser, **Password** to a strong password, and **Hosts** to **Any**.
4. Click the **Create** button.

Granting user access to database

In order to grant user access to database, perform the following steps:

1. Navigate to **Servers | MySQL Database Server | Database Permissions**.
2. Click the **Create new database permissions** link.
3. In the **Databases** line, choose **Selected** and select your testdb database.
4. Set **Username** to the name of the created user, that is, dbuser.
5. Set **Hosts** to **Any** to allow the user to connect from anywhere.

 For added security, you should specify an IP address or domain name from which the user will be able to connect. You can use % as part of the address to specify a wildcard. For example, 192.168.0.% would denote the entire 192.168.0.1/24 subnet, while %.example.com would include all hosts within a domain.

6. Select all the permissions in the **Permissions** list.
7. Click the **Create** button.

Testing the connection

Try to connect to your database server from a second machine on the network. If your other machine has the MySQL command-line client installed, you can test the connection by typing in this command at the terminal, but substitute mysql-host with the IP or domain name of your MySQL server:

```
$ mysql -u dbuser -p -h mysql-host -D testdb
```

If the connection is successful, you will see the following welcome message including the server's MySQL version:

```
Welcome to the MySQL monitor.  Commands end with ; or \g.
Your MySQL connection id is 58
Server version: 5.5.31-0+wheezy1 (Debian)
mysql> exit
Bye
```

When you arrive at the `mysql>` prompt, you can start executing SQL commands. Type `exit` and press *Enter* to disconnect.

How it works...

In order to allow the MySQL server to accept incoming network connections, Webmin edits your server's configuration file (usually located in `/etc/my.cnf`, `/var/db/mysql/my.cnf` or `/etc/mysql/my.cnf`).

There are two lines in the server's configuration that specify what connections the server will accept. For instance, if we only want to accept local connections, these lines could read like the following:

```
socket=/var/lib/mysql/mysql.sock
bind-address=127.0.0.1
```

The first line instructs MySQL to create a local Unix socket for communication with other programs on the same machine, while the second line instructs it to listen for incoming connections on the local loopback interface (`127.0.0.1`). In order to make the server listen to incoming network connections on all interfaces, Webmin simply removes the `bind-address` line.

We tested our connection by issuing the following command on another computer attached to the same network:

```
$ mysql -u dbuser -p -h mysql-host -D testdb
```

This command starts the MySQL command-line client. The options specified are as follows:

- `-u`: This option specifies which user is trying to connect to the server
- `-p`: This option states that we want to be prompted for a password
- `-h`: This option specifies the host to which we're trying to connect
- `-D`: This option states which database we want to use once we are connected

In order to create database users and grant them permissions, Webmin operates directly on the data stored in MySQL's internal configuration databases. If you wanted to perform the same operations manually, you could connect to the MySQL server by using the command-line client and issuing the following commands.

First, connect to the local database server as `root`:

```
$ mysql -u root -p
```

Next, issue the following MySQL commands:

```
mysql> CREATE USER 'dbuser'@'%' IDENTIFIED BY 'strongpassword';
mysql> GRANT ALL PRIVILEGES ON testdb.* TO 'dbuser'@'%';
mysql> FLUSH PRIVILEGES;
```

The first command creates a user named `dbuser`, while the second gives this user complete access to the `testdb` database. The final command forces your MySQL server to reload information about users and privileges so that the new user can connect.

> The MySQL command-line client stores a history of all the entered commands in a file. If we execute the commands listed earlier, the history file will contain the password of our newly created user. To avoid this, we can instruct MySQL not to save history during this session by issuing the following command before connecting to the server:
>
> `$ export MYSQL_HISTFILE=/dev/null`

There's more...

This recipe allows a user to access a single database remotely. For security reasons, the primary management account (`root`) should not be allowed to connect to your server from another computer. If you would nevertheless like to allow some remote management of the database server (creating databases, users, and so on), you can perform the following outlined steps.

Managing databases remotely

Follow these steps to create an account that you will use for remote administration:

1. Navigate to **Servers | MySQL Database Server | User Permissions**.
2. Click the **Create new user** link.
3. Set **Username** to an administrative account name. Try to choose a username that will be harder to guess than `admin`.
4. Set **Password** to a very strong password.
5. Set **Hosts** to the IP address range from which your administrative user will connect.
6. From the **Permissions** list, carefully choose only those permissions that you are sure you need to access remotely.

More information about the significance of each permission can be found in the *Privileges Provided by MySQL* section of MySQL's documentation at the following link:

```
http://dev.mysql.com/doc/refman/5.6/en/privileges-
provided.html
```

7. Click the **Create** button.

   You should now be able to connect to your server (`mysql-host`) from a remote client computer. You do not need to specify a database name when you connect:

   ```
   $ mysql -u administrative_user -p -h mysql-host
   ```

See also

In order to make remote access and management of your MySQL databases more secure, you can tunnel your connection over SSH.

▸ Take a look at the *Accessing your MySQL server over an SSH tunnel* recipe of this chapter for instructions.

Accessing your MySQL server over an SSH tunnel

If your server is hosting a website on the Internet and running a database system on the same machine, it is safer to disable remote network access to MySQL. On the other hand, you may still want to manage your databases remotely, and you can do so by tunneling MySQL traffic over an SSH connection.

One of the most important aspects of a database system is the speed with which it can find and return the data that you ask for. Tunneling traffic over SSH will add significant overhead to this communication. This solution is great for intermittent management tasks, but is typically not suitable as a replacement for a direct connection to your database system.

Getting ready

The server you want to connect to must run both the MySQL server and an SSH server. The remote client machine must have an SSH client and MySQL client software installed. Make a note of the IP address or domain name of the server (`mysql-host`), the SSH username (`ssh-user`), MySQL user (`mysql-user`), and database name (`database-name`). Substitute them in this recipe.

How to do it...

In order to create an SSH tunnel for MySQL, follow these steps:

1. Issue the following command on your client machine:

   ```
   $ ssh -L 15000:localhost:3306 ssh-user@mysql-host
   ```

   This creates a tunnel between the port `15000` on your client machine and the port `3306` of the server. You can now access the remote database by making a MySQL connection to your client computer's local port `15000`.

2. Issue the following command on the client system to test the connection:

   ```
   $ mysql -u mysql-user -p  -D database-name -h 127.0.0.1 -P 15000
   ```

How it works...

The SSH client acts as an intermediator in communication between a MySQL client running on your machine and the remote server. It opens port `15000` and listens for incoming connections. All packets arriving at port `15000` are encrypted and forwarded over SSH to the server. On the server side, SSH receives the packets, decrypts them, and sends them to port `3306`. Answers are sent back in the opposite direction over the same channel.

You can find more information about SSH tunnels in the *Connecting to Webmin securely over an SSH tunnel* recipe in *Chapter 3, Securing Your System*.

There's more...

Some MySQL clients incorporate the ability to set up an SSH tunnel when connecting to a remote database.

Making an SSH tunnel in MySQL Workbench

Popular GUI clients such as MySQL Workbench or Sequel Pro allow you to specify the SSH connection settings in the same window as the database connection settings. The procedure is similar in all cases. In MySQL Workbench you would set up the connection as follows:

1. Run MySQL Workbench on your client computer.

2. Select **Connect to database** from the **Database** menu.

3. Set **Connection Method** to **Standard TCP/IP over SSH**.

4. Set **SSH Hostname** to the remote server's IP address or domain name.

5. Set **SSH Username** to a system user with SSH access.

6. Set **MySQL Hostname** to `127.0.0.1`.

7. Set **MySQL Server Port** to `3306`.

8. Set **Username** to the name of a MySQL user.

9. Click the **Test Connection** button. Consider the following screenshot:

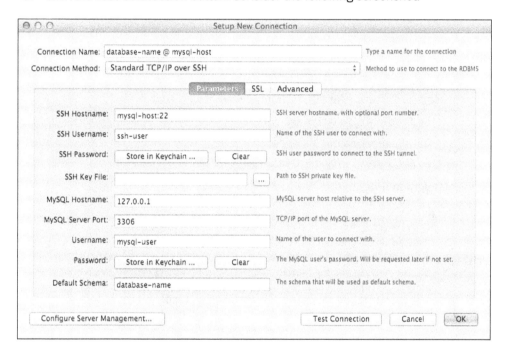

You will be asked for the password of the SSH user and then the password of the MySQL user. If all goes well, you will see a message indicating that the connection parameters are correct.

See also

▶ There are many tools that allow you to connect to and control your MySQL databases. Webmin provides a wide range of tools to perform most of the common tasks, and these are described in recipes later in this chapter. An even more powerful web-based solution that is dedicated to MySQL is phpMyAdmin. It is discussed in the *Installing phpMyAdmin* recipe of this chapter.

- ► You can download the GUI clients mentioned in this recipe from the following sites:

    - ❏ **MySQL Workbench**: `http://dev.mysql.com/downloads/tools/workbench`.

    - ❏ **Sequel Pro (OS X only)**: `http://www.sequelpro.com/download`.

- ► More information about SSH tunnels is provided in the *Connecting to Webmin securely over an SSH tunnel* recipe in *Chapter 3, Securing Your System*.

Creating a new database

Creating a new MySQL database through Webmin's interface is very quick and simple.

How to do it...

Follow these steps to create a new database:

1. Navigate to **Servers | MySQL Database Server**.
2. Click the **Create a new database** link.
3. Enter **Database name**, for instance, `new_db`.
4. Set **Character set** to **utf8 (UTF-8 Unicode)**.
5. Set **Collation order** to **utf8_unicode_ci (UTF-8 Unicode)**.

> The character set specifies how letter characters are stored in your database and the `utf8` character set contains all the letters of most alphabets. The collation order, on the other hand, specifies what order the letters should be placed in when sorting alphabetically. The `utf8_unicode_ci` collation aims to be universal, but there may be regional variations that make a local collation such as `utf8_polish_ci` more appropriate for your situation.

6. Set **Initial table** to **None**.
7. Click the **Create** button.

How it works...

Webmin takes the information that you provide and creates a new database by connecting to the MySQL server and executing the following command:

```
mysql> CREATE DATABASE `new_db` CHARACTER SET utf8 COLLATE utf8_unicode_ci;
```

> ▶ In order to make the database useful, you would want to grant users permissions to access it. Take a look at the *Creating users and granting permissions to databases* recipe of this chapter for instructions.

> ▶ If you have an initial database structure or contents, you can upload them to the server using a SQL commands file. Take a look at the *Executing custom SQL commands* recipe of this chapter for more information.

> ▶ More information about character sets and collations can be found in MySQL's manual at the following link:
> `https://dev.mysql.com/doc/refman/5.7/en/charset-charsets.html`

Creating users and granting permissions to databases

Because of MySQL's client-server architecture, the server may accept connections from multiple clients. The connecting clients authenticate themselves to MySQL using a username and password. Information about user accounts and privileges is stored in an internal database called `mysql`.

MySQL accounts are separate from system accounts, which is usually a good thing because more often than not they represent applications running on your server rather than actual users. Each application connecting to your database server should have its own user account, with access privileges limited to only those databases which are needed for the application to run. It would be a bad idea to allow an application root-level access. This is because if the application is compromised, an attacker could steal or damage all databases on your system.

In addition to a username and password, MySQL accounts are also described by the host from which a user is allowed to connect. This means that `'user'@'localhost'` is a different account than `'user'@'remotehost'` and these accounts may have different access privileges.

Unfortunately, this means that multiple accounts have to be created if a user should have access from multiple hosts, or worse yet, if the location of the user changes as he roams around the network. In such cases, you may specify `%` as part of the host address as a wildcard. For example, `192.168.0.%` would specify the entire `192.168.0.1/24` subnet and `%.example.com` would specify all hosts within a domain.

If the location of your users cannot be narrowed down to a network or range of IP addresses, you should consider using SSH tunnels instead of opening access to your database server from the entire Internet. See the *Accessing your MySQL server over an SSH tunnel* recipe in this chapter for more information.

Getting ready

You should remove MySQL's anonymous accounts unless you have a particular reason to use them. Anonymous accounts are created by default for testing purposes, but they may cause difficulties in debugging problems with user privileges.

Let's say, for example, that you have a user account with access from any location: `'user'@'%'`, but you also have an anonymous account with access from the local host `@'localhost'`. If you try to connect as `user` from the local host, MySQL will first check the privileges entry that specifies the incoming connection's host more precisely (`@'localhost'` is more specific then `@'%'`). This will cause `user` to be assigned privileges of the anonymous account rather than the expected `'user'@'%'` account. You can check what user you are connected as by issuing the following MySQL command:

```
mysql> SELECT CURRENT_USER();
```

You will get the following output:

```
+----------------+
| CURRENT_USER() |
+----------------+
| @localhost     |
+----------------+
```

The output shows that we are being treated as an anonymous user `@'localhost'`. The solution to this situation is to add a second account for `user` as `'user'@'localhost'`. Then, when we log in again, we will see the following output of the same command:

```
+----------------+
| CURRENT_USER() |
+----------------+
| user@localhost |
+----------------+
```

If you don't need them for any specific purpose, it's safer and more convenient to remove anonymous accounts altogether.

How to do it...

In this recipe, we will create a user named `dbuser` with access from the local machine to the database `testdb`. The user will have to authenticate using a strong password. Prepare the username, database name, and password for your particular case.

Creating a user account

In order to create a user account, perform the following steps:

1. Navigate to **Servers | MySQL Database Server | User Permissions**.
2. Click the **Create new user** link.
3. Set **Username** to dbuser.
4. Set **Password** to a strong password.
5. Set **Hosts** to localhost.
6. In the **Permissions** list, do not select any permissions.

 We do not need to grant any global permission to the account, as the user will have access limited to a specific database.

7. Click the **Create** button.

Granting privileges

In order to grant privileges, perform the following steps:

1. Navigate to **Servers | MySQL Database Server | Database Permissions**.
2. Click the **Create new database permissions** link.
3. Set **Databases** to **Selected** and choose **testdb** from the list.
4. Set **Username** to dbuser.
5. Set **Hosts** to localhost.
6. In the **Permissions** list, select all permissions as shown in the following screenshot:

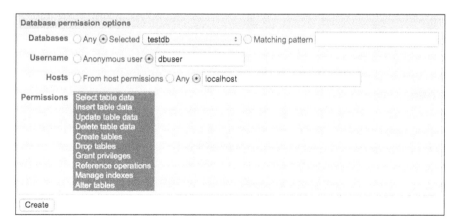

7. Click the **Create** button.

The created account and privileges will allow dbuser to connect to and have full control over the testdb database when connecting to the local MySQL server.

 The MySQL server will use accounts associated with the localhost when a client connects from the local machine, regardless of whether the connection is made over a socket or TCP. However, if you create an account associated with 127.0.0.1, it will be used when connecting over TCP, but not when connecting on a socket. When connecting over TCP using IPv6, a third option comes into play, namely the IPv6 address of the local machine ::1. It's best to set up accounts for localhost to avoid this confusion.

How it works...

Webmin creates accounts and grants privileges by manipulating the mysql database directly. In particular, it adds a row to the user and db tables and then executes the FLUSH PRIVILEGES command.

If you wanted to perform the same operations manually, you could connect to the MySQL server using its command-line client and issue the following commands.

First connect to the local database server as root:

```
$ mysql -u root -p
```

Next issue the MySQL commands:

```
mysql> CREATE USER 'dbuser'@'localhost' IDENTIFIED BY 'strongpassword';
mysql> GRANT ALL PRIVILEGES ON testdb.* TO 'dbuser'@'localhost';
mysql> FLUSH PRIVILEGES;
```

The first command creates a user named dbuser, the second gives this user complete access to the testdb database. The final command forces your MySQL server to reload information about users and privileges so that the new user can connect.

There's more...

Webmin allows you to specify more granular access permissions—at the level of a database table or even a specific column within a database table. It also allows you to automatically create MySQL accounts for the new system users that are created via Webmin.

Granting permissions to a specific database table

In order to grant permissions to a specific database table, perform the following steps:

1. Navigate to **Servers | MySQL Database Server | Table Permissions**.
2. Select a database from the list and click the **Add new permissions in database** button.
3. Select a database **Table** from the list.
4. Set **Username** to the name of a previously defined MySQL user.
5. Set **Host** to the name of the host associated with the user account.
6. Select the permissions you wish to grant from the **Table permissions** and **Field permissions** lists as shown in the following screenshot:

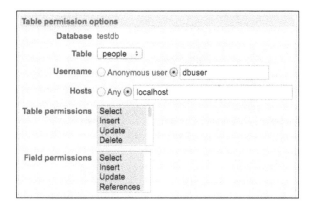

7. Click the **Create** button.

Granting permissions to a specific column in a database table

To grant permissions to a specific column in a database table, perform the following steps:

1. Navigate to **Servers | MySQL Database Server | Field Permissions**.
2. Select a database and table from the list and click the **Add new permissions in database and table** button.
3. Select a database table **Field** from the list.
4. Set **Username** to the name of a previously defined MySQL user.
5. Set **Host** to the name of the host associated with the user account.
6. Select the permissions you wish to grant from the **Permissions** list.
7. Click the **Create** button.

Automatically granting new system users access to MySQL

To automatically grant all system users access to MySQL, perform the following steps:

1. Navigate to **Servers | MySQL Database Server | User Permissions**.

2. Select all three checkboxes in the **When to synchronize** section.

3. Select permissions in the **Permissions for new users** list. For instance, if you want every user of your system to be a MySQL administrator, select all permissions. Use this with caution.

4. Set **Create new users with hosts** to **Specific host** and enter localhost.

The options below configure synchronization between Unix users created through Webmin and MySQL users.

When to synchronize	☑ Add a new MySQL user when a Unix user is added
	☑ Update a MySQL user when the matching Unix user is modified.
	☑ Delete a MySQL user when the matching Unix user is deleted.
Permissions for new users	Select table data
	Insert table data
	Update table data
	Delete table data
	Create tables
Create new users with hosts	○ All hosts ⊙ Specific host localhost

Save

5. Click the **Save** button.

From now on, every new user account created through Webmin will automatically receive a corresponding MySQL account with the same password as the system password. Passwords will be updated if changed through Webmin, and the MySQL account will be deleted if the corresponding system account is also deleted through Webmin.

Creating a backup of your database

Webmin can help you make backups of your MySQL databases. With just a few clicks, you can make a backup of any database. Webmin can also help you set up cron jobs to create backups automatically on a regular schedule.

Getting ready

Before starting, create a directory to store local backup files. You can keep these files in /backups in the root directory /root/backups, or in any location that you find convenient.

Backup files created by Webmin will be readable by all users of your system. This may be a security risk, since database backups often contain sensitive data such as hashed user passwords. You should remove all permissions on the backups directory for users outside of root's group. You can do that by issuing the following command:

```
$ sudo chmod o-rwx /backups
```

If your file system supports access control lists, you can additionally set the default mask for newly created files in this directory in such a way that they are not readable by users outside of the group. You can set the default ACL for `/backups` by issuing the following command:

```
$ sudo setfacl -d -m other:- /backups
```

Take a look at the *Changing file ownership and permissions* recipe in *Chapter 6, Managing Files on Your System*, for more information.

How to do it...

Follow these steps to create a database backup:

1. Navigate to **Servers | MySQL Database Server**.
2. Click the icon that represents the database you would like to back up.
3. Click the **Backup Database** button.
4. Set **Backup to file** to a path such as `/backups/database-name.sql.bz2`.
5. Set **Tables to backup** to **All tables**.
6. Open the **Other backup options** section.
7. Set **Add drop table statements to backup?** to **Yes**.

This helps you import the created backup into an existing database. Tables with the same names will be deleted (dropped) before importing the ones stored in the backup.

8. Set **Character set for backup** to **UTF-8 Unicode**.
9. Choose **Compression format** to **Bzip2**.

Bzip2 gives really good compression for text such as SQL command files.

10. Click the **Backup Now** button.

How it works...

Webmin executes the `mysqldump` command to output a series of SQL commands that would be needed to create the entire database. The database "dump" is then piped through the bzip2 compression algorithm and saved to an output file. If you wanted to do the same kind of backup in the terminal, you could run a command similar to the following (make sure you set the `mysqldump` options correctly):

```
$ mysqldump --add-drop-table --routines database-name | bzip2 -c > /
backups/database-name.sql.bz2
```

There's more...

Webmin is quite a capable tool for making backups. Here are a few other, easily accessible functions.

Backing up all databases automatically

Webmin can help you make an automated backup of some or all databases hosted by your server. These backups will be executed on a regular schedule by cron. For more information about scheduling commands take a look at the *Scheduling a command to run regularly with cron* recipe in *Chapter 4, Controlling Your System*. In order to back up all databases automatically, perform the following steps:

1. Navigate to **Servers | MySQL Database Server**.
2. Click the **Backup Databases** button.
3. Set **Backup to directory** to the location of your backup directory, for instance, `/backups`.
4. Open the **Other backup options** section.
5. Set **Add drop table statements to backup?** to **Yes**.
6. Set **Character set for backup** to **UTF-8 Unicode**.
7. Set **Compression format** to **Bzip2**.
8. Open the **Backup schedule** section.
9. Set **Send backup status email to** to your e-mail address.
10. Set **Scheduled backup enabled?** to **Yes, at times chosen below**, set **Simple schedule** and select **Daily (at midnight)**.

Note that many things may be scheduled to start at midnight on your system, so you can choose another time if your system resources are limited. Choose a more complex schedule by marking the minutes, hours, and days of the month at which the job is to be performed.

11. Click the **Save** button.

Exporting a database table to CSV

Webmin can export a single table of your database into a **comma-separated-values** (**CSV**) file that can be opened by spreadsheet programs, such as Excel, Calc, or Gnumeric. To export a database table to CSV, perform the following steps:

1. Navigate to **Servers | MySQL Database Server**.
2. Click the icon of the database, which contains the table.
3. Click the icon of the table you would like to export.
4. Click the **Export to CSV** button.
5. Set **File format** to **CSV with quotes**.
6. Set **Include column names in CSV?** to **Yes**.
7. Set **Export destination** to **Display in browser**.
8. Click the **Export Now** button.

See also

▶ You can easily perform backups to a remote host by using a network file sharing protocol such as NFS or CIFS. You start by creating a network volume on the remote server, and then mount the volume on your server. You can then back up to directories on the remote system just as easily as if they were stored locally. Take a look at *Chapter 6, Managing Files on Your System*, for instructions on the setting up of network file sharing using NFS or CIFS.

▶ Another way to store spare copies of your databases remotely is to send your backup directory to a remote server using the SSH protocol. Take a look at the *Backing up to a remote host* recipe in *Chapter 7, Backing Up Your System*, for more information.

Executing custom SQL commands

Webmin provides a simple interface to your MySQL database server that allows you to execute arbitrary SQL commands. This can be a useful feature when you want to quickly find something in a database or perform a bulk update of multiple rows of data.

How to do it...

Follow these steps to execute an SQL command on your database:

1. Navigate to **Servers | MySQL Database Server**.
2. Click the icon that represents the database you would like to use, for instance, `mysql`.

3. Click the **Execute SQL** button.

4. Enter an SQL command in the text area, for instance:

   ```
   SELECT host,user FROM user;
   ```

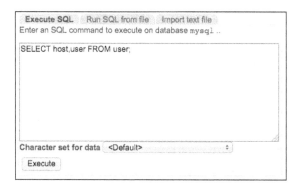

5. Click the **Execute** button.

You will be presented with a sortable display of data returned by the SELECT command.

How it works...

Webmin simply passes the SQL command to the database server. If the command returns an error, it will be displayed on screen. If the command returns rows of data, Webmin will convert them into an HTML page and display them on screen. Please note that Webmin is running as the root user, so caution should be used when executing commands.

See also

▶ Webmin can also help you to execute an entire SQL script saved in a file. See the *Restoring database from the backup* recipe of this chapter for more information.

▶ You can save commands you execute often in an easy-to-use control panel in Webmin. Take a look at the *Creating a panel with the database commands that you execute often* recipe in *Chapter 4, Controlling Your System*, for more information.

▶ If you find that you need a more full-fledged, web-based MySQL management tool, consider installing phpMyAdmin. This is described in the *Installing phpMyAdmin* recipe in this chapter.

Restoring database from the backup

Databases may be stored as text files that contain SQL instructions which rebuild them. If you have a SQL backup file, you can use Webmin to restore it.

Getting ready

Large backups should be uploaded to the server before being executed. If your backup file is large, upload it to the server and note its location. Take a look at the *Uploading files to the server* recipe in *Chapter 6, Managing Files on Your System*, for more information.

We will restore the backup to an existing database. If you haven't created the database yet, follow instructions in the *Creating a new database* recipe before starting.

How to do it...

Follow these steps to restore a database from backup or execute a SQL script saved in a file:

1. Navigate to **Servers | MySQL Database Server**.
2. Click the icon that represents the database you would like to restore the backup to.
3. Click the **Execute SQL** button.
4. Select the **Run SQL from file** tab.
5. If you have uploaded the file onto the server, select **From local file** and enter the file's location in the text box. Otherwise, select **From uploaded file** and choose a file from your disk.

 Webmin can handle SQL files that are compressed using gzip or bzip2.

6. Click the **Execute** button.

How it works...

Webmin pipes the entire SQL instructions file into the MySQL server. The server executes every instruction stored in the file, rebuilding the database line by line.

If you wanted to perform the same task in the terminal, you could use the following command:

```
$ mysql database-name < backup-file.sql
```

There's more...

Webmin can import a single table into your database from a CSV file that can be created by a spreadsheet program such as Excel, Calc, or Gnumeric.

Follow these steps to import a CSV file:

1. Navigate to **Servers** | **MySQL Database Server**.
2. Click the icon that represents the database to which you would like to restore the backup.
3. Click the **Execute SQL** button.
4. Select the **Import text file** tab.
5. If you have uploaded the file onto the server, select **From local file** and enter the file's location in the text box. Otherwise, select **From uploaded file** and choose a file from your disk.
6. Select a table from the **Table to import data into** dropdown.
7. Set **Character set** to **utf8 (UTF-8 Unicode)**.
8. Click the **Execute** button.

You will be presented with an information screen that describes how many rows were successfully imported or what errors were encountered.

Editing the structure of your database

Webmin allows you to quickly modify the structure of tables in your MySQL database through an easy-to-use interface. In this recipe, we will demonstrate how to perform the following list of tasks:

- Create a table in a database
- Add a column to a database table
- Edit a column
- Create an index
- Delete an index
- Delete a column
- Delete a table from the database

Getting ready

For demonstration purposes, we will be using a database called testdb. You can create a database with this name through Webmin by following the steps described in the *Creating a new database* recipe of this chapter.

How to do it...

In the testdb database, we'll create a table called people and add a column called name to the table. We'll then change the width of the field, turn it into a unique index, and finally delete the index, field, and table from the database.

Creating a table in a database

To create a table in a database, perform the following steps:

1. Navigate to **Servers | MySQL Database Server**.

2. Click the icon that represents the `testdb` database.

3. Click the **Create a new table** button.

4. Specify `people` as **Table name**.

5. Set **Type of table** to **myisam**.

 The table type option specifies which storage engine is used by this table. This determines what features are available for your table, for instance **myisam** allows for full-text search indexes, while **innodb** supports transactions. You can find more information on storage engines in MySQL's manual:

`http://dev.mysql.com/doc/refman/5.6/en/storage-engines.html`

6. Provide the definition of one field that will be the primary key for this table. Fill in the following field definitions:

   - **Field name**: `id`
   - **Data type**: **int**
   - **Type width**: `11`
   - **Key**: **Yes**
   - **Auto increment**: **Yes**
   - **Allow nulls**: **No**

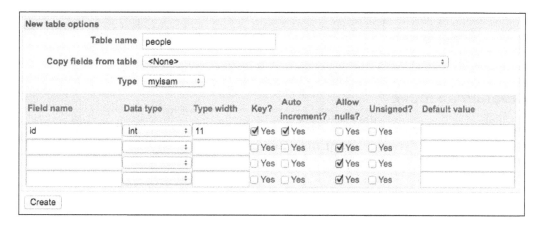

New table options

| Table name | people | | | | | | |

| Copy fields from table | <None> | | | | | | |

| Type | myisam | | | | | | |

Field name	Data type	Type width	Key?	Auto increment?	Allow nulls?	Unsigned?	Default value
id	int	11	☑ Yes	☑ Yes	☐ Yes	☐ Yes	
			☐ Yes	☐ Yes	☑ Yes	☐ Yes	
			☐ Yes	☐ Yes	☑ Yes	☐ Yes	
			☐ Yes	☐ Yes	☑ Yes	☐ Yes	

Create

7. Click the **Create** button.

Adding a field to a database table

In order to add a field to the database table, perform the following steps:

1. Navigate to **Servers | MySQL Database Server**.
2. Click the icon that represents the `testdb` database.
3. Click the icon that represents the `people` table.
4. Select `varchar` from the types drop-down menu and click the **Add field of type** button.
5. Fill in the following field definitions:

   - **Field name**: `name`
   - **Type width**: `80`
   - **Type options: Case insensitive**
   - **Allow nulls: Yes**
   - **Default value: NULL**
   - **Part of primary key?: No**

6. Click the **Create** button.

Editing a field

To edit a field, perform the following steps:

1. Navigate to **Servers | MySQL Database Server**.
2. Click the icon that represents the `testdb` database.
3. Click the icon that represents the `people` table.
4. Click the link for field `name`.
5. Set **Type width** to `128`.
6. Click the **Save** button.

Creating an index

To create an index, perform the following steps:

1. Navigate to **Servers | MySQL Database Server**.
2. Click the icon that represents the `testdb` database.
3. Click the icon that represents the `people` table.
4. Click the **Create Index** button.
5. Set **Index name** to `unique_name`.
6. Select the field `name` in the **Fields in index** list.

7. Set **Index type** to **Unique**.

8. Click the **Create** button.

Deleting an index

To delete an index, perform the following steps:

1. Navigate to **Servers | MySQL Database Server**.

2. Click the icon that represents the `testdb` database.

3. Click the icon that represents the `unique_name` index.

4. Click the **Delete** button.

Deleting a field

In order to delete a field, perform the following steps:

1. Navigate to **Servers | MySQL Database Server**.

2. Click the icon that represents the `testdb` database.

3. Click the icon that represents the `people` table.

4. Click the link for `name` field.

5. Click the **Delete** button.

Deleting a table from the database

To delete a table from the database, perform the following steps:

1. Navigate to **Servers | MySQL Database Server**.

2. Click the icon that represents the `testdb` database.

3. Click the icon that represents the `people` table.

4. Click the **Drop table** button and confirm on the screen that follows it.

How it works...

Webmin prepares the syntax for the appropriate CREATE, DROP, and ALTER TABLE SQL commands to perform all of the earlier mentioned actions, and then executes those commands on your MySQL server as the `root` user.

See also

▶ If you find that you need a more full-fledged, web-based MySQL management tool, consider installing phpMyAdmin. This is described in the *Installing phpMyAdmin* recipe

Editing records in a database

Webmin allows you to quickly edit data in your MySQL database through a simple interface. In this recipe, we will demonstrate how to add, edit, and delete records in a database table.

Getting ready

In this recipe, we will use examples based on the `testdb` database created in the *Creating a new database* and *Editing the structure of your database* recipes of this chapter.

How to do it...

We'll add a record to the `people` table of the `testdb` database; we'll edit the same record, and finally delete it to show how to perform these actions in Webmin.

Adding a row to database table

In order to add a row to the database table, perfom the following steps:

1. Navigate to **Servers | MySQL Database Server**.
2. Click the icon that represents the `testdb` database.
3. Click the icon that represents the `people` table.
4. Click the **View Data** button.
5. Click the **Add row** button.
6. Fill in a name in the textbox.
7. Click the **Save** button.

Editing a row

In order to edit a row, perform the following steps:

1. Navigate to **Servers | MySQL Database Server**.
2. Click the icon that represents the `testdb` database.
3. Click the icon that represents the `people` table.
4. Click the **View Data** button.
5. Mark the checkbox next to the record you would like to edit.
6. Click the **Edit selected rows** button.
7. Change the name value in the text box.
8. Click the **Save** button.

Deleting a row

In order to delete a row, perform the following steps:

1. Navigate to **Servers | MySQL Database Server**.

2. Click the icon that represents the `testdb` database.

3. Click the icon that represents the `people` table.

4. Click the **View Data** button.

5. Mark the checkbox next to the record you would like to delete.

6. Click the **Delete selected rows** button.

How it works...

Webmin prepares the syntax for the appropriate `INSERT`, `UPDATE`, and `DELETE` SQL commands to perform the preceding actions and executes those commands on your MySQL server as the `root` user.

See also

▸ If you find that you need a more full-fledged, web-based MySQL management tool, consider installing phpMyAdmin. This is described in the *Installing phpMyAdmin* recipe

Checking who is using your database server

You may wish to check who is connected to your database server when debugging network connectivity, auditing security, or simply if you're curious. In Webmin, this information is just a few clicks away.

How to do it...

Follow these steps:

1. Navigate to **Servers | MySQL Database Server**.

2. Click the **Database Connections** icon.

You will see a list of active connections or a message that no clients other then Webmin are connected to the database at this time. Consider the following screenshot:

ID	Username	Client host	Database	Mode	Connected	Running query
☐ 5797	root	localhost		Sleep	00:00:05	

Select all. | Invert selection.

Kill Selected Connections

How it works...

Webmin queries your MySQL server for information about active client connections. You could gain the same information by running the SQL command SHOW PROCESSLIST in a MySQL client:

```
mysql> SHOW PROCESSLIST;
```

You will get the following output:

```
+------+------+-----------+------+---------+------------------+
| Id   | User | Host      | db   | Command | Info             |
+------+------+-----------+------+---------+------------------+
| 5797 | root | localhost | NULL | Query   | SHOW PROCESSLIST |
+------+------+-----------+------+---------+------------------+
1 row in set (0.00 sec)
```

There's more...

Webmin also makes it easy to close any unnecessary connections. The clients will have to re-establish their connections to continue using the database.

Follow these steps to close a connection:

1. Navigate to **Servers | MySQL Database Server**.
2. Click the **Database Connections** icon.
3. Mark the checkbox next to the description of an active connection.
4. Click the **Kill Selected Connections** button.

Installing phpMyAdmin

phpMyAdmin is a commonly used database administration tool for MySQL. It is a web-based application, like Webmin itself, but dedicated to all tasks related to the administration of a MySQL server. It's easy to use and can be a helpful tool for your database users and administrators.

> System packages are configured to run phpMyAdmin on Apache. The Apache web server and PHP are installed as package dependencies. If you're not already using Apache and PHP, this exposes a potential attack vector on your database server. Consider the security implications of installing phpMyAdmin and keep it up to date.

How to do it...

Follow these steps to set up phpMyAdmin on your system:

1. Install the package named `phpmyadmin` (or `phpMyAdmin` depending on your system). Refer to the *Installing software packages* recipe in *Chapter 1, Setting Up Your System*, for more information.

> On some systems, you may need to add an additional repository to install the package. For instance, if you're running a Linux distribution from the RedHat family (RHEL, CentOS, Fedora, and so on), you should add the **Extra Packages for Enterprise Linux** (**EPEL**) repository. Information about the setting up of EPEL can be found in the *Giving users access to your server via FTP* recipe in *Chapter 6, Managing Files on Your System*.

2. Since phpMyAdmin runs on top of Apache, you should make sure that this server is installed on your system and is accessible to a browser. Follow the *Installing Apache on your system* recipe in *Chapter 8, Running an Apache Web Server*, to get Apache up and running.

3. Navigate to the following URL, but substitute `webmin-host` for the IP or domain name of your server: `http://webmin-host/phpmyadmin`.

On some systems, phpMyAdmin is configured to be accessible to connections that originate from the local host only. If you wish to change this behavior, go to **Servers | Apache Webserver | Default Server**, select **Per-Directory Options** for phpMyAdmin's directory, and change its **Access Control** settings. More information is provided in the *Setting options for directories, files, and locations* recipe in *Chapter 8, Running an Apache Web Server*.

Information about additional steps that may be necessary to set up phpMyAdmin in your system distribution can be found in package documentation files. Refer to the *Reading the documentation of the installed software* recipe in *Chapter 1, Setting Up Your System*.

4. You can now log in using the username and password of a MySQL account.

phpMyAdmin will log you in as if you were connecting from the local machine, so privileges assigned to an account on `localhost` will be used.

How it works...

phpMyAdmin is an application written in PHP. The main configuration file of phpMyAdmin is named `config.inc.php`, and it is usually installed inside the `/etc/` directory. Example locations for different distributions are listed in the following table. The code of the application itself is stored in the form of PHP script files in a directory named phpMyAdmin.

Because phpMyAdmin is served by Apache, the installation package includes an application-specific configuration file that will be loaded by the web server. This file informs Apache where phpMyAdmin is stored on the disk and which of its directories should be made available on the web.

File	OS / distro	Location
phpMyAdmin configuration	Debian	`/etc/phpmyadmin/config.inc.php`
	CentOS	`/etc/phpMyAdmin/config.inc.php`
	OpenSUSE	`/etc/phpMyAdmin/config.inc.php`
phpMyAdmin files	Debian	`/usr/share/phpmyadmin`
	CentOS	`/usr/share/phpMyAdmin`
	OpenSUSE	`/srv/www/htdocs/phpMyAdmin`
Apache configuration file for phpMyAdmin	Debian	`/etc/phpmyadmin/apache.conf`
	CentOS	`/etc/httpd/conf.d/phpMyAdmin.conf`
	OpenSUSE	`/etc/apache2/conf.d/phpMyAdmin.conf`

Regardless of how package maintainers decided to prepare it, you can tweak the Apache configuration for phpMyAdmin by going to **Servers | Apache Webserver | Default Server** and selecting **Per-Directory Options** for the phpMyAdmin directory.

There's more...

phpMyAdmin is a very capable tool and you can find detailed information about how it can be used in its documentation at: `http://docs.phpmyadmin.net/en/latest/`

10
Running a PostgreSQL Database Server

In this chapter, we will cover the following recipes:

- ▶ Installing the PostgreSQL database server
- ▶ Locating the PostgreSQL server configuration files
- ▶ Allowing access to PostgreSQL over the network
- ▶ Accessing the PostgreSQL server over an SSH tunnel
- ▶ Creating a new database
- ▶ Creating users and granting permissions
- ▶ Creating a backup of your database
- ▶ Executing custom SQL commands
- ▶ Restoring a database from backup
- ▶ Editing the structure of your database
- ▶ Editing records in a database
- ▶ Installing phpPgAdmin

Introduction

PostgreSQL is a powerful open source relational **database management system** (**DBMS**). It features a powerful type system and advanced programming functions. This allows it to store and perform calculations on complex values, such as geographic coordinates, JSON objects, and arrays.

PostgreSQL uses a distributed client-server architecture, which means that the database server and client applications can run on separate machines. If the client and server are running on the same system, they can communicate using Unix sockets; otherwise, they communicate over the network by using TCP sockets. The Postgres server uses port number 5432 by default, but this setting can be changed if needed.

 Unix domain sockets are channels used for inter-process communication. Different programs running on the same machine can read and write information to a socket, enabling communication between the programs. Unix sockets are represented as nodes of the filesystem, so you can find a socket by listing the contents of a directory in which it was created.

The PostgreSQL DBMS is very popular and most operating system distributions provide packages for its easy installation. Each Postgres server hosts a database **cluster** that consists of a collection of databases, associated configuration files, and running processes. On some systems, the cluster must be initiated after package installation. Initiation creates the directory structure of the cluster and fills it with standard databases. The standard database, `template1`, plays a special role, because all new databases are created as its copies by default.

Installation of the Postgres system involves the creation of a special user, usually named `postgres`. This user has complete administrative control over your databases, and Webmin will run most database commands and scripts as this user.

Webmin allows you to perform many tasks related to the running of the Postgres database server. In this chapter, we will demonstrate how Webmin can help you install PostgreSQL, set up access to the server over a network, manage user accounts, create databases, and edit their structure and data. We'll also demonstrate how to automatically back up databases and restore backup files. If you find that you need an even more advanced web-based management tool, we will demonstrate how to set up phpPgAdmin on your server.

Installing the PostgreSQL database server

Most operating systems that come with a package management solution for open source software make PostgreSQL packages available for installation. In this recipe, we will install PostgreSQL from a package and set it up on your system. Installing the server package automatically installs the PostgreSQL command-line client package, as well.

How to do it...

Perform the following steps to install the PostgreSQL database server:

1. Follow the steps described in the _Installing software packages_ recipe in _Chapter 1, Setting Up Your System_, to find and install the PostgreSQL database server package.

    In most package repositories, the PostgreSQL server package is simply named `postgresql-server`. If your distribution allows you to select among different versions of PostgreSQL, the package names will contain version numbers such as `postgresql-9.1` or `postgresql93-server`. Pick the package with the latest version unless you have reasons to stick with an older one.

2. Click the **Refresh Modules** link at the bottom of Webmin's main menu and reload the browser to update the menu.

3. Navigate to **Servers | PostgreSQL Database Server**. You should see a screen that lists installed databases. It should include the default databases such as `postgresql` and `template1`.

4. If you do not see the list of databases, but instead a message which indicates that the database system has not yet been initialized, click the **Initialize Database** button.

    At the bottom of the screen, if you see the message, **Warning: The Perl modules DBI and DBD::Pg are not installed on your system**, click the link and follow Webmin's instructions to install the missing Perl modules.

5. Navigate to **System | Bootup and Shutdown** and verify that the init script, `postgresql`, is set to start at boot. If it isn't, select its checkbox and click the **Start Now and On Boot** button.

How it works...

Webmin helps you find and install the `postgresql-server` package from your distribution's repositories. The package installs the database server, client, and an init script that starts the server during system boot.

Before Postgres can be used to manage databases, a new cluster must be created. A PostgreSQL cluster is a collection of databases managed by a single server. Creating the cluster involves the creation of a directory in which the database files will be stored, and filling it with a few standard databases. The standard database named `template1` plays a special role, because all new databases in the cluster will be made by copying this template.

If your package installation script does not initialize a database cluster for you, you can ask Webmin to do it by clicking the **Initialize Database** button. This runs the following subcommand of the init script:

```
/etc/rc.d/init.d/postgresql initdb
```

See also

▶ If you want to allow other computers to access your databases, take a look at the recipe, *Allowing access to PostgreSQL over the network*.

Locating the PostgreSQL server configuration files

The main configuration file of the PostgreSQL server is usually named `postgresql.conf`, and is stored in the database cluster data directory by default. Various system distributions move this configuration outside of the data directory and place it in a different location, for example, in the `/etc/` directory. In this recipe, we will demonstrate how to find the `postgresql.conf` and change it to modify the server's configuration. Webmin does not assist you in the modification of the basic settings of PostgreSQL, so you will need to edit the configuration file manually.

Getting ready

Make sure that the PostgreSQL server is installed and running, and that you are able to connect to it via Webmin before starting. The recipe, *Installing the PostgreSQL database server*, provides more information.

How to do it...

Follow these steps to locate PostgreSQL's main configuration file on your system:

1. Navigate to **Servers | PostgreSQL Database Server**.
2. Click the icon of the default database, `postgres`.
3. Click the **Execute SQL** button.
4. Enter the following SQL command in the provided text area:

   ```
   SHOW config_file;
   ```

5. Click the **Execute** button and you will see the output of the SQL command, which provides the full path to the main server configuration file, as shown in the following screenshot:

How it works...

When an init script starts the PostgreSQL server, it may specify the location of the database cluster's data directory or the location of the server's main configuration file (customarily called `postgresql.conf`). By default, the main configuration file is stored inside of the data directory, but package maintainers often move it to a different location (such as `/etc/`) to keep system configuration files in order. The SQL command, `SHOW config_file;`, can be used to check where the main configuration file is located.

There's more...

The location of other configuration files and the values of other settings can also be displayed using the SQL `SHOW` command.

Determining location of other configuration files and data files

Use the following commands to check where other configuration files are located:

Setting	Command
Main configuration file (`postgresql.conf`)	`SHOW config_file;`
Data directory	`SHOW data_directory;`
Host-based access configuration file (`pg_hba.conf`)	`SHOW hba_file;`
Identity mapping file (`pg_ident.conf`)	`SHOW ident_file;`
Directory where the Unix-domain socket will be created	`SHOW unix_socket_directory;`

Checking values of other settings

You can also reveal the values of all settings by issuing the following command:

```
SHOW all;
```

Allowing access to PostgreSQL over the network

Programs that access PostgreSQL databases, which are called clients, may be running on the same machine as the server. In this case, the client and server will communicate most efficiently using a Unix-domain socket, a channel of inter-process communication accessed through the filesystem such as a file or directory. Access to a socket is controlled by filesystem permissions.

Other client programs may be able to communicate only over TCP network sockets. These clients may connect to the local server using the loopback interface and IP address of `127.0.0.1`.

However, if a client program is located on a machine other than the server, then communication between them must take place over the network using the TCP protocol. There are a number of ways to set up network connections for PostgreSQL. The most efficient but least secure method is to use a direct unencrypted connection between the client and server. This method has the drawback that unencrypted information could potentially be eavesdropped upon or even modified in transit over the network. Because database systems are usually designed to be as efficient as possible, this type of communication is used often, but should only be deployed inside of a secure network. We will describe how to enable this type of communication in this recipe.

In order to make network access to your PostgreSQL server more secure, you can choose to encrypt the transferred information using SSL. This prevents eavesdropping and man-in-the-middle attacks, but leaves the PostgreSQL server's network port exposed and potentially vulnerable to brute-force password guessing and other attacks.

If you really need security, for instance, to access your database server over the Internet, you should probably choose a third option: send the PostgreSQL traffic over an encrypted SSH tunnel. This is the least efficient of the described transmission methods, but it generates the fewest security concerns. For more information, take a look at the recipe, *Accessing the PostgreSQL server over an SSH tunnel*.

Getting ready

In this recipe, we will prepare your PostgreSQL server to accept incoming network connections. In order to test the connection, we will need access to two computers attached to the same network: the server and a client machine. Make note of the server and client's IP or domain name before starting.

How to do it...

The steps in this recipe will be divided into five sections:

- First, we'll instruct PostgreSQL to listen for incoming network connections on the standard port (5432).

- Next, we'll create a database user named dbuser.

- Then, we will create a database named testtdb.

- We will allow remote access to the database.

- And finally, we will test the setup by connecting to our server from a secondary client machine.

Perform the following steps to instruct the PostgreSQL server to listen for network connections:

1. Follow steps described in the recipe, *Allowing access to a service through the firewall* in *Chapter 3*, *Securing Your System*, to allow incoming TCP traffic to port 5432 through your firewall.

2. Find the location of the PostgreSQL main server configuration file (postgresql.conf). Refer to the recipe, *Locating the PostgreSQL server configuration files*, for detailed instructions.

3. Within the `postgresql.conf` file, find the line with the `listen_addresses` directive. This line may be commented out (start with the # character). Change the line to the following:

```
listen_addresses = '*'
```

 The most effective way to edit files on your server is to use an editor such as Vim or Nano in a terminal session (for example, over SSH). But to make a small change in a configuration file, you do not need to leave Webmin. Take a look at the *Editing a file on the server* section of the *Managing files and directories on the server* recipe from *Chapter 6, Managing Files on Your System*.

4. We must restart the server after making configuration changes. Navigate to **Servers | PostgreSQL Database Server**, click the **Stop PostgreSQL Server** button, and then click the **Start PostgreSQL Server** button.

Your PostgreSQL server will now listen for incoming network connections on port 5432.

Perform the following steps to create a new user:

1. Navigate to **Servers | PostgreSQL Database Server | PostgreSQL Users**.
2. Click the **Create new user** link.
3. Set **Username** to dbuser and assign a strong password in the **Password** field.
4. Answer **No** to the **Can create databases?** and **Can create users?** questions.
5. Set **Valid until** to **Forever**:

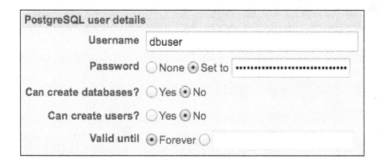

6. Click the **Create** button.

Perform the following steps to create a database:

1. Navigate to **Servers | PostgreSQL Database Server**.

2. Click the **Create a new database** link.

3. Set **Database name** to testdb.

4. Set **Owned by user** to dbuser.

5. Set **Template database** to template1:

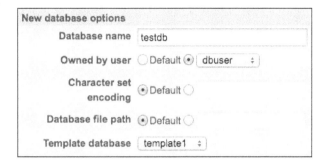

6. Click the **Create** button.

Perform the following steps to grant a user remote access to the database:

1. Navigate to **Servers | PostgreSQL Database Server**.

2. Click the **Allowed Hosts** icon.

3. Click the **Create a new allowed host** link.

4. Set **Host address** to **Single host** and enter the IP address of the client computer (for example, 10.10.10.100).

 If the client can connect from more then one IP, you can specify a subnet by providing a network and netmask or CIDR length. For instance, to grant access to all computers in the 10.10.10.* subnet, you could specify the network as 10.10.10.0 and either the netmask as 255.255.255.0 or the CIDR length as 24.

5. Set **SSL connection required?** to **Yes**.

 You can shave off a little performance overhead by not using SSL, but you should only do that on entirely trusted networks.

6. Set **Database** to `testdb`.

7. Set **Users** to **Listed users** and enter `dbuser`.

8. Set **Authentication mode** to **MD5 encrypted password**:

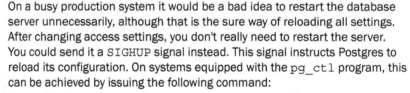

9. Click the **Create** button.

10. We'll need to restart the server one more time to load the new access configuration. Navigate to **Servers | PostgreSQL Database Server**, click the **Stop PostgreSQL Server** button, and then click the **Start PostgreSQL Server** button.

On a busy production system it would be a bad idea to restart the database server unnecessarily, although that is the sure way of reloading all settings. After changing access settings, you don't really need to restart the server. You could send it a `SIGHUP` signal instead. This signal instructs Postgres to reload its configuration. On systems equipped with the `pg_ctl` program, this can be achieved by issuing the following command:

```
$ sudo pg_ctl reload
```

On systems with the `pg_ctlcluster` command, you will need to specify the server version and cluster name, for example:

```
$ sudo pg_ctlcluster 9.1 main reload
```

Testing the connection

Try to connect to your database server from the client machine that uses the IP we specified. If your other machine has the PostgreSQL command-line client installed, you can test the connection by typing in this command at the terminal. However, substitute `postgresql-host` with the IP or domain name of your Postgres server as follows:

```
$ psql -h postgresql-host -U dbuser testdb
testdb=# \q
```

If the connection is successful, you should arrive at the PostgreSQL prompt (`testdb=#`). Type `\q` and press *Enter* to exit.

How it works...

In order to enable network access to the PostgreSQL database server, we needed to modify two configuration files. We edited the main configuration file (`postgresql.conf`) manually to instruct the server to listen for incoming network connections on all network interfaces. The second file, which was edited through Webmin's interface, is the host-based authentication configuration (`pg_hba.conf`). This file instructs the server which users should be allowed to connect from which network hosts and how they should be required to authenticate.

Webmin added the following line to `pg_hba.conf`:

```
hostssl testdb dbuser 10.10.10.100 255.255.255.255 md5
```

The preceding line instructs the server to accept SSL connections to the `testdb` database by the `dbuser` user if the connection originated from the IP address `10.10.10.100`. The user should be asked to provide an MD5-encrypted password for authentication.

Another line in `pg_hba.conf` can look like the following:

```
local    all    postgres    peer
```

This line instructs the server to accept connections made locally over the Unix socket. These connections use the `peer` authentication method, which checks the username of the system account running the connecting client program. If the system username matches a Postgres account name, then the connection is considered authenticated. Password checking is not performed in `peer` authentication. The preceding line of code will allow the system account `postgres` to access `all` databases.

See also

 ▸   In order to make remote access and management of your PostgreSQL databases more secure, you can tunnel your connection over SSH. Take a look at the recipe, *Accessing the PostgreSQL server over an SSH tunnel*, for instructions.

Accessing the PostgreSQL server over an SSH tunnel

If your server is hosting a website on the Internet and running a database system on the same machine, it is safer to disable remote network access to the database. On the other hand, you may still want to manage your databases remotely. You can do so by tunneling PostgreSQL traffic over an SSH connection.

 One of the most important aspects of a database system is the speed with which it can find and return the data that you ask for. Tunneling traffic over SSH will add significant overhead to this communication. This solution is great for intermittent management tasks, but not suitable as a replacement for a direct connection to your database system.

Getting ready

Before you can access the PostgreSQL server through an SSH tunnel, you will need to make sure that an allowed hosts entry exists in the pg_hba.conf file. This entry should allow users from the loopback IP 127.0.0.1 to authenticate using MD5-encrypted passwords. Take a look at the recipe, *Allowing access to PostgreSQL over the network*, for more information. This is what the appropriate line in pg_hba.conf would look like:

```
# IPv4 local connections:
host    all    all    127.0.0.1/32    md5
```

The server you want to connect to must run both the PostgreSQL server and an SSH server. The remote client machine must have an SSH client and PostgreSQL client software installed. Make a note of the IP address or domain name of the server (postgresql-host), the SSH username (ssh-user), the PostgreSQL user (postgresql-user), and the database name (database-name). Substitute them in the following recipe.

How to do it...

In order to create an SSH tunnel for PostgreSQL, follow these steps:

1. Issue the following command on your client machine:

    ```
    $ ssh -N -L 15000:localhost:5432 ssh-user@postgresql-host
    ```

    This creates a tunnel between port 15000 on your client machine and port 5432 of the server. You can now access the remote database by making a PostgreSQL connection to your client computer's local port 15000.

2. Issue the following command on the client system to test the connection:

```
$ psql -h 127.0.0.1 -p 15000 -U postgresql-user database-name
```

How it works...

The SSH client acts as an intermediary in the communication between the PostgreSQL client running on your machine and the remote server. It opens port `15000` on the client machine and listens for incoming connections. All packets arriving at port `15000` are encrypted and forwarded over SSH to the server. On the server side, SSH receives the packets, decrypts them, and sends them to port `5432`. Answers are sent back in the opposite direction over the same channel.

See also

▸ There are many tools that allow you to connect to and control your PostgreSQL databases. Webmin provides a wide range of tools to perform most common tasks, and these are described in recipes in this chapter.

▸ An even more powerful web-based solution dedicated to PostgreSQL is phpPgAdmin. It is discussed in the recipe, *Installing phpPgAdmin*.

▸ More information about SSH tunnels is provided in the recipe, *Connecting to Webmin securely over an SSH tunnel*, in *Chapter 3, Securing Your System*.

Creating a new database

Creating a new PostgreSQL database through Webmin's interface is very quick and simple.

How to do it...

Follow these steps to create a database:

1. Navigate to **Servers | PostgreSQL Database Server**.
2. Click the **Create a new database** link.
3. Enter a **Database name**, for instance, `new_db`.
4. Select the user who will have administrative rights to the database from the **Owned by user** dropdown.
5. Leave **Character set encoding** and **Database file path** set to **Default**.
6. Set **Template database** to `template1`.
7. Click the **Create** button.

How it works...

Webmin takes the information you provide and creates a new database by connecting to the PostgreSQL server and executing the following command:

```
CREATE DATABASE new_db WITH OWNER="dbuser" TEMPLATE = template1;
```

Postgres creates the new database by making a copy of a selected template. The database, `template1`, is installed by default to serve as a source of default settings for newly created databases. If you want new databases to have different settings, for instance, character set and collation, you can introduce these changes to your template database.

Another way to create a database is to execute the `createdb` command as the user, `postgres`, for instance:

```
postgres@postgresql-host:~$ createdb --owner dbuser new_db
```

See also

▶   If you have an initial database structure or contents, you can upload them to the server using an SQL commands file. Take a look at the recipe, *Executing custom SQL commands*, for more information.

Creating users and granting permissions

Creating PostgreSQL users through Webmin is very simple. Users can be designated as owners of newly created databases and will have complete access and administrative rights to the databases they own. Users may also be granted limited privileges on specific database tables.

How to do it...

In this recipe, we will create a new user called `dbuser` and grant selected privileges on a table named `dbtable` in a database called `testdb`.

Perform the following steps to create a user:

1.   Navigate to **Servers | PostgreSQL Database Server | PostgreSQL Users**.
2.   Click the **Create new user** link.
3.   Set **Username** to `dbuser` and set a strong password in the **Password** field.
4.   Answer **No** to the **Can create databases?** and **Can create users?** questions.
5.   Set **Valid until** to **Forever**.
6.   Click the **Create** button.

Perform the following steps to grant user privileges on a database table:

1. Navigate to **Servers | PostgreSQL Database Server**.

2. Click the **Granted Privileges** icon.

3. Click the name of the database object for which you want to modify permissions (for instance, the table name, dbtable).

4. Select the user, dbuser, from the **User** dropdown.

5. Mark the checkboxes next to the privileges you would like to grant:

6. Click the **Save** button.

How it works...

Webmin creates a new database user by connecting to the PostgreSQL server and executing the following command:

```
CREATE USER 'dbuser' WITH PASSWORD '***' NOCREATEDB NOCREATEUSER;
```

Another way to create a database user is to execute the createuser command as the user postgres, for instance:

```
postgres@postgresql-host:~$ createuser dbuser
Shall the new role be a superuser? (y/n) n
Shall the new role be allowed to create databases? (y/n) n
Shall the new role be allowed to create more new roles? (y/n) n
```

Privileges are assigned to users through the GRANT command, for instance:

```
GRANT SELECT,UPDATE,INSERT,DELETE ON "public"."dbtable" to 'dbuser';
```

The PostgreSQL manual provides the following definitions of privileges:

Privilege	Definition
SELECT	This allows SELECT from any column of the specified table.
UPDATE	This allows UPDATE of any column of the specified table.
INSERT	This allows INSERT of a new row into the specified table.
DELETE	This allows DELETE of a row from the specified table.
RULE	This allows the creation of a rule on the table.

Privilege	Definition
REFERENCES	To create a foreign key constraint, it is necessary to have this privilege on both the referencing and referenced tables.
TRIGGER	This allows the creation of a trigger on the specified table.

There's more...

PostgreSQL does not make it easy to grant privileges to an entire database. In order to grant the user named dbuser access to all the tables defined in the public schema, execute the following command:

```
GRANT ALL PRIVILEGES ON ALL TABLES IN SCHEMA public TO 'dbuser';
```

 Postgres databases may be subdivided into **schemas**. Each schema contains its own set of tables independent of other schemas and may use different user privileges. By default, each database contains only one schema called public, and all tables are assigned to it.

Inserting new objects also requires access to sequence objects, which may be granted as follows:

```
GRANT ALL PRIVILEGES ON ALL SEQUENCES IN SCHEMA public TO dbuser;
```

Unfortunately, when you add new tables to the database or add another schema, you will have to execute the commands again. Another option is to set default permissions for the objects by using the ALTER DEFAULT PRIVILEGES command:

```
ALTER DEFAULT PRIVILEGES IN SCHEMA public GRANT ALL PRIVILEGES ON TABLES TO 'dbuser';
```

```
ALTER DEFAULT PRIVILEGES IN SCHEMA public GRANT ALL PRIVILEGES ON SEQUENCES TO 'dbuser';
```

See also

- ▶ Refer to the recipe, *Executing custom SQL commands*, for information about executing commands.
- ▶ You can find more information about granting privileges in the PostgreSQL manual:
  - ❏ http://www.postgresql.org/docs/9.3/static/sql-grant.html
  - ❏ http://www.postgresql.org/docs/9.3/static/sql-alterdefaultprivileges.html

Creating a backup of your database

Webmin can help you make backups of your PostgreSQL databases. With just a few clicks, you can make a backup of any database. Webmin can also help you set cron jobs to create backups automatically on a regular schedule.

Getting ready

Before starting, create a directory to store local backup files. You can keep these files in /backups in the root directory, /root/backups, or in any location you find convenient.

The backup directory should be owned by and be accessible only to the postgres user. Take a look at the recipe, *Changing file ownership and permissions,* in *Chapter 6, Managing Files on Your System*, for more information.

To get general background information about backups, refer to *Chapter 7, Backing Up Your System* .

How to do it...

Follow these steps to create a backup of a database:

1. Navigate to **Servers | PostgreSQL Database Server**.
2. Click the icon that represents the database you would like to back up.
3. Click the **Backup** button.
4. Set **Backup file path** to /backups/database-name.sql.
5. Set **Backup file format** to **Plain SQL Text**.

 The backup will be stored as a series of SQL statements in plain text. If you are exporting a large database, use the compressed **Custom archive** format.

6. Set **Tables to backup** to **All tables**.
7. Click the **Backup Now** button.

How it works...

Webmin executes the `pg_dump` command to output a series of SQL commands that would be needed to recreate the entire database. The command is run as a user who has administrative access to the database. On most systems, the user is called `postgres`.

The database dump is saved to the specified output file. If you wanted to do the same kind of backup in the terminal, you could run a command similar to the following:

```
postgres@postgresql-host:~$ pg_dump -U postgres -f /backups/database-
name.sql database-name
```

There's more...

Webmin is quite a capable tool to create backups. Here are a few other easily accessible functions.

Backing up all databases automatically

Webmin can help you make an automated backup of some or all databases hosted by your server. These backups will be executed on a regular schedule by cron.

1. Navigate to **Servers | PostgreSQL Database Server**.

2. Click the **Backup Databases** button.

3. Set **Backup to directory** to the location of your backup directory, for instance, `/backups`.

4. Set **Backup file format** to **Custom archive**.

> The custom archive format is compressed to save the disk space. It's also very flexible and allows manual selection of archived items during the restore phase.

5. Open the **Backup schedule** section.

6. Set **Scheduled backup enabled?** to **Yes, at times chosen below**; set **Simple schedule** and select **Daily (at midnight)**.

> Note that many things may be scheduled to start at midnight on your system, so you can choose another time if your system resources are limited. Choose a more complex schedule by marking the minutes, hours, and days of the month at which the job is to be performed.

7. Click the **Save** button.

Exporting a database table to CSV

Webmin can export a single table of your database into a CSV file that can be opened by spreadsheet programs such as Excel, Calc, or Gnumeric:

1. Navigate to **Servers | PostgreSQL Database Server**.
2. Click the icon of the database, and then click the icon of the table you would like to export.
3. Click the **Export as CSV** button.
4. Set **File format** to **CSV with quotes**.
5. Set **Include column names in CSV?** to **Yes**.
6. Set **Export destination** to **Display in browser**.
7. Click the **Export Now** button.

See also

▶ You can easily perform backups to a remote host using a network file sharing protocol such as NFS or CIFS. You start by creating a network volume on the remote server and then mount the volume on your server. You can then back up to directories on the remote system just as easily as if they were stored locally. Take a look at *Chapter 6, Managing Files on Your System*, for instructions to set up network file sharing using NFS or CIFS.

▶ Another way to store spare copies of your databases remotely is to send your backup directory to a remote server using the SSH protocol. Take a look at recipe, *Backing up to a remote host*, in *Chapter 7, Backing Up Your System*, for more information.

Executing custom SQL commands

Webmin provides a simple interface to your Postgres database server, which allows you to execute arbitrary SQL commands. This can be a useful feature when you want to quickly find something in a database or perform a bulk update of multiple rows of data.

How to do it...

Perform the following steps to execute custom SQL commands:

1. Navigate to **Servers | PostgreSQL Database Server**.
2. Click the icon that represents the database you would like to use.
3. Click the **Execute SQL** button.

4. Enter SQL commands in the text area, for instance:

```
CREATE TEMPORARY TABLE IF NOT EXISTS films (
    title varchar(40)
);
INSERT INTO films(title) VALUES ('Bananas'), ('Yojimbo');
SELECT * FROM films;
```

5. Click the **Execute** button.

You will be presented with a sortable display of data returned by the SELECT command. The presented data will come from a temporary films table created by the first command. Temporary tables are not stored when the client who created them disconnects, so you will not see this table in your database later.

How it works...

Webmin simply passes the SQL commands to the database server. If the command returns an error, it will be displayed on screen. If the command returns rows of data, Webmin will convert them into an HTML page and display them on screen. Please note that Webmin is running as the administrative user (postgres), so caution should be used when executing commands.

There's more...

Webmin also allows you to execute the SQL scripts saved in files. These can be used to restore databases from plain SQL text backups.

Executing a SQL script from a file

Perform the following steps to execute a SQL script from a file:

1. Navigate to **Servers | PostgreSQL Database Server**.
2. Click the icon that represents the database you would like to use.
3. Click the **Execute SQL** button.
4. Select the **Run SQL from file** tab.

5. If you uploaded the file onto the server, select **From local file** and enter the file's location in the text box. Otherwise, select **From uploaded file** and choose a file from your disk.

6. Click the **Execute** button.

See also

▶ You can save the commands that you execute often in an easy-to-use control panel in Webmin. Take a look at the recipe, *Creating a panel with the database commands that you execute often*, in *Chapter 4, Controlling Your System*, for more information.

▶ If you find that you need a more full-fledged, web-based PostgreSQL management tool, consider installing phpPgAdmin. This is described in the *Install phpPgAdmin* recipe.

Restoring a database from backup

Backups of Postgres databases are created using the pg_dump command that can output a variety of formats. By default, backups are created as plain text SQL scripts, but a compressed custom PostgreSQL format is more efficient. Webmin helps you to create backups in both of these formats as well as in the TAR format.

The method of restoring your database will depend on the file format chosen during backup. If you chose the plain SQL text format, then simply running your backup script will restore the database. Take a look at the recipe, *Execute custom SQL commands,* for more information.

If you chose the custom archive or TAR file format, you should use the procedure described in this recipe.

How to do it...

Follow these steps to restore a database from backup:

1. Navigate to **Servers | PostgreSQL Database Server**.

2. Click the icon that represents the database you would like to restore.

3. Click the **Restore** button.

4. Choose **Restore from Uploaded file**, click **Browse**, and choose the file from your computer.

 If the backup file is larger then a few MB, it will be safer to upload the file to the server first, before running the restore. Take a look at the recipe, *Uploading files to the server*, in *Chapter 6, Managing Files on Your System*, for more information.

5. Set **Only restore data, not tables?** to **No**.
6. Set **Delete tables before restoring?** to **Yes**.
7. Set **Tables to restore** to **All in backup file**.
8. Click the **Restore** button.

How it works...

Webmin uploads your file onto your server and then executes the `pg_restore` command to load contents of the backup into a database. If you wanted to restore a backup in the terminal, you could run a command similar to the following:

```
postgres@postgresql-host:~$ pg_restore -c -d database-name backup-file.
post
```

Command-line options are as specified:

▸ `-c`: This option drops database objects before recreating them
▸ `-d`: This option specifies the database you want to restore

There's more...

Webmin can import data into a table of your database from a CSV file that can be created by spreadsheet programs such as Excel, Calc, or Gnumeric.

Follow these steps to restore a database table from a properly formatted CSV file:

1. Navigate to **Servers | PostgreSQL Database Server**.
2. Click the icon that represents the database to which you would like to import data.
3. Click the **Execute SQL** button.
4. Select the **Import text file** tab.
5. If you uploaded the file onto the server, select **From local file** and enter the file's location in the text box. Otherwise, select **From uploaded file** and choose a file from your disk.
6. Select a table from the **Table to import data into** dropdown.
7. Set **Delete data in table first** to **No**.
8. Set **Ignore duplicate rows** to **Yes**.
9. Set **File format** to **CVS with quotes**.

You will have to select the same format when exporting data from your spreadsheet program. Experiment with the other formats if you run into problems.

10. Click the **Execute** button.

You will be presented with an information screen that describes how many rows were successfully imported or what errors were encountered.

Editing the structure of your database

Webmin allows you to quickly modify the structure of tables in your PostgreSQL database through an easy-to-use interface. In this recipe, we will demonstrate how to perform the following list of tasks:

▸ Create a table in a database

▸ Add a field to a database table

▸ Create an index

▸ Delete an index

▸ Delete a field

▸ Delete a table from the database

Getting ready

For demonstration purposes, we will be using a database called testdb. You can create a database with this name through Webmin by following steps described in the recipe, *Creating a new database*.

How to do it...

In the testdb database, we'll create a table called people and add a field called name to the table. We'll then change the name of the field, add a unique index, and finally delete the index, field, and table from the database.

Perform the following steps to create a table in a database:

1. Navigate to **Servers | PostgreSQL Database Server**.

2. Click the icon that represents the testdb database.

3. Click the **Create Table** button.

4. Specify `people` as the **Table name**.

5. Provide the definition of the field that will be the primary key for this table. Fill in the following field definition:

   ❑ Type `id` in **Field name**.

   ❑ Type `serial` in **Data type**.

   ❑ Check the boxes **Primary key** and **Unique**.

   ❑ Uncheck the boxes **Array** and **Allow nulls**:

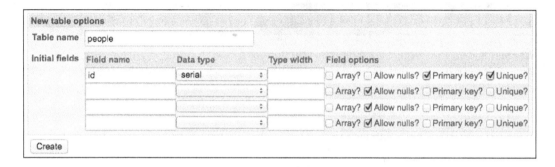

6. Click the **Create** button.

Perform the following steps to add a field to a database table:

1. Navigate to **Servers | PostgreSQL Database Server**.

2. Click the icon that represents the `testdb` database.

3. Click the icon representing the `people` table.

4. Select **varchar** from the types dropdown and click the **Add field of type** button.

5. Fill in the following field definition:

   ❑ **Field name**: `name`

   ❑ **Type width**: `80`

   ❑ **Array field**: `No`

6. Click the **Create** button.

Perform the following steps to create an index:

1. Navigate to **Servers | PostgreSQL Database Server**.

2. Click the icon that represents the `testdb` database.

3. Click the icon that represents the `people` table.

4. Click the **Create Index** button.

5. Set **Index name** to unique_name.

6. Select the field name, in the **Fields in index** list.

7. Set **Index type** to **Unique**.

8. Click the **Create** button.

Perform the following steps to delete an index:

1. Navigate to **Servers | PostgreSQL Database Server**.

2. Click the icon that represents the testdb database.

3. Click the icon that represents the unique_name index.

4. Click the **Delete** button.

Perform the following steps to delete a field:

1. Navigate to **Servers | PostgreSQL Database Server**.

2. Click the icon that represents the testdb database.

3. Click the icon that represents the people table.

4. Mark the checkbox next to the name field.

5. Click the **Delete Selected Fields** button.

Perform the following steps to delete a table from the database:

1. Navigate to **Servers | PostgreSQL Database Server**.

2. Click the icon that represents the testdb database.

3. Click the icon that represents the people table.

4. Click the **Drop Table** button and confirm on the screen that follows.

How it works...

Webmin prepares syntax for the appropriate CREATE, DROP, and ALTER TABLE SQL commands to perform all of the preceding actions and executes those commands on your PostgreSQL server as the postgres user.

See also

▸ If you find that you need a more full-fledged, web-based PostgreSQL management tool, consider installing phpPgAdmin. This is described in the *Installing phpPgAdmin* recipe

Editing records in a database

Webmin allows you to quickly edit data in your PostgreSQL database through a simple interface. In this recipe, we will demonstrate how to add, edit, and delete records in a database table.

Getting ready

In this recipe, we will use examples based on the `testdb` database and `people` table created in the recipe, *Editing the structure of your database*.

How to do it...

We'll add a record to the `people` table of the `testdb` database; we'll edit the same record, and finally delete it to show how to perform these actions in Webmin.

Perform the following steps to add a row to a database table:

1. Navigate to **Servers | PostgreSQL Database Server**.
2. Click the icon that represents the `testdb` database.
3. Click the icon that represents the `people` table.
4. Click the **View Data** button.
5. Click the **Add row** button.
6. Fill in a numeric `id` and type in a `name` in the text box.
7. Click the **Save** button.

Perform the following steps to edit a row:

1. Navigate to **Servers | PostgreSQL Database Server**.
2. Click the icon that represents the `testdb` database.
3. Click the icon that represents the `people` table.
4. Click the **View Data** button.
5. Mark the checkbox next to the record you would like to edit.
6. Click the **Edit selected rows** button.
7. Change the `name` value in the text box.
8. Click the **Save** button.

Perform the following steps to delete a row:

1. Navigate to **Servers | PostgreSQL Database Server**.

2. Click the icon that represents the `testdb` database.

3. Click the icon that represents the `people` table.

4. Click the **View Data** button.

5. Mark the checkbox next to the record you would like to edit.

6. Click the **Delete selected rows** button.

How it works...

Webmin prepares syntax for the appropriate `INSERT`, `UPDATE`, and `DELETE` SQL commands to perform the preceding actions and executes those commands on your PostgreSQL server as the `postgres` user.

See also

▶   If you find that you need a more full-fledged, web-based PostgreSQL management tool, consider installing phpPgAdmin. This is described in the *Installing phpPgAdmin* recipe.

Installing phpPgAdmin

phpPgAdmin is a database administration tool for PostgreSQL. It is a web-based application, like Webmin itself, but dedicated to all tasks related to the administration of a PostgreSQL server. It's easy to use and can be a helpful tool for your database users and administrators.

 System packages are configured to run phpPgAdmin on Apache. The Apache web server and PHP are installed as package dependencies. If you're not already using Apache and PHP, this exposes a potential attack vector on your database server. Consider the security implications of installing phpPgAdmin and keeping it up to date.

How to do it...

Perform the following steps to install phpPgAdmin:

1. Install the package named `phpPgAdmin` (or `phppgadmin` depending on your system). Refer to the recipe, *Installing software packages*, in *Chapter 1, Setting Up Your System* for more information.

> On some systems, you may need to add an additional repository to install the package. For instance, if you're running a Linux distribution from the RedHat family (RHEL, CentOS, Fedora, and so on), you should add the **Extra Packages for Enterprise Linux** (**EPEL**) repository. Information about setting up EPEL can be found in the recipe, *Giving users access to your server via FTP,* in *Chapter 6, Managing Files on Your System.*

2. Since phpPgAdmin runs on top of Apache, you should make sure that this server is installed on your system and accessible to a browser. Follow the steps in the recipe, *Installing Apache on your system,* from *Chapter 8, Running an Apache Web Server,* to get Apache up and running.

3. Navigate to the following URL, but substitute webmin-host for the IP or domain name of your server: http://webmin-host/phppgadmin or http://webmin-host/phpPgAdmin (depending on distribution).

> On some systems, phpPgAdmin is configured to be accessible to connections originating from the local host only. If you wish to change this behavior, go to **Servers | Apache Webserver | Default Server,** select the **Per-Directory Options** for phpPgAdmin's directory, and change its **Access Control** settings. More information is provided in the recipe, *Setting options for directories, files, and locations,* in *Chapter 8, Running an Apache Web Server.*
>
> Information about additional steps that may be necessary to set up phpPgAdmin in your system distribution can be found in package documentation files. Refer to the recipe, *Reading documentation of installed software* in *Chapter 1, Setting Up Your System.*

4. You can now log in using the username and password of a PostgreSQL account.

Depending on the how phpPgAdmin's configuration is defined, it will connect to your Postgres server over a Unix socket or TCP network socket. The following line in config.inc.php decides how connections are established:

```
$conf['servers'][0]['host'] = 'localhost';
```

If the host value for a server is set to 'localhost', connections are made over a network socket. If the value is set as an empty string ' ', then connections are made over a Unix socket.

Your Postgres server must be set up to handle the chosen type of connection and allow users to authenticate using a password. Take a look at the recipe, *Allowing access to PostgreSQL over the network,* for more information.

If you are running a RedHat-based system with **Security Enhanced Linux** (**SELinux**), you may have to allow Apache to connect to databases by setting the following flag:

```
$ sudo setsebool -P httpd_can_network_connect_db 1
```

How it works...

phpPgAdmin is an application written in PHP. The main configuration file of phpPgAdmin is named `config.inc.php`, and is usually installed inside the `/etc/` directory. Example locations for different distributions are listed in the following table. The code of the application itself is stored in the form of PHP script files in a directory named `phpPgAdmin`.

Because phpPgAdmin is served by Apache, the installation package includes an application-specific configuration file that will be loaded by the web server. This file informs Apache where phpPgAdmin is stored on disk and which of its directories should be made available on the Web:

File	OS / distro	Location
phpPgAdmin configuration	Debian	`/etc/phppgadmin/config.inc.php`
	CentOS	`/etc/phpPgAdmin/config.inc.php`
	OpenSUSE	`/etc/phpPgAdmin/config.inc.php`
phpPgAdmin files	Debian	`/usr/share/phppgadmin`
	CentOS	`/usr/share/phpPgAdmin`
	OpenSUSE	`/srv/www/htdocs/phpPgAdmin`
Apache configuration file for phpPgAdmin	Debian	`/etc/apache2/conf.d/phppgadmin`
	CentOS	`/etc/httpd/conf.d/phpPgAdmin.conf`
	OpenSUSE	`/etc/apache2/conf.d/phpPgAdmin.conf`

Regardless of how the package maintainers decided to prepare it, you can tweak the Apache configuration for phpPgAdmin by going to **Servers | Apache Webserver | Default Server** and selecting the **Per-Directory Options** for the phpPgAdmin directory.

11
Running Web Applications

In this chapter, we will cover the following:

- ▸ Generating dynamic pages using CGI
- ▸ Installing PHP
- ▸ Changing PHP configuration settings
- ▸ Displaying PHP errors while debugging
- ▸ Logging in PHP
- ▸ Installing WordPress on your server
- ▸ Installing Drupal on your server
- ▸ Installing a Django-based application using `mod_wsgi`

Introduction

Internet sites may be roughly divided into two categories: static and dynamic. When a web server hosts a static site, its role is very limited. The server waits for incoming requests, maps every request to a file on its disk, and sends contents of the file as its response. All pages of such a site have to be prepared ahead of time, and they don't change automatically between visits. The functionality of such sites may seem limited, but they do have a number of advantages. Since the server doesn't do any computational work, static sites can be very fast and can serve large numbers of requests. Such sites are also easy to index by search engines. The fact that a site is static does not mean that it can't be interactive. JavaScript components allow the browser to provide the user with a graphical interface, through which he or she may interact with our website. In the end though, if the user provides us with information we would like to store, we will need a dynamic component to process incoming data.

On a dynamic website, incoming requests are not mapped directly to files on a disk; instead, they are handed over to programs that process each request and produce a response. Processing usually involves interacting with a database to look up or store information; the response is generated on the fly and may be different each time. Dynamic websites are an essential component of the modern Internet, and Apache is a server that can host most available dynamic technologies.

In *Chapter 8, Running an Apache Web Server,* we demonstrated how Webmin can help you set up a web server to host static websites. In this chapter, we will dive into topics related to various dynamic website solutions. We will start with CGI, the classic way to serve dynamic websites using programs written in any language. To illustrate the point, we will demonstrate how to set up a simple dynamic website powered by a Bash script. We will then proceed to demonstrate how more efficient language-specific technologies can be hosted. Most of this chapter is focused on the PHP language, but the final recipe demonstrates how applications written in Python may be hosted using the Apache module `mod_wsgi`.

Generating dynamic pages using CGI

Since the earliest days of the World Wide Web, it was possible to generate web pages dynamically using a standard method called the **Common Gateway Interface** (**CGI**). With the use of CGI, an Apache web server can generate dynamic content by executing any program installed on the same machine as long as that program generates the text of a properly formatted HTTP response. The main advantage of this method is its universality, as CGI scripts may be written in any programming language. In this recipe, we will demonstrate how to write a simple Hello World script in the shell scripting language, Bash, but the same principles would apply to any other programming language.

The main disadvantage of the CGI protocol is the fact that the web server must invoke a new process for each incoming request. This solution does not scale very well and is therefore applicable to low traffic sites only. The other disadvantage of using CGI directly is that the protocol is very basic and parsing of incoming requests has to be done manually by your scripts.

Basic CGI is superseded by technologies that do not require a new process to be invoked for every incoming request but have a component loaded into memory, ready to process requests. These solutions are usually language specific and may come as Apache modules, for instance `mod_perl`, `mod_php` or `mod_python`. Some of these technologies are described in subsequent recipes in this chapter.

The method described in this recipe is still suitable for small tasks. If you have a web server and wish to return a simple status page but don't want the overhead (and potential security risks) associated with installing a technology such as PHP, you could use this basic method of generating dynamic web pages.

CGI scripts are regular programs from the perspective of your Unix system, and they have access to the underlying machine with the same privileges as the web server process. If a CGI script accepts user input, great care should be taken to verify and clean up incoming data. Mistakes in input handling often become security vulnerabilities, which can be exploited.

Getting ready

This recipe involves the configuration of an Apache web server. Information about installing and configuring Apache can be found in *Chapter 8, Running an Apache Web Server*.

Checking what user and group Apache is running as

The Apache web server accesses your system as a special user, usually called `apache`, `www-data`, `wwwrun`, `httpd`, or something similar. In order to complete this recipe, you'll need to know the username and group of this Apache user. This can be easily checked through Webmin, as follows:

1. Navigate to **Servers | Apache Webserver | Global configuration**.

2. Click on the **User and Group** icon. You will see the following screen:

The Apache username will be displayed in the **Run as Unix user** field and the group in the **Run as Unix group** field. Both values are set to `www-data` in the preceding image. Make a note of your system's configuration.

How to do it...

This recipe will consist of two sections. First, we'll create a CGI script and then the Apache configuration needed to display the web page it generates.

Follow these steps to create a CGI-compatible shell script:

1. Create the directory that will contain your web-accessible CGI scripts, for instance, in `/usr/lib/cgi-bin`.

It is not a good idea to store CGI scripts in the `DocumentRoot` directory from which regular HTML pages are served. Incorrect configuration of the server could expose the source code of your scripts, run scripts that should not be executed, or make the directory writeable, which would constitute a serious security vulnerability.

2. Create a shell script file named `/usr/lib/cgi-bin/hello.sh`. Enter the following code in this file:

```
#!/bin/bash

echo "Content-type: text/plain"
echo "" # End of headers, start of response body

echo "Hello World!"
echo "The current date is:"
date

exit 0
```

3. Set the group owner of the script to the name of the group that Apache runs as. If Apache runs as `www-data` on your system, you can do this by executing the following command:

```
$ sudo chgrp www-data /usr/lib/cgi-bin/hello.sh
```

4. Allow the group read and execute privileges to the file, full access to the owner, and no access to other users. You can do this by executing the following command:

```
$ sudo chmod 750 /usr/lib/cgi-bin/hello.sh
```

Information about manipulating files and changing ownership and permissions can be found in the *Manage files and directories on the server* recipe in *Chapter 6, Managing Files on Your System.*

Follow these steps to create the Apache configuration:

1. Navigate to **Servers | Apache Webserver**.

2. Click on the icon of the virtual server you wish to configure or click on **Default Server**.

3. Click on the **CGI Programs** icon.

4. Create a CGI directory alias by setting the **From** value to `/cgi-bin/` and the **To** value to `/usr/lib/cgi-bin/`:

CGI Programs for *:80

CGI directory aliases	From	To
	/cgi-bin/	/usr/lib/cgi-bin/

---

5. Click the **Save** button.

6. Under **Create Per-Directory, Files or Location Options**, select **Directory** and create a configuration for the path, `/usr/lib/cgi-bin`.

7. Click the icon for the directory, `/usr/lib/cgi-bin`.

8. Click the **Document Options** icon.

9. Under **Directory options**, choose **Selected below..**, set **Execute CGI programs** to **Yes**, and set all other options to **No**.

10. Under **Options file can override..**, set **Selected below...** and leave all checkboxes unmarked. Consider the following screenshot:

Document Options for Directory /usr/lib/cgi-bin

Directory options ○ Default ◉ Selected below..

Option	Set for directory	Merge with parent
Execute CGI programs	◉ Yes ○ No	○ Enable ○ Disable
Follow symbolic links	○ Yes ◉ No	○ Enable ○ Disable
Server-side includes and execs	○ Yes ◉ No	○ Enable ○ Disable
Server-side includes	○ Yes ◉ No	○ Enable ○ Disable
Generate directory indexes	○ Yes ◉ No	○ Enable ○ Disable
Generate Multiviews	○ Yes ◉ No	○ Enable ○ Disable
Follow symbolic links if owners match	○ Yes ◉ No	○ Enable ○ Disable

Options file can override.. ○ Default ◉ Selected below...

☐ Authentication options
☐ MIME types and encodings
☐ Indexing and index files
☐ Hostname access control
☐ Directory options

Generate MD5 digests

○ Yes ○ No ◉ Default

Generate ETag header from ◉ Default ○ Selected attributes : ☐ INode number ☐ Last modified time ☐ File size

Error message footer [Default ÷]

[Save]

---

11. Click the **Save** button.

12. Click the **Access Control** icon.

13. Under **Restrict access**, select **Allow then deny** and set only one entry, as follows:
Action to **Allow** and **Condition** to **All requests**. Consider the following screenshot:

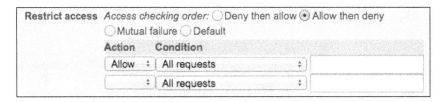

14. Click the **Save** button.

You may wish to restrict access to specific client IPs if the presented data must not be made public. The location can also be protected with a password.

15. Click the **Apply Changes** link.

To see the result, navigate to the URL, `http://your-server/cgi-bin/hello.sh`, where `your-server` is the IP or domain name of your Apache server machine.

You should see a webpage with the words, **Hello World**, and the current date. Your shell script executed by Apache through the common gateway interface generated this text dynamically.

How it works...

When a browser requests a URL with a path matching `/cgi-bin/hello.sh`, Apache recognizes it as an alias to the script, `/usr/lib/cgi-bin/hello.sh`. Apache prepares an execution environment in which various request parameters, such as HTTP headers and the query string, are set as environment variables and then executes the script in this environment. The body of the request is passed to the script over the standard input stream.

The script we wrote creates the HTTP response, which will be sent back to the browser. The response consists of two parts: headers and the response body. We send only one header informing the browser that `Content-type` for our response is `text/plain`. This tells the browser that the response should be displayed as text rather than downloaded as a file. We then send an empty line to end the headers section and proceed to send the response body, which consists of the words, "Hello World!", and the current date.

The Apache configuration we created informs the server that all requests to paths starting with `/cgi-bin/` should be treated as aliases to files in the directory, `/usr/lib/cgi-bin/`. We also informed Apache to execute scripts found in the directory and to allow access from all clients. This is equivalent to creating the following configuration fragment:

```
ScriptAlias /cgi-bin/ /usr/lib/cgi-bin/
<Directory "/usr/lib/cgi-bin">
  AllowOverride None
  Options ExecCGI
  Order allow,deny
  Allow from all
</Directory>
```

All CGI scripts must be executable and the Apache user must have the ability to run them in order to use them. To achieve this, we gave the file to a group that Apache belongs to and assigned read and execute permissions to this group. Assigning permissions in this way allows Apache to run the script but not modify it. If the Apache user were able to modify CGI scripts, a compromised server could be used as a means of taking control of the server.

There's more...

Programs running over the CGI can output data as described earlier, but they can also read incoming headers and content of submitted forms. The CGI protocol was standardized and is described in the *RFC3875* document, which can be found at `http://tools.ietf.org/html/rfc3875`.

Displaying incoming request headers

Incoming HTTP request headers and many other useful pieces of information described by the CGI protocol are available to the script as environment variables. In order to display them, you could use the `printenv` command, as in the following script:

```
#!/bin/bash
echo "Content-type: text/plain"
echo ""
printenv
exit 0
```

Displaying incoming request body

The incoming request body (which contains, for example, values of `HTTP POST` forms) is passed to the script over the standard input stream. In order to display the body of the request, you could add the following code to your script:

```
while read LINE; do
    echo ${LINE}  # perform operations on request body
done
```

See also

We can also refer to the following sections:

- ▶ The *Installing Apache on your system* recipe in *Chapter 8, Running an Apache Web Server*
- ▶ The *Creating a virtual host* recipe in *Chapter 8, Running an Apache Web Server*
- ▶ The *Setting options for directories, files, and locations* recipe in *Chapter 8, Running an Apache Web Server*
- ▶ The *Installing PHP* recipe in this chapter
- ▶ The *Installing a Django-based application using mod_wsgi* recipe in this chapter

Installing PHP

PHP is currently among the most popular programming languages for the Web. Many of the largest and most popular sites are powered by software written in PHP, including Facebook, Yahoo!, Wikipedia, and Wordpress.com. PHP started as a set of simple tools for designing dynamic personal home pages, but it quickly grew in popularity and evolved into a modern, object-oriented programming language. The open source community that grew around the language created many useful libraries and added support for multiple platforms, databases, and so on.

PHP is quite powerful, yet very easy to use. Deployment of a PHP application usually boils down to placing source code files in a directory on a server. It's also very easy to start programming with PHP—its code can be embedded directly within standard HTML. PHP makes programming for the Web very simple by abstracting away details of the HTTP protocol. For example, form values are available directly as data structures inside scripts, simple functions allow headers to be read and written, support for cookies and user sessions is built in, and so on.

PHP's ease of use may in fact be too great as it has allowed many to develop for the Web without fully understanding its underlying protocol. If you find a PHP application ready to install on your server, make sure to read its reviews to make sure it doesn't pose any serious security or stability issues.

In this recipe, we will demonstrate how to install PHP and then write and deploy a simple Hello World script.

Getting ready

This recipe involves the configuration of an Apache web server. Information about installing and configuring Apache can be found in *Chapter 8, Running an Apache Web Server*.

How to do it...

Follow these steps to install PHP and verify that it works on your system:

1. Follow the instructions in the *Installing software packages* recipe in *Chapter 1, Setting Up Your System*, and install the PHP package for your system. The package may simply be named `php` or `php5`.

2. Navigate to **Servers | Apache Webserver | Global configuration**.

3. Click the **Configure Apache Modules** icon.

4. Mark the checkbox next to the `php5` module and click the **Enable Selected Modules** button.

> The **Configure Apache Modules** screen may not be present in your system. If you installed PHP from a package, then in all likelihood, it enabled the module for you already. Follow the rest of this recipe to test that.

5. Navigate to **Servers | Apache Webserver**.

6. Click the icon of the virtual server you wish to configure, or the default server.

7. Click the **Document Options** icon and note what the document root directory of the server is.

8. Create a file named `hello.php` in the document root directory.

9. Enter the following code into this `hello.php` file:

```php
<?php
    echo "Hello World!";
?>
```

To see the result, navigate to the URL, `http://your-server/hello.php`, where `your-server` is the IP or domain name of your Apache server machine. You should see a web page with the words **Hello World!** generated by PHP.

> If you end up seeing the PHP code instead of Hello World!, you will have to enable the PHP module manually. Take a look at the *How it works section* for information about instructions that you'll have to add to the Apache configuration file, and read your package's documentation for directions.

How it works...

Practically all server OS distributions offer a PHP package for installation from their repositories. There are a few different ways to install PHP, and it's a good idea to install the standard system package as this will ensure that it is optimized for your version of Apache and will be kept up to date by package maintainers.

Installation of the package not only places PHP executables and documentation on your disk but also modifies configuration of the Apache web server. Introduced changes include the following:

- A line that loads the PHP interpreter module when Apache starts, such as this:

```
LoadModule php5_module /path/to/libphp5.so
```

- Lines that instruct Apache to pass PHP files to the interpreter, such as this:

```
SetHandler application/x-httpd-php
```

Or

```
AddHandler php5-script .php
```

- An instruction to use the index.php files for directory indexes:

```
DirectoryIndex index.html index.php
```

See also

We can also refer to the following sections.

- The *Installing Apache on your system* recipe in *Chapter 8, Running an Apache Web Server*
- The *Creating a virtual host* recipe in *Chapter 8, Running an Apache Web Server*
- The *Setting options for directories, files, and locations* recipe in *Chapter 8, Running an Apache Web Server*
- The *Changing PHP configuration settings* recipe in this chapter
- The *Viewing PHP error logs* recipe in this chapter

Changing PHP configuration settings

The PHP interpreter allows you to specify values of numerous settings, which determine how PHP applications behave on your system. This configuration affects how errors are logged or displayed, how input data is handled, what resources are allocated to the interpreter, and settings for extension modules bundled with PHP.

PHP's configuration file is traditionally called `php.ini`, and its location depends on your operating system distribution and version of PHP. Common locations of the `php.ini` file include: `/etc/`, `/etc/php5/apache2/`, and `/usr/local/etc/`. The `php.ini` file contains master setting values, but some settings may be overwritten locally with a PHP script or Apache configuration for a directory.

In this recipe, we will demonstrate how to check values of currently used configuration settings and how they can be modified.

Getting ready

Assuming you already have Apache and PHP installed, prepare a directory that is exposed through the web server and ready to serve PHP scripts. We will refer to this directory as the `DocumentRoot` directory in this recipe.

How to do it...

The first part of this recipe will check currently defined settings, which we will then proceed to modify.

Follow these steps to check current PHP settings:

1. Create a file named `phpinfo.php` in the `DocumentRoot` directory of your web server.

2. Enter the following code into the `phpinfo.php` file:

```php
<?php
    phpinfo();
?>
```

3. Navigate to the URL of the `phpinfo.php` file: `http://your-server/phpinfo.php`.

4. Make a note of the location of the **Loaded Configuration File**.

 This informs us where the main PHP configuration file (`php.ini`) is located.

5. Make a note of the `memory_limit` value.

 Note that there are two columns. They specify the local value and the master value of this setting. The master value is specified in `php.ini`, but the local value is currently in use. The local value may be different from the master value if it is overridden. See the *There's more* section of this recipe.

Follow these steps to change the master PHP settings:

1. Find the location of the global PHP configuration (`php.ini`) file as described earlier.
2. Navigate to **Others | PHP Configuration**.
3. Click **Manage** in the line corresponding to the global PHP configuration file.
4. Click **Resource Limits**.
5. Change **Maximum memory allocation** to 260M:

Memory and transfer limit options		
Maximum memory allocation ○Default ⊙ `260M`	Maximum HTTP POST size ○Default ⊙ `8M`	
Maximum file upload size ○Default ⊙ `2M`	Maximum execution time ○Default ⊙ `30` seconds	
Maximum input parsing time ○Default ⊙ `60` seconds		

6. Click **Save**.
7. Navigate to **Servers | Apache Webserver**.
8. Click the **Apply Changes** link.
9. Navigate once again to the URL, `http://your-server/phpinfo.php`.

Check the `memory_limit` value. Its master value should now be changed to 260M.

 Leaving the `phpinfo.php` file on your server is a bad idea as it unnecessarily exposes information about your system to the public. Delete the file when you're done using it.

How it works...

Apache loads the global PHP configuration (`php.ini`) file every time the server is started. In this recipe, we modified this file through Webmin. In particular, we changed the line that determines how much memory the PHP interpreter will be able to use to the following:

```
memory_limit = 260M
```

After we modified the file, we went to Webmin's interface to apply the configuration changes by restarting Apache.

There's more...

PHP settings may be set locally in scripts and in Apache's per-directory configuration files.

Modifying PHP settings for a directory using .htaccess files

In order to modify PHP settings through .htaccess files, we must instruct Apache to allow local option overrides for the directory that contains our PHP script. Take a look at the *Setting options for directories, files, and locations* recipe in *Chapter 8, Running an Apache Web Server*, for more information. Perform the following steps:

1.   Navigate to **Servers | Apache Webserver**.
2.   Click the icon of the virtual server you wish to configure or the default server.
3.   Click or create directory settings for the directory that contains your PHP script.
4.   Click **Document Options**.
5.   In the **Options file can override** section, mark **Selected below** and select **Directory options**.

 This is equivalent to adding the following line to Apache's configuration for the directory:

```
AllowOverride Options
```

6.   Click the **Save** button.
7.   Click the **Apply Changes** link.
8.   Create a file named .htaccess in the same directory.
9.   Place the following instruction in the .htaccess file to locally change the memory limit to 32MB:

```
php_value memory_limit 32M
```

 The directive, php_value, is used to configure settings which accept parameter values. Boolean parameters, which only accept the values on and off, are set with the php_flag directive. More information can be found in PHP's online manual at http://php.net/manual/configuration.changes.php.

Verify the change in local settings using the phpinfo() function, as described earlier.

Modifying PHP settings dynamically inside script code

Prepare a `phpinfo.php` file as described in this recipe, but add the following code to it:

```php
<?php
  ini_set('memory_limit', '64M');
  phpinfo();
?>
```

Navigate to the URL of the `phpinfo.php` file to verify the change in local settings.

See also

> ► Take a look at the *Setting options for directories, files, and locations* recipe in *Chapter 8, Running an Apache Web Server*, for more information about changing Apache settings locally

Displaying PHP errors while debugging

While writing code in PHP or installing a downloaded application, you may find yourself staring at a blank browser screen with no hint as to why it isn't working as expected. This is caused by the default PHP configuration that hides error messages from prying eyes. Error messages could reveal information about your server, so this is a good idea in production, but makes resolving problems more difficult. During development, you can enable PHP's friendly error messages by following this recipe.

How to do it...

Follow these steps to execute this recipe:

1. Let's start by writing a PHP script that will cause an error. The script could contain the following broken code:

```php
<?php
    echo "Hello World!";
    syntax!error
?>
```

2. Save the script to a file on your server and navigate to the file's public URL on your web server. If error displaying is turned off, you should see a blank screen.

3. Navigate to **Others | PHP Configuration**.

4. Click **Manage** in the line corresponding to the global PHP configuration file.
5. Click **Error Logging**.
6. Set **Display error messages?** to **Yes**.
7. Click **Save**.
8. Navigate to **Servers | Apache Webserver**.
9. Click the **Apply Changes** link.

After changing the setting, navigate to your broken script's URL once again. You should now see an error message like this:

Parse error: syntax error, unexpected '!' in /var/www/index.php on line 3

How it works...

PHP's `display_errors` setting is responsible for whether the interpreter displays error messages on the screen or hides them.

In this recipe, we enabled PHP's error reporting globally by turning on the `display_errors` configuration flag. To achieve this, we changed the `display_errors` line in `php.ini` to the following and restarted Apache:

```
display_errors = Off
```

You can also set the flag locally for a chosen directory by adding the following line to a `.htaccess` file. Make sure that Apache allows local overrides in this directory:

```
php_flag display_errors on
```

Don't use the `ini_set` function to turn on displaying errors, as some errors will prevent the script from being parsed and the setting will not be able to take effect.

See also

▸ The *Changing PHP configuration settings* recipe in this chapter
▸ The *Logging in PHP* recipe in this chapter

Logging in PHP

Applications written in PHP generate log messages whenever an error occurs. These messages may be saved to a log file, passed to syslog, or ignored, depending on the configuration settings of the interpreter. Ignoring error messages is a bad idea as it prevents you from detecting problems occurring on your server.

On the other hand, saving every message to a file can cause your logs to grow very quickly, especially on high-traffic sites. Fortunately, PHP allows you to configure which errors are logged quite precisely. All PHP errors are assigned a level value; most severe errors are marked as E_ERROR, less severe as E_WARNING, even less severe as E_NOTICE, and so on. A complete list of error levels can be found in the PHP manual at http://php.net/errorfunc.constants.php.

It is recommended to log all errors during development, but in production, all errors should be logged, except E_DEPRECATED (deprecation warnings) and E_STRICT (code style suggestions). We will set this level of logging in this recipe.

Getting ready

To complete this recipe, we will need to know what user and group Apache is running as. You can find instructions on obtaining this information in the *Getting ready* section of the *Generating dynamic pages using CGI* recipe of this chapter.

How to do it...

Instruct PHP to keep a log of error messages by following these steps:

1. Create an empty file to store your PHP error log in a location of your choosing, for example, in /var/log/php_errors.log.

2. Change the owner of the file to the Apache user. If your web server runs as the www-data user, you can do this by issuing the following command:

   ```
   $ sudo chown www-data /var/log/php_errors.log
   ```

    Information about manipulating files and changing ownership and permissions can be found in the *Managing files and directories on the server* recipe in *Chapter 6, Managing Files on Your System*.

3. Make sure that the owner (Apache) has write access to the file:

   ```
   $ sudo chmod u+w /var/log/php_errors.log
   ```

4. Navigate to **Others | PHP Configuration**.

5. Click **Manage** in the line corresponding to the global PHP configuration file.

6. Click **Error Logging**.

7. Set **Display error messages?** to **Yes**.

8. Set **Write error messages to log?** to **Yes**.

9. Set **Expression for error types** to E_ALL & ~E_DEPRECATED & ~E_STRICT.

10. Set **Log file for errors** to **Other file** and enter /var/log/php_errors.log in the text field, as shown in the following screenshot:

Error message display and logging options

Display error messages? ○ Yes ⊙ No		Write error messages to log? ⊙ Yes ○ No
Ignore repeated errors? ○ Yes ⊙ No		Ignore source when checking for repeats? ○ Yes ⊙ No
Expression for error types ○ Default ⊙ E_ALL & ~E_DEPRECATED & ~E_STRICT		
Maximum size of logged errors ○ Unlimited ⊙ 1024		
Log file for errors ○ None ○ Syslog ⊙ Other file /var/log/php_errors.log		

11. Click **Save**.

12. Navigate to **Servers | Apache Webserver**.

13. Click the **Apply Changes** link.

From now on, you should see error messages appear in PHP's log file.

How it works...

In order to enable PHP error logging, we set the following master values in your php.ini file:

```
log_errors = On
error_reporting = E_ALL & ~E_DEPRECATED & ~E_STRICT
error_log = /var/log/php_errors.log
```

The preceding settings turn on PHP's error logging (log_errors) and specify which file the errors should be saved in (error_log).

The error_reporting instruction specifies which messages are saved and which ones are ignored. This line accepts a complex syntax in which ampersand signs (&) allow you to specify different levels of messages to log and tilde characters (~) that negate a given class. This allows us to log errors of all levels (E_ALL), but not deprecation warnings (& ~E_DEPRECATED) or style suggestions (& ~E_STRICT).

Refer to the *Changing PHP configuration settings* recipe in this chapter for more information about ways of changing the configuration of PHP.

There's more...

PHP can also output error messages to the system log (syslog). If you wish to use syslog, change the `error_log` line as follows:

```
error_log = syslog
```

PHP errors are output to the syslog facility named `user`, and unfortunately, this cannot be changed through the PHP configuration at this time.

 Modern syslog implementations (such as rsyslog, syslog-ng) can filter messages based on the command that generated them.

Refer to the *Saving syslog messages to a file* recipe in *Chapter 5, Monitoring Your System*, for more information about syslog.

See also

For more information about using system logs, take a look at the following recipes:

▶ The *Viewing and searching through system logfiles* recipe in *Chapter 5, Monitoring Your System*

▶ The *Adding other logfiles to Webmin* recipe in *Chapter 5, Monitoring Your System*

▶ The *Configuring logfile rotation* recipe in *Chapter 5, Monitoring Your System*

Installing WordPress on your server

WordPress is a very popular open source blogging platform. The software is very easy to use yet versatile enough to serve a variety of purposes, such as running informational websites or even simple e-commerce shops. WordPress is written entirely in PHP, which makes it quite easy to install.

This recipe pulls together strands from various preceding chapters. We will demonstrate how to use the recipes provided in this book to set up a working web server hosting a website powered by the WordPress blogging platform.

Package repositories of many operating system distributions host a package for WordPress. You may choose to install the package if you don't intend to customize your site or host multiple different versions of the software. Note that WordPress may be updated more frequently than packages in your OS repository, which could possibly lead you to use an insecure version of the software. Look for documentation contained within the package for more information if you choose this route.

How to do it...

This recipe is divided into a number of sections. We will prepare the server first by installing the required software packages. You may skip these steps if you have the software mentioned installed on your server already. We will then create a MySQL database and user for our WordPress installation. Finally, we'll create an Apache virtual host and install WordPress.

Please follow these steps to prepare the server:

1. Install the Apache web server by following the *Installing Apache on your system* recipe in *Chapter 8, Running an Apache Web Server*.

2. Install the MySQL database server by following the *Installing the MySQL database server* recipe in *Chapter 9, Running a MySQL Database Server*.

3. Install PHP by following the *Installing PHP* recipe in this chapter.

In order for PHP applications to communicate with MySQL, you will need to install an additional PHP module, which is available as a package on most OS distributions. You can check to see if this module is already installed by looking at the output of the phpinfo() function, as described in the *Changing PHP configuration settings* recipe of this chapter. If you find an information section named **mysql**, then the php-mysql module is installed.

4. Install the system package named php-mysql, php5-mysql, or something similar.

More information about installing packages can be found in the *installing software packages* recipe in *Chapter 1, Setting Up Your System*.

5. Install the php-gd module that allows PHP applications to manipulate graphic images in common formats such as PNG and JPEG. Install a system package named php-gd, php5-gd, or something similar.

6. Make sure that the rewrite module of Apache (mod_rewrite) is installed and enabled. Take a look at the *Enabling Apache modules* recipe in *Chapter 8, Running an Apache Web Server*, for more information.

Creating a database

We will create a database and user named `wordpress`. You should probably use a more informative name, especially if you plan to use more than one instance of WordPress. Please follow these steps to create a database:

1. Create a new MySQL database and user, both named `wordpress`. The user should use a strong password and be allowed to connect from the local machine (`localhost`).

2. Grant the `wordpress` user connecting from `localhost` all permissions on the `wordpress` database.

> Information about creating MySQL databases and granting permissions can be found in the *Creating a new database* and *Creating users and granting permissions to databases* recipes in *Chapter 9, Running a MySQL Database Server*.

> If you are running a system with **Security Enhanced Linux (SELinux)**, you will have to allow Apache to connect to databases by setting the following flag:
>
> ```
> $ sudo setsebool -P httpd_can_network_connect_db 1
> ```

Creating a virtual host and installing WordPress

In order to create a virtual host and install WordPress, perform the following steps:

1. Follow the *Creating a virtual host* recipe in *Chapter 8, Running an Apache Web Server*, to create a website serving files from the document root, `/var/www/blog.example.com`, with the server name, `blog.example.com`.

2. Download the latest version of WordPress from the following URL and extract the archive into the `/var/www/blog.example.com` directory: `http://wordpress.org/latest.tar.gz`

> When the extraction is complete, WordPress's `index.php` file should have the following path: `/var/www/blog.example.com/index.php`.

3. Create an `.htaccess` file in the same directory and enter the following rewrite rules to enable WordPress's clean URLs:

```
<IfModule mod_rewrite.c>
RewriteEngine On
RewriteBase /
RewriteRule ^index\.php$ - [L]
RewriteCond %{REQUEST_FILENAME} !-f
```

```
RewriteCond %{REQUEST_FILENAME} !-d
RewriteRule . /index.php [L]
</IfModule>
```

> Apache's virtual host or directory configuration must allow options to be overridden by the `.htaccess` files (`AllowOverride All`). For more information, take a look at the *Setting options for specific directories, files, and locations* recipe in *Chapter 8, Running an Apache Web Server*.

4. Navigate to the URL of your new WordPress site: `http://blog.example.com/`.

5. A setup screen will appear. Follow instructions there and enter the created database name, username, and password, as shown in the following screenshot:

6. WordPress setup will generate the contents of a configuration file, which you should save as `/var/www/blog.example.com/wp-config.php`.

You can now navigate to the URL of your WordPress site and follow onscreen instructions to finish setup and start using the site.

How it works...

WordPress uses technologies described throughout this book. In order to set up our server for the application, we need to install Apache, MySQL, and PHP. We also need a number of additional PHP modules to allow WordPress to communicate with the database and manipulate image files.

Every instance of WordPress requires access to a database. The table prefix is added to the name of every database table, which allows multiple installations of WordPress to share a single database. We left the prefix set at its default value of `wp_`. Since we are running our own server, we can create as many databases as we need; therefore, there is no need to share databases. In fact, we also created a dedicated database user for this application with access to one database only.

The virtual host configuration we created allows us to run WordPress on one subdomain (`blog.example.com`), leaving us free to run other software on the main domain or other subdomains.

The `.htaccess` file we created is designed to allow WordPress to use clean URLs. Thanks to this function, pages may have URLs such as `http://blog.example.com/hello-world/` instead of `http://blog.example.com/?p=1`.

 More information about clean URLs, called permalinks in WordPress, is available in its documentation at `http://codex.wordpress.org/Using_Permalinks`.

We finished the installation by allowing WordPress to create the contents of its main configuration file (`wp-config.php`) for us. We needed to provide database connection details into a form, and WordPress prepared the configuration file itself. In addition to storing database connection details, the installer also generated pseudo-random cryptographic salt strings, which help keep WordPress secure. Salt strings are also stored in the configuration file and should be kept secret and changed occasionally.

 To keep the WordPress configuration file safe, make sure its permissions are set correctly. It has to be readable for Apache, but not anyone else. Take a look at the *Getting ready* section of the *Generating dynamic pages using CGI* recipe in this chapter to find the name of the Apache user, as well as the *Managing files and directories on the server* recipe in *Chapter 6, Managing Files on Your System*, for information about setting permissions.

Also, make sure that any backup copies of this file are stored in a safe way.

See also

▶ More information about the process of installing WordPress can be found in its manual at `http://codex.wordpress.org/Installing_WordPress`

Installing Drupal on your server

Drupal is a powerful open source **content management system** (**CMS**). It is highly modular, which means it can be customized to perform nearly any task by installation of additional plugins. Drupal is written entirely in PHP, which makes it quite easy to install.

This recipe pulls together strands from various preceding chapters. We will demonstrate how to use recipes provided in this book to set up a working web server hosting a website powered by the Drupal CMS platform.

 Package repositories of many operating system distributions host a package for Drupal. You may choose to install the package if you don't intend to host multiple different versions of the software. Note that Drupal may be updated more frequently than packages in your OS repository, which could possibly lead to using an insecure version of the software. Look for documentation contained within the package for more information if you choose this route.

Getting ready

To complete this recipe, we will need to know what user and group Apache is running as. You can find instructions on obtaining this information in the *Getting ready* section of the *Generating dynamic pages using CGI* recipe in this chapter.

How to do it...

This recipe is divided into a number of sections. We will prepare the server first by installing required software packages. You may skip these steps if you already have the software mentioned installed on your server. We will then create a MySQL database and user for our Drupal installation. Finally, we'll create an Apache virtual host and install Drupal.

Follow these steps to prepare the server:

1. Install the Apache web server by following the *Installing Apache on your system* recipe in *Chapter 8, Running an Apache Web Server*.

2. Install the MySQL database server by following the *Installing the MySQL database server* recipe in *Chapter 9, Running a MySQL Database Server*.

3. Install PHP by following the *Installing PHP* recipe in this chapter.

4. In order for PHP applications to communicate with MySQL, you will need to install an additional PHP module, which is available as a package on most OS distributions. Install the system package named `php-mysql`, `php5-mysql`, or something similar.

More information about installing packages can be found in the *Installing software packages* recipe in *Chapter 1, Setting Up Your System*.

5. Install the `php-gd` module that allows PHP applications to manipulate graphic images in common formats such as PNG and JPEG. Install a system package named `php-gd`, `php5-gd`, or something similar.

6. Make sure that the rewrite module of Apache (`mod_rewrite`) is installed and enabled. Take a look at the *Enabling Apache modules* recipe in *Chapter 8, Running an Apache Web Server*, for more information.

Creating a database

We will create a database and user named `drupal`. You should probably use a more informative name, especially if you plan to use more than one instance of Drupal. Please follow these steps:

1. Create a new MySQL database and user, both named `drupal`. The user should use a strong password and be allowed to connect from the local machine (`localhost`).

2. Grant the `drupal` user connecting from `localhost` all permissions on the `drupal` database.

 Information about creating MySQL databases and granting permissions can be found in the *Creating a new database* and *Creating users and granting permissions to databases* recipes in *Chapter 9, Running a MySQL Database Server*.

 If you are running a system with **Security Enhanced Linux** (**SELinux**), you will have to allow Apache to connect to databases by setting the following flag:

```
$ sudo setsebool -P httpd_can_network_connect_db 1
```

Creating a virtual host and installing WordPress

Follow these steps to create a virtual host and install Drupal:

1. Follow the *Creating a virtual host* recipe in *Chapter 8, Running an Apache Web Server*, to create a website serving files from the document root, `/var/www/cms.example.com`, with the server name, `cms.example.com`.

2. Find and download the latest version of WordPress from the following URL and extract the archive into the `/var/www/cms.example.com` directory: `https://drupal.org/download`.

When the extraction is complete, Drupal's `index.php` file should have this path: `/var/www/cms.example.com/index.php`.

 Drupal comes bundled with an `.htaccess` file. Make sure that the file was properly extracted to `/var/www/cms.example.com/.htaccess`.

Apache's virtual host or directory configuration must allow options to be overridden by `.htaccess` files (`AllowOverride All`). For more information, take a look at the *Setting options for specific directories, files, and locations* recipe in *Chapter 8, Running an Apache Web Server*.

3. Create a directory (`sites/default/files`) in which Drupal will store uploaded and temporary files. The directory is relative to the root Drupal directory, so its full path in our case would be `/var/www/cms.example.com/sites/default/files`.

4. Change the owner of the `sites/default/files` directory to the Apache user and make sure the owner has read and write permissions for the directory.

 Information about manipulating files and changing ownership and permissions can be found in the *Managing files and directories on the server* recipe in *Chapter 6, Managing Files on Your System*.

5. Create Drupal's configuration file in `sites/default/settings.php` by making a copy of the default settings file, `sites/default/default.settings.php`.

6. Temporarily allow all users to write to the `settings.php` file by changing its permissions to `666`.

7. Visit the URL of your new Drupal site: `http://cms.example.com/`.

8. A setup screen will appear. Follow the instructions on this screen and enter the created database, username, and password.

9. When the installer is finished modifying your settings file, it will inform you that you should now change permissions to remove write access to the `settings.php` file:

 All necessary changes to *sites/default* and *sites/default/settings.php* have been made, so you should remove write permissions to them now in order to avoid security risks. If you are unsure how to do so, consult the online handbook.

You can now navigate to the URL of your Drupal site and follow onscreen instructions to finish setup and start using the site.

How it works...

Drupal uses technologies described throughout this book. In order to set up our server for the application, we need to install Apache, MySQL, and PHP. We also need a number of additional PHP modules to allow Drupal to communicate with the database and manipulate image files.

After the initial server setup was complete, we created a virtual host, which allows us to run a Drupal site on a subdomain (cms.example.com), leaving us free to run other software on the main domain or other subdomains.

With everything prepared, we copied Drupal files to the domain directory, created the files and folder that Drupal needs for installation, and then allowed Drupal's installer to guide us through the remaining steps. Drupal filled its settings file with the information necessary to connect to the database and initialized the website. After installation, it's important to remove write permissions from the settings file.

See also

   ▶   More information about the process of installing Drupal can be found in its manual at
       https://drupal.org/documentation/install

Installing a Django-based application using mod_wsgi

Django is a versatile web development framework written in the Python programming language. The framework allows for rapid development while encouraging good coding practices. Applications written in Django can be hosted on Apache with the use of the mod_wsgi module.

This recipe will demonstrate how to set up your server to host a Django application. Other Python applications supporting mod_wsgi can be set up in a similar fashion. This includes applications such as MoinMoin, PyBlosxom, Trac, and other frameworks such as CherryPy, Pylons, TurboGears, Pyramid, web.py, Werkzeug, Web2Py, and Zope.

How to do it...

Install the Apache web server by following the *Installing Apache on your system* recipe in *Chapter 8, Running an Apache Web Server*.

   1.   Install Python Version 2.7 using a system package. The package will be named
        python, python2.7, python-2.7, or something similar.

As of Version 1.5, Django supports Python 3, and setup is the same as in the newer version. You just need to substitute Python 2.7 with Python 3, and packages for `pip` and `mod_wsgi` with their Python 3 equivalents.

2. Install `pip`—the Python package installer—from a system package. The package will be named `python-pip` or something similar.

On some systems, you may need to add an additional repository to install the package. For instance, if you're running a Linux distribution from the RedHat family (RHEL, CentOS, Fedora, and so on), you should add the **Extra Packages for Enterprise Linux** (**EPEL**) repository. Information about setting up EPEL can be found in the *Giving users access to your server via FTP* recipe in *Chapter 6, Managing Files on Your System*.

3. Install `mod_wsgi`, a module that enables Apache to host Python applications, from a system package. The package will be named `mod_wsgi`, `apache2-mod_wsgi`, `libapache2-mod-wsgi`, or something similar.

4. Follow the steps in the *Enabling Apache modules* recipe in *Chapter 8, Running an Apache Web Server*, to enable the `mod_wsgi` module (`wsgi`).

5. Install Django using `pip` by issuing the following command:

```
$ sudo pip install django
```

You can modify the preceding command to install a particular version of Django. For instance, to install Django 1.6.2, use the following command:

```
$ sudo pip install django==1.6.2
```

6. Make a directory for web applications in `/srv/webapps/`.

7. Create a project structure for your application by issuing the following command. This will create a directory in `/srv/webapps/hello` to store your application. Execute the following command:

```
$ cd /srv/webapps/ && django-admin.py startproject hello
```

Instead of starting a new project in `hello`, you can upload a Django application to another directory. Make a note of the application path and substitute it for `/srv/webapps/hello` in subsequent steps.

8. Make directories for static and media files used by your application, for instance, in `/srv/webapps/hello/static/` and `/srv/webapps/hello/media/`.

9. In Webmin, navigate to **Servers | Apache Webserver** and click **Create virtual host**. You don't need to specify a document root; just set **Server Name** to `hello.example.com`.

>
>
> More information about setting up virtual servers can be found in the *Createing virtual host* recipe in *Chapter 8, Running an Apache Web Server*. This recipe also explains how to set up a mock DNS record in `/etc/hosts` if you don't have another way to point subdomains to your server.

10. Click the icon for the newly created virtual server.

11. Click the **Edit Directives** icon.

12. Enter the following configuration directives in the text area and click **Save**:

```
ServerName hello.example.com

WSGIDaemonProcess hello python-path=/srv/webapps/hello/
processes=3 threads=1
WSGIProcessGroup hello
WSGIScriptAlias / /srv/webapps/hello/hello/wsgi.py

Alias /favicon.ico /srv/webapps/hello/static/favicon.ico
Alias /static/ /srv/webapps/hello/static/
Alias /media/ /srv/webapps/hello/media/
```

Consider the following screenshot:

Module Index	Edit Directives

Edit Directives

For hello.example.com:80

Use the text box below to manually edit the Apache directives in `/etc/apache2/sites-available/hello.example.com.conf` that apply to this virtual server, directory or files.

```
ServerName hello.example.com

WSGIDaemonProcess hello python-path=/srv/webapps/hello/ processes=5 threads=1
WSGIProcessGroup hello
WSGIScriptAlias / /srv/webapps/hello/hello/wsgi.py

Alias /favicon.ico /srv/webapps/hello/static/favicon.ico
Alias /static/ /srv/webapps/hello/static/
Alias /media/ /srv/webapps/hello/media/
```

Save

13. Click the **Apply Changes** link.

Now, when you navigate to `http://hello.example.com`, you should be greeted by Django's welcome screen served by Apache.

 If you're using SELinux, you may run into problems because the location `/srv/webapps` is not accessible to Apache. Disable SELinux temporarily to see if that solves your problem, and then refer to the following documentation page for information on how to fix the issue:

`https://code.google.com/p/modwsgi/wiki/ApplicationIssues#Secure_Variants_Of_UNIX`

How it works...

Web Server Gateway Interface (**WSGI**) is a low-level interface between web servers and web applications or frameworks written in Python. Apache is able to serve such applications through a module named `mod_wsgi`.

The configuration we created instructs Apache to create a number of daemon processes (`processes=3`) that reside in memory ready to process HTTP requests coming from the web server. The number of processes and threads started within each process determines how much of the system's resources are assigned to the application, which in turn decides how many requests it can handle simultaneously. These parameters should be tweaked to your specific needs.

The `python-path` parameter tells Python where it can find additional application modules. Our application is placed in `/srv/webapps/hello/`, which is not on the standard list of places Python searches when it looks for modules; therefore, we specify its location explicitly.

The `WSGIScriptAlias` directive instructs Apache to serve all requests coming in to the root URL of the domain (/) to be handled by Django. `Alias` directives instruct Apache that requests to places such as `/static/` should be served directly from disk. You can combine the `Alias` and `WSGIScriptAlias` directives to specify which parts of a domain are served by an application and which parts Apache should serve directly.

See also

▶ More information about serving Django through mod_wsgi can be found in its manual at `https://docs.djangoproject.com/en/dev/howto/deployment/wsgi/modwsgi/`.

▶ Even more detailed information can be found in the `mod_wsgi` documentation at `https://code.google.com/p/modwsgi/wiki/InstallationInstructions`.

12
Setting Up an E-mail Server

In this chapter, we will cover:

- ▸ Setting up your server to send and receive e-mails
- ▸ Setting up secure IMAP access to mailboxes
- ▸ Setting up a secure SMTP relay for users
- ▸ Controlling the mail queue
- ▸ Reading and writing e-mails on the server
- ▸ Configuring e-mail aliases
- ▸ Filtering incoming mail using Procmail and SpamAssassin
- ▸ Debugging e-mail-related problems

Introduction

E-mail is a standard means of communication on the Internet. As a way to send messages to anyone in the world, instantly and for free, it became one of the first killer features of the Internet and a harbinger of many things to come.

E-mail is an old technology, designed in the early, naive days of the Internet. Initially, every mail server accepted all messages from anyone and forwarded them on to any destination. E-mail accounts were protected by passwords, but those were symbolic—sent as plain text over unencrypted connections, and the word, "spam" was still associated mainly with the Monty Python sketches.

Unfortunately, as more and more people came online, many malicious users started to abuse the e-mail system. E-mail became a free way to send marketing information with the ability to reach every person on the planet. This caused an explosion of unwanted e-mail messages, most commonly called **spam**, which, at its peak, made up more than 95 percent of e-mail traffic. These days, the problem is slowly subsiding as administrators valiantly fight against the spam tide. On a properly configured system, spam is no longer the nuisance it once was, but there is no single foolproof solution. If you decide to host your own mail server, be aware that you will have to put in a substantial bit of work to get everything working properly.

 You may decide to let someone else host mail for your domain. For example, Google provides a commercial version of its Gmail service to businesses as Google Apps for Business. Many companies offer similar services.

Because e-mail is such a complex topic, one book chapter will only get you started. If you follow these recipes, you will end up with a working, but very basic, e-mail system. If e-mail is important to your enterprise, you should proceed to read other material on this topic. There is a benefit of starting here, as we will demonstrate how helpful Webmin can be in administering a mail server.

In this chapter, we will set up Postfix, a popular open source mail transfer agent. Its alternatives, such as exim and sendmail, are also supported by Webmin but are not covered here.

Setting up your server to send and receive e-mails

To handle e-mail, your server needs to run a service called a **Mail Transfer Agent** (**MTA**) that is capable of:

 ▸ Receiving incoming e-mail and placing it in the user's local mail spool
 ▸ Sending e-mail to other MTAs for delivery to users on remote systems

MTAs exchange messages using **Simple Mail Transfer Protocol** (**SMTP**). A mail server listens for connections on port 25 and accepts incoming e-mail messages from anywhere on the Internet. If the message is addressed to a valid local address, it should be delivered to the destination mailbox.

When a user of our server decides to send an e-mail, the MTA picks up the message, checks where it is addressed to, and forwards it to the MTA associated with the destination domain.

 MTAs can also relay e-mails—forward e-mails coming in over SMTP but bound for other destinations. This is discussed in the *Setting up a secure SMTP relay for users* recipe later in this chapter.

In this recipe, we will set up the Postfix mail transfer agent on your server.

Getting ready

E-mail addresses are based on the following structure: `mailbox@fqdn`, where `mailbox` uniquely identifies a user or alias and `fqdn` uniquely identifies a mail system through a fully qualified domain name (FQDN). You will need to assign an FQDN to your server in order to make use of the e-mail system.

 To make sure that your server is assigned an FQDN, check that your domain's DNS A or MX (Mail eXchange) record points to the IP of your mail server. A DNS MX record allows you to host mail on a machine other than the one indicated by the basic A record.

Throughout this recipe, we will assume that your server's FQDN is `mailserver.example.com`, which makes `mailserver` its hostname and `example.com` its domain. Replace these with your real values.

How to do it...

Follow these steps to set up Postfix on your server:

1. Follow the instructions contained in the *Installing software packages* recipe from *Chapter 1*, *Setting Up Your System*, and install the `postfix` package for your system.

    A system can have only one MTA installed at any time. If another MTA was installed on your system, you will need to uninstall it. If you're installing from a system package, this should be done automatically.

2. To receive mail, your server will need to answer incoming SMTP connections on TCP port 25. Follow the steps described in the *Allowing access to a service through the firewall* recipe in *Chapter 3*, *Securing Your System*, to allow incoming TCP traffic to port 25 through your firewall.

3. Navigate to **System | Bootup and Shutdown**, check the box next to `postfix`, and click the **Start Now and On Boot** button.

4. Navigate to **Servers | Postfix Mail Server | General Options**.

5. Set **What domain to use in outbound mail** to **Use domainname**.

6. Set **What domains to receive mail for** to **Whole domain**.

7. Set **Internet hostname of this mail system** to `mailserver.example.com`.

8. Set **Local internet domain name** to **Default**. This sets the mail domain to the hostname without the first component. In our case, this would be `example.com`.

9. Set **Network interfaces for receiving mail** to **All**.

10. Click the **Save and Apply** button.

11. Click the **Stop Postfix** and then the **Start Postfix** buttons to restart the mail system.

Your system should now be able to send and receive e-mail messages. Test the ability of the server to send e-mail, and its ability to receive it, by following the steps in the *Debugging e-mail related problems* recipe later in this chapter.

How it works...

In this recipe, we installed the popular open source MTA called Postfix on your system. In order to receive mail, we opened port 25 in your firewall, and we also made sure that the service is started during system boot.

We then proceeded to configure the mail system's basic settings. Postfix keeps settings in a text file located in the path `/etc/postfix/main.cf`. Posfix's default configuration is very close to what a working system requires, so we only needed to specify which domain we are going to handle mail for and instruct Postfix to listen for connections on all network interfaces.

More information about each setting we modified is available in Webmin. Just click the label of any form field to get a detailed description.

See also

Now that you have gotten your feet wet, you should probably read all recipes in this chapter:

▶ In particular, take a look at the *Debugging e-mail related problems* recipe

▶ To allow users to pick up e-mail from your server, refer to the recipe, *Setting up secure IMAP access to mailboxes*

▶ To allow users to send e-mails through your system, refer to the recipe, *Setting up a secure SMTP relay for users*

Setting up secure IMAP access to mailboxes

Mail received by your MTA is delivered to a queue directory on your server. Recipients are expected to pick up messages from here and store them in their own mailboxes. If users connect to your server by SSH, they may use terminal applications such as `mutt` or `alpine` and store messages in home directories. Another access method you can provide is a web mail application such as Roundcube, which runs on Apache with PHP. Webmin's companion product, Usermin, also provides basic mail functionality for users. See the *Installing Usermin* recipe in *Chapter 2, User Management*, for more information.

You can find more information on each of these programs online, but most system distributions offer convenient packages, which make installation very easy:

Roundcube: `http://www.roundcube.net`

Alpine, the successor to Pine: `https://www.washington.edu/alpine/`

Mutt: `http://www.mutt.org`

The standard method of picking up e-mail, however, is to use a **Mail User Agent** (**MUA**), more commonly referred to as an e-mail client or e-mail reader. Programs such as Thunderbird, KMail, Evolution, Apple Mail, Outlook, and many others, serve this role for desktop users. These programs expect to talk to your server using the IMAP, POP3, and SMTP protocols.

Protocol	Function
POP3	Used to pick up messages from the server by downloading the entire mailbox.
IMAP	Used to download new mail and manages message on the server.
SMTP	Used to submit mail for delivery to others.

In this recipe, we'll demonstrate how to set up IMAP access to your Postfix server using a companion server named Dovecot. We'll make sure that access is secured using a TLS encrypted connection. In the next recipe, *Setting up a secure SMTP relay for users*, we'll demonstrate setting up SMTP.

The POP3 protocol is becoming obsolete, so in this recipe, we'll focus on IMAP. If you need it, enabling POP3 using the described software is simple.

Getting ready

In this recipe, we're building on basic Postfix MTA setup described in *Setting up your server to send and receive e-mails*. Make sure your Postfix is working properly before starting with this recipe.

We will need to know the location of your Postfix mail queue directory. Check it by following these steps:

1. Navigate to **Servers** | **Postfix Mail Server** | **General Options**.
2. Make a note of the **Mail queue directory** value.

How to do it...

Follow these steps to set up the Dovecot IMAP service:

1. Follow the instructions contained in the *Installing software packages* recipe from *Chapter 1, Setting Up Your System,* and install Dovecot Version 2. The package should be named `dovecot`, but on some (Debian-based) systems you may need to install a number of smaller packages such as `dovecot-common`, `dovecot-imapd`, and optionally, `dovecot-pop3d`.

2. Your server will need to answer incoming IMAP connections on TCP ports 143 and 993. Follow the steps described in the *Allowing access to a service through the firewall* recipe in *Chapter 3, Securing Your System,* to allow incoming TCP traffic to ports `143` and `993` through your firewall.

3. Navigate to **System | Bootup and Shutdown**, check the box next to `dovecot`, and click the **Start Now and On Boot** button.

4. Navigate to **Servers | Dovecot IMAP/POP3 Server | Networking and Protocols**.

5. In the **Serve mail protocols**, select **IMAP**.

6. Click **Save**.

7. Navigate to **Servers | Dovecot IMAP/POP3 Server | Mail Files**.

8. Set mail location and reading options to **Other Dovecot** location, and enter a string based on the location of your Postfix mail queue directory. For example, if the location is `/var/spool/postfix`, enter the following:

    `mbox:~/mail:INBOX=/var/spool/postfix/%u`

9. Set **UIDL format** to **Other**, and enter `%08Xu%08Xv` in the text field.

10. Click **Save**.

11. Navigate to **Servers | Dovecot IMAP/POP3 Server | SSL Configuration**.

12. Set **Disallow plaintext authentication in non-SSL mode?** to **Yes**.

13. Click **Save**.

14. Click the **Apply Configuration** button.

Users will now be able to connect to your server to receive mail via IMAP. Test the configuration by creating an account in your e-mail client program with the following settings:

*   **IMAP server**: The hostname of your mail server
*   **Port**: `143` or `993`
*   **Require SSL**: **Yes**
*   **Username**: Your system username
*   **Password**: Your system password

If you're having trouble connecting, look for debugging information in your server's mail log. If you see an error message resembling `Operation not permitted (egid=500(username), group based on /var/spool/mail/username)`, then you will need to change the group permissions of files in your mail spool directory. You can do that by issuing the following command:

```
$ sudo find /var/spool/mail -type f -exec
  chmod 0600 '{}' \; -print
```

Paste the error messages you encounter into a search engine to find resolutions of other problems.

How it works...

Dovecot was designed to be secure and easy to configure. During installation, it generates a self-signed SSL certificate to encrypt communication with clients. This is very important because without encryption, your system username and password travels in plain text throughout the Internet and may be read by every ISP along the way. E-mail clients will complain that no recognized certificate authority signed your certificate. You may purchase a signed certificate and replace the self-signed certificate that Dovecot generated to get rid of these error messages. Take a look at the *There's more* section for more information.

Dovecot listens for IMAP connections on ports 143 or 993. Traditionally, port 143 was used for unencrypted IMAP connections and port 993 for SSL/TLS encrypted connections. Dovecot allows both ports to use encryption; in fact, we specifically instructed it to reject authentication attempts in non-SSL mode. Leaving both ports open makes it easier for users to configure their e-mail clients, which attempt to guess IMAP ports.

There's more...

Professional e-mail services use commercially signed SSL certificates. To replace your certificate, follow these steps:

1. Upload your purchased certificate, private key, and the certificate of your certificate authority to a folder on your server.

2. Make sure that the private key is protected and not readable by users other than root.

3. Navigate to **Servers | Dovecot IMAP/POP3 Server | SSL Configuration**.

4. Specify the paths to each of the uploaded files in the text fields labeled **SSL certificate file**, **SSL private key file**, and **SSL CA certificate file**.

5. If your key is password protected, enter the password in the **Password for key file** field.

6. Click the **Save** button.

▸ For more information about working with SSL certificates, take a look at the *Setting up encrypted websites with SSL* recipe in *Chapter 8, Running an Apache Web Server.*

▸ Your users will need to send e-mail through your server via SMTP. Take a look at the next recipe, *Setting up a secure SMTP relay for users*, for information about that.

▸ As with every recipe in this chapter, if you run into problems, take a look at the *Debugging e-mail-related problems* recipe in this chapter.

Setting up a secure SMTP relay for users

Users who employ a mail client program will want to send messages through your server using the SMTP protocol. Since we set up an MTA, your server already supports SMTP connections, but only to receive e-mail destined for your domain. Messages submitted anonymously for destinations other than your domain should be rejected. Otherwise, we would create a so-called **open relay**, and spammers would quickly abuse your server. Anti-spam filters would then put your server on blacklists, and other mail servers would stop accepting messages from your users.

In order to avoid creating an open relay, and yet allow remote users to send mail to other domains, we need to require user authentication. We will allow authenticated users to submit mail bound for any domain but reject outbound mail submitted anonymously.

The SMTP protocol supports a method of authentication called **Simple Authentication and Security Layer** (**SASL**), which allows users to specify their username and password before submitting e-mail.

In this recipe, we will use a combination of Postfix and Dovecot to set up SASL authentication for your SMTP server. Sensitive information should not be sent using an unencrypted connection, so we will also provide a layer of TLS encryption for SMTP connections.

Getting ready

This recipe builds on the groundwork performed in the previous recipes, *Setting up your server to send and receive e-mails* and *Setting up secure IMAP access to mailboxes*. Make sure your Postfix and Dovecot are working properly before starting with this recipe.

We will need to know the name of your Postfix user name and group. Check it by following these steps:

1. Navigate to **Servers | Postfix Mail Server | General Options**.
2. Make a note of the **Mail owner** value; this is the Postfix user name.
3. Navigate to **System | Users and Groups**, and check the primary group of this user.

How to do it...

Follow these steps to set up a secure SMTP relay for your users:

1. Navigate to **Servers | Postfix Mail Server | SMTP Authentication And Encryption**.

2. Set **Require SASL SMTP authentication?** to **Yes**.

3. Set **Disallow SASL authentication over insecure connections?** to **Yes**.

4. Set **Handle non-compliant SMTP clients?** to **Yes**.

5. Under **SMTP security options**, check the box labeled **Reject anonymous logins**.

6. Under **SMTP relaying restrictions**, check the boxes marked as follows:

   ❏ **Allow connections from same network**

   ❏ **Allow authenticated clients**

   ❏ **Reject email to other domains**

7. Set **Enable TLS encryption?** to **If requested by client**.

8. You should use the same SSL certificates that the Dovecot server uses. Provide a path to your **TLS certificate file**, **TLS private key file**, and optionally to your **TLS certificate authority file**:

9. Click **Save and Apply**.

10. Navigate to **Servers | Postfix Mail Server | Edit Config Files**.

11. Select `main.cf` from the **Edit config file** dropdown.

12. Click the **Edit** button.

13. Scroll down to the end of the configuration file, and add the following settings:

```
smtpd_sasl_type = dovecot
smtpd_sasl_path = private/auth
```

14. Click **Save**.

15. Navigate to **Servers | Dovecot IMAP/POP3 Server | Edit Config Files**.

16. Select `10-master.conf` from the **Edit config** file dropdown.

17. Click the **Edit** button.

18. Find the configuration section for the `auth` service, and uncomment lines related to the socket. Specify the username and group name of your Postfix user. The section should look something like the following code when finished:

```
service auth
{
...
  # Postfix smtp-auth
  unix_listener /var/spool/postfix/private/auth
  {
    mode = 0660
    user = postfix
    group = postfix
  }
...
}
```

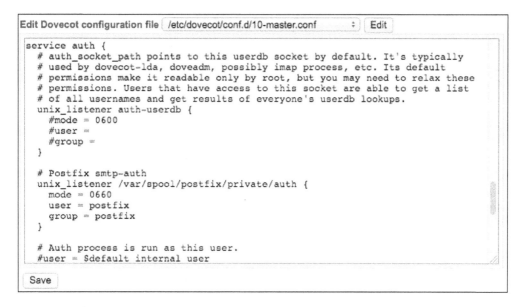

```
service auth {
  # auth_socket_path points to this userdb socket by default. It's typically
  # used by dovecot-lda, doveadm, possibly imap process, etc. Its default
  # permissions make it readable only by root, but you may need to relax these
  # permissions. Users that have access to this socket are able to get a list
  # of all usernames and get results of everyone's userdb lookups.
  unix_listener auth-userdb {
    #mode = 0600
    #user =
    #group =
  }

  # Postfix smtp-auth
  unix_listener /var/spool/postfix/private/auth {
    mode = 0660
    user = postfix
    group = postfix
  }

  # Auth process is run as this user.
  #user = $default_internal_user
```

Save

19. Click **Save**.

20. Click the **Stop Dovecot Server** button and then the **Start Dovecot Server** button to restart the daemon.

Users will now be able to connect to your server and send mail via SMTP. Test the configuration by creating an account in your e-mail client program with the following settings:

▸ **SMTP server**: The hostname of your mail server
▸ **Port**: 25

 Some users may have problems using port 25. Take a look at the *There's more...* section for instructions on adding the alternate SMTP port number 587.

▸ **Require SSL**: **Yes**
▸ **Username**: Your system username
▸ **Password**: Your system password

 If you're having trouble connecting, look for debugging information in your server's mail log. Refer to the *Using Telnet to test SMTP authentication* section of the *Debugging e-mail related problems* recipe for a way to manually test your server. Paste any error messages you encounter into a search engine to find solutions.

How it works...

Dovecot and Postgres work together to provide an authenticated SMTP server. Dovecot provides the SASL authentication service, which is accessible via a UNIX socket. The configuration file, `10-master.conf`, tells Dovecot which services to launch when starting. We edited this file to instruct Dovecot to start the SASL service (named `auth`). We specified the location of the socket (`/var/spool/postfix/private/auth`) and which user and group may connect to it (`postfix`).

We also edited the main configuration file of Postfix called `main.cf`. The changes we made cause Postfix to require SASL authentication over an encrypted connection for submission of messages for relaying. We also told Postfix which type of authentication backend to use (`dovecot`) and the location of the socket relative to its mail queue directory (`private/auth`).

There's more...

Some Internet service providers block traffic on port 25 to prevent machines infected by viruses and worms from abusing the e-mail system. Your server can provide the SMTP service at an alternate port 587. This will allow users from such ISPs to send mail through your server.

Follow these steps to instruct Postfix to listen for SMTP connections on port 587:

1. Navigate to **Servers | Postfix Mail Server | Server Processes**.
2. Click **Add a new server process**.
3. Set **Transport type** to **Internet**.
4. Set **Server name/port** to `587`.
5. Set **Process command** to `smtpd`.
6. Set **Enabled?** to **Yes**.
7. Set **Listen on host address** to **Any address**.
8. Set **Private to mail system?** to **No**.

Postfix server process details

Transport type	Internet ⏷	Enabled?	⦿ Yes ◯ No
Server name/port	587	Listen on host address	⦿ Any address ◯
Process command	smtpd		

Private to mail system?	◯ Yes ⦿ No ◯ Default (Yes)	Run as Postfix user? ◯ Yes ◯ No ⦿ Default (Yes)
Chroot to mail queue directory?	◯ Yes ◯ No ⦿ Default (Yes)	
Automatically wake up process?	⦿ Default ◯ Unlimited ◯ After [ ] seconds (☐ Only if actually used)	
Maximum processes	⦿ Default ◯ Unlimited ◯ At most [ ]	

9. Click **Create**.

10. Navigate to **Servers | Postfix Mail Server | Server Processes**.

11. Click **Stop Postfix** and then **Start Postfix** to restart the service.

See also

To find more detailed information about this setup, refer to the Postfix and Dovecot manuals:

  ▸ `http://wiki2.dovecot.org/HowTo/PostfixAndDovecotSASL`

  ▸ `http://www.postfix.org/SASL_README.html`

Controlling the mail queue

Messages that your mail server is going to send are placed in a mail queue. Normally, they don't stay there very long as the server deletes them as soon as they are sent. However, if for any reason a message cannot be sent, it may stay stuck in the queue.

Inspecting the mail queue will give you important information about the health of your mail system. Webmin provides a convenient graphical user interface to view and control the queue.

Getting ready

In this recipe, we are going to control the Postfix MTA's mail queue. Refer to the *Setting up your server to send and receive e-mails* recipe in this chapter for information about its installation.

How to do it...

1. Navigate to **Servers | Postfix Mail Server | Mail Queue**.
2. If no messages are currently queued for delivery, Webmin will inform you of that. Otherwise, you will see a list of messages resembling the following screenshot:

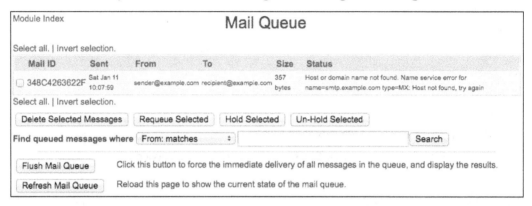

3. To delete a message from the queue, mark the checkbox next to its ID, and click **Delete Selected Messages**.

How it works...

Webmin controls the Postfix mail queue by issuing appropriate Postfix superintendent (`postsuper`) or Postfix queue control (`postqueue`) commands. The following table lists the functions of commands that Webmin allows you to execute:

Command	Function
Delete message	This removes the message from the queue without sending it.
Requeue message	This moves the message to a new queue file, and restarts the delivery attempt.
Hold message	This puts the message *on hold* and does not attempt to deliver it.
Un-Hold message	This removes the hold on a message and attempts to deliver it.
Flush queue	This attempts to deliver all queued messages.
Refresh queue	This updates the information about the queue.

Reading and writing e-mails on the server

Webmin gives you a convenient interface to read and write messages as any user of your system. This can be very useful when debugging mail problems, for instance, to check if a particular message reached a particular mailbox. Keep your users' privacy in mind of course.

How to do it...

1. Navigate to **Servers | Read User Mail**.
2. Click on the name of the user whose mailbox you would like to visit.
3. You will be presented with a graphical interface similar to any mail program, which allows you to read the user's e-mail messages:

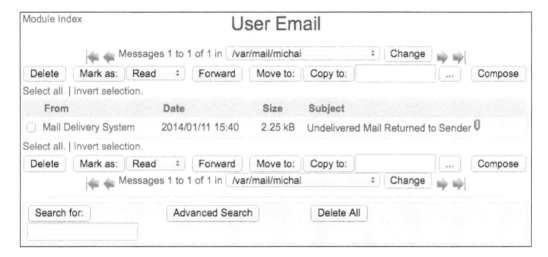

4. Click the **Compose** button to see an interface for writing and sending a new message.
5. Enter a destination address, message subject, and body.
6. Click the **Send Mail** button.

How it works...

Webmin features a basic mail client program written in Perl. Thanks to this functionality, Webmin is able to read and write messages in your users' mailboxes.

Configuring e-mail aliases

Each e-mail address is normally associated with a single user's mailbox on your server. In some situations, however, it's beneficial to forward incoming mail to multiple users or to an address on another server. This can be achieved by using mail aliases, which Postfix supports and Webmin makes easy to administer.

There are a number of aliases which every mail server should define. For instance, mail to the `root` mailbox should always reach an actual person. If you're running a mail server, you should also define aliases named `postmaster` and `abuse` through which people can report mail-related issues. If you wish to read mail sent in reply to automated messages from your MTA, define an alias for `mailer-daemon`.

More information about common mailbox names may be found in the RFC2142 document at `http://tools.ietf.org/html/2142`.

Postfix aliases allow you to not only forward mail to other addresses, but also save their content to files or pipe them to other applications. Sensitive data such as password verification codes are often sent via e-mail, so keep the security of such destinations in mind.

In this recipe, we demonstrate how easy it is to configure Postfix mail aliases using Webmin.

How to do it...

For configuring e-mail aliases, perform the following steps:

1. Navigate to **Servers | Postfix Mail Server | Mail Aliases**.
2. Click **Create a new alias**.
3. In the **Address** field, enter a local e-mail address without the domain, that is, for `mailbox@example.com`, enter just `mailbox`.
4. Set **Enabled?** to **Yes**.
5. Set **Alias to** to **Email address**, and enter a full e-mail address or a local mailbox name in the text field provided.
6. Click **Save**.

How it works...

Whenever Postfix encounters an incoming message, it checks whether the destination address is contained amongst defined aliases. The main list of aliases is stored in a text file named /etc/aliases on most systems. Because this file can grow quite large, it isn't used directly in its text format. Instead, it's converted to an indexed binary file, which allows quick lookups. Every time the alias file is modified, Webmin executes a command named postalias, which creates the binary index. The command will resemble the following with paths adjusted for your system:

```
/usr/sbin/postalias -c /etc/postfix /etc/aliases
```

Postfix aliases may serve a number of different functions listed in the following table. Webmin allows you to not only create all of these, but also others that may not be supported by your MTA. This table lists examples of different ways to define the alias test (as in test@ example.com) and what function they may serve:

Alias syntax	Function
test: user	This forwards the message to another local mailbox.
test: user@remotedomain.com	This forwards the message to a remote e-mail address.
test: "/path/to/file"	This appends incoming messages to a file.
test: "|/usr/local/bin/mailhelper"	This pipes incoming messages to a program.
test: user, root, user@remotedomain.com	This forwards the message to a list of recipients.
test: :include:/path/to/aliases	This forwards the message to destinations listed in /path/to/aliases.

There's more...

There are many interesting ways to use mail aliases, for instance, to create a basic mailing list. Users can also influence how their mail is forwarded by creating a special file in their home directory.

Creating a simple mailing list

You can create a basic mailing list by creating an address and assigning it to forward mail to addresses defined in a text file. You can then manage subscriptions by editing the file. For example, you could create a mailing list, `students@yourdomain.com`, by following these steps:

1. Create a file `/etc/postfix/list-students.txt`.

2. Enter e-mail addresses of all list members in the file, one address per line.

3. Navigate to **Servers | Postfix Mail Server | Mail Aliases**.

4. Click the **Create a new alias** link.

5. In the **Address** field, enter the mailing list address without the domain, for example, `students`.

6. Set **Enabled?** to **Yes**.

7. Set **Alias to** to **Addresses in file**, and enter `/etc/postfix/list-students.txt` in the provided text field.

8. Click **Save**.

> This type of mailing list provides only the most basic functionality. Users cannot manage their mailing preferences or sign out. There are multiple applications dedicated to running full-featured mailing lists. Take a look at Mailman (`http://www.list.org`) and Sympa (`http://www.sympa.org`).

Using .forward files

Users can also control their own mail-forwarding preferences by placing a file named `.forward` in their home directory. Before Postfix delivers mail to a user, it will check if this file exists, and if it does, Postfix will obediently forward the message to addresses specified in the file. Other types of alias behaviors can also be specified in `.forward` files.

See also

▶   Find more information about Postfix aliases in its manual at
    `http://www.postfix.org/aliases.5.html`.

Filtering incoming mail using Procmail and SpamAssassin

E-mail gives us the ability to send free messages to nearly everyone in the world. Unfortunately, some people decided to abuse this system and send unsolicited mass mail (spam) in hopes of making money through advertising or fraud. So many people were tempted by this possibility that, at some point, spam made up over 95 percent of e-mail traffic. This would make e-mail practically unusable, but thankfully, anti-spam filters make this problem more manageable.

Spam fighting is a large and complex topic. In this recipe, we will demonstrate an effective yet basic technique based on the programs Procmail and SpamAssassin. If your site handles a large volume of e-mail, you will probably need a more efficient solution.

How to do it...

This recipe is divided into two parts. First, we instruct our Postfix MTA to hand incoming messages to a filtering program called Procmail. Next, we create a filter, which pipes messages through SpamAssassin and sends spam to a separate mailbox.

First, let's start with setting up Procmail filters in Postfix:

1. Follow instructions contained in the *Installing software packages* recipe from *Chapter 1, Setting Up Your System,* and install Procmail. The package should simply be named `procmail`.

2. Determine the location of the `procmail` binary by issuing the following command:

   `$ which procmail`

   The output of this command will give you the location of the binary, as follows:

   `/usr/bin/procmail`

3. Navigate to **Servers | Postfix Mail Server | Local Delivery**.

4. Enter the following command in the **External command to use instead of mailbox delivery** text field. Replace `/usr/bin/procmail` with your location if it's different.

   `/usr/bin/procmail -a "$EXTENSION"`

5. Click **Save and Apply**.

Now, let's set up SpamAssassin filters in Procmail:

1. Install SpamAssassin its package should simply be named `spamassassin`.

2. Determine the location of the `spamassassin` binary by issuing the following command:

   ```
   $ which spamassassin
   /usr/bin/spamassassin
   ```

3. Navigate to **Servers | Procmail Mail Filter**.

4. Click the **Add a new filter action** link.

5. Set **Delivery mode** to **Feed to program**, and enter the path to the `spamassassin` binary in the text field.

6. Mark the checkboxes, **Action program is a filter** and **Wait for action program to finish, and check result**.

7. Set **Delivery lock file** to **Specific file**, and enter `spamassassin.lock` in the text field.

8. Don't set any action conditions; we want to run all mail through SpamAssassin:

Delivery action details

Delivery mode [Feed to program ⬍] [/usr/bin/spamassassin]

☐ Apply conditions to headers   ☐ Apply conditions to body
☐ Case-sensitive matching   ☐ Feed headers to destination
☐ Feed body to destination   ☐ Continue processing even if conditions match
☑ Wait for action program to finish, and check result   ☐ Wait for action program to finish, but ignore result
☐ Ignore write errors on delivery   ☐ Write out mail in raw mode
☑ Action program is a filter

Delivery lock file   ○ None ○ Default ⦿ Specific file [spamassassin.lock]

Action conditions

For the above action to be carried out, all the conditions below must match. If there are no conditions, the action will always be executed.

Condition type	Regular expression or command
[⬍]	[ ]
[⬍]	[ ]

---

9. Click **Create**.

Let's create a second filter now, which will move all spam messages to another folder called `Junk`.

1. Click the **Add a new filter action** link.
2. Set **Delivery mode** to **Append to file**, and enter `$HOME/mail/Junk` in the text field.
3. Set **Delivery lock file** to **Default**.
4. Under **Condition type**, select **Matches regular expression**, and enter `^X-Spam-Status: Yes:`

Delivery action details

Delivery mode [Append to file ⇕] [$HOME/mail/Junk]

☐ Apply conditions to headers   ☐ Apply conditions to body
☐ Case-sensitive matching   ☐ Feed headers to destination
☐ Feed body to destination   ☐ Continue processing even if conditions match
☐ Wait for action program to finish, and check result ☐ Wait for action program to finish, but ignore result
☐ Ignore write errors on delivery   ☐ Write out mail in raw mode
☐ Action program is a filter

Delivery lock file ○ None ⦿ Default ○ Specific file [   ]

Action conditions

For the above action to be carried out, all the conditions below must match. If there are no conditions, the action will always be executed.

Condition type	Regular expression or command
Matches regular expression ⇕	^X-Spam-Status: Yes
⇕	
⇕	

---

5. Click **Create** .

Incoming mail should now be passed to SpamAssassin. Detected spam messages should not be delivered to your users' regular mailboxes but to files named `~/mail/Junk` in their home directories.

How it works...

This recipe attempts to filter out spam by passing incoming messages through two programs. The first is Procmail, a mail delivery agent (MDA). Postfix hands messages off to the MDA for delivery to mailboxes. Procmail has the added functionality of passing mail through a series of configurable filters. A Procmail filter inspects the headers or body of a message and decides what to do with the message based on its content.

> Procmail is a stable software installed by default on many operating systems. Unfortunately, it's no longer maintained, so no new features will be added in the future. The **maildrop** program is often recommended as a newer replacement for Procmail, but Webmin does not currently support it. More information is available at http://www.courier-mta.org/maildrop/.

In our example, we set up two Procmail filters. The first has no conditions, which means that it applies to every message, and it hands the message off to yet another program for spam analysis. SpamAssassin inspects every part of the message, looks up DNS records of MTAs the message was relayed through, and checks them against spam blacklist and other sources of information about spammers. It uses all this data to perform statistical and artificial intelligence analysis and ends up giving every message a score. If the score is high, the message should probably be considered spam. SpamAssassin writes its report in the headers of the messages and hands it back to Procmail.

Our second Procmail filter inspects message headers to check if SpamAssassin decided that the message is spam (X-Spam-Status: Yes). These messages will not be delivered to a user's inbox but instead appended to a secondary inbox called Junk (~/mail/Junk).

> If your system is going to handle a lot of mail, then invoking SpamAssassin for every message can create a serious bottleneck. It could slow down your server significantly and cause problems. There is a way to optimize SpamAssassin's performance by running it as a background daemon. Look for it in its manual.

There's more...

Once you have everything set up, you should test your anti-spam configuration. There is a way to trigger an automatic SpamAssassin high score. Just enter the following string in a message, and it will be marked as spam:

```
XJS*C4JDBQADN1.NSBN3*2IDNEN*GTUBE-STANDARD-ANTI-
UBE-TEST-EMAIL*C.34X
```

You can find more information about this technique, called **Generic Test for Unsolicited Bulk E-mail** (**GTUBE**), in SpamAssassin's manual at `http://spamassassin.apache.org/gtube/`.

See also

▶ Find more information about the type of setup we created in the SpamAssassin manual, which contains a slightly more complex set of Procmail filters that solves some common bugs you may encounter, at the following URL: `http://wiki.apache.org/spamassassin/UsedViaProcmail`.

Debugging e-mail-related problems

You will learn most about your mail server by talking to it directly in SMTP through a Telnet session. At the same time, you should be monitoring mail logfiles for any messages that occur while you're performing your tests.

In this recipe, we cover a number of techniques for testing and debugging e-mail systems. We will demonstrate how to test your system's ability to:

▶ Receive e-mail by submitting a message directly over SMTP

▶ Send e-mail by sending a message though the mail command

▶ Authenticate users

We'll also mention the location of mail logs, various ways of sending e-mail, debugging SMTP authentication, and other topics. Read on; this recipe should give you a way to find the solution to your problem.

Getting ready

We will be testing the mailing capabilities of a system located at the `mailserver.example.com` domain name. Our test will be performed from another machine (the client).

Before starting, make sure that you have the Telnet program installed on the client machine. A Telnet client is installed by default on most systems and can be installed from a package named `telnet` on others.

 On some systems, the Netcat (nc) program may be a better alternative to using Telnet. You can find out more about it on its website: `http://nc110.sourceforge.net`.

How to do it...

Follow these steps to submit an e-mail message directly to your server using Telnet:

1. On the client machine, open a terminal, and type in the following command to start a Telnet client and connect to port 25 of the `mailserver.example.com` system:

   `$ telnet mailserver.example.com 25`

   The mail server should respond with its greeting banner.

2. Type in the `EHLO` command followed by the fully qualified domain name of your client system. When you press *Enter*, the server should reply with a list of `250` messages:

   `EHLO localhost.localdomain`

   > If your client system isn't a mail server in its own right, it may not have an FQDN. In this situation, use `localhost.localdomain`, but note that most mail servers will reject your message if it comes from a misidentified sender. Look for information about the `XCLIENT` command in the Postfix manual if this is causing a problem for you.

3. Type in the `MAIL FROM` command to specify the sender's e-mail address. The server should respond with a `250 OK` message for the following command:

   `MAIL FROM: user@localhost.localdomain`

4. Type in the `RCPT TO` command to specify the recipient's e-mail address. The server should respond with a `250 OK` message for the following command:

   `RCPT TO: user@example.com`

5. Type in the `DATA` command to start the message body.

6. Optionally, type in e-mail headers. For instance, enter a `Subject:` header to specify the message subject, as shown in the following command:

   `Subject: Test`

7. Enter a blank line to close the headers section and start the message body.

8. Type in a message, and end by entering a dot (`.`) on a single line. The server should respond with a `250 OK` message and indicate that the message was queued for delivery.

9. Type `QUIT` to finish the SMTP session.

The complete Telnet session may look something like the following commands. Your commands are highlighted.

```
$ telnet mailserver.example.com 25
Trying 10.10.10.200...
Connected to mailserver.example.com.
Escape character is '^]'.
220 mailserver.example.com ESMTP Postfix (Debian/GNU)
EHLO localhost.localdomain
250-mailserver.example.com
250-PIPELINING
250-SIZE 10240000
250-VRFY
250-ETRN
250-STARTTLS
250-ENHANCEDSTATUSCODES
250-8BITMIME
250 DSN
MAIL FROM: user@localhost.localdomain
250 2.1.0 Ok
RCPT TO: user@example.com
250 2.1.5 Ok
DATA
354 End data with <CR><LF>.<CR><LF>
Subject: Test

This is the message body.
.
250 2.0.0 Ok: queued as DBE6040983
QUIT
221 2.0.0 Bye
Connection closed by foreign host.
```

How it works...

The Telnet client allows you to establish an interactive TCP connection to your server. When you successfully connect to port 25, the SMTP service answers with code 220 and a welcome message. You can then type text commands, which will be sent to the server when you press *Enter*. The server's answers are displayed inline, and you can proceed to send the next command. This technique may be used to debug any text-based protocol running over TCP such as HTTP, FTP, POP, or IMAP.

Simple Mail Transfer Protocol (SMTP) is as simple as the name promises. The only commands you need to send an e-mail are EHLO, MAIL FROM, RCPT TO, and DATA.

The EHLO command used to be called HELO. It was substituted in the current extended version of the protocol (ESMTP). Using EHLO indicates that you are ready to use this protocol version.

Other information about the message is provided in an envelope, which consists of a number of headers. Each header is provided on a separate line consisting of the header name, colon, and header content. This section ends with an empty line.

More information about e-mail formats may be found in RFC 2822: http://tools.ietf.org/html/rfc2822

The message body ends when a line with a single dot character (.) is sent. This finishes the submission of this message, and the server will answer with 250 OK and information that the message was queued for delivery or an error message. The fact that a message was queued is not a guarantee of its delivery. The e-mail system will scan it for viruses, analyze if it isn't spam, and may decide not to deliver (bounce) the message. In most cases, the sender of the message will be notified by a response e-mail if the message could not be delivered. This may not be true if the message was classified as spam.

Using Telnet to analyze what your e-mail server is doing is a great way to see what errors others who try to send you mail may encounter. Note that not all diagnostic messages are displayed as SMTP responses. You should keep an eye on the server's mail log for additional details if you see any errors.

There's more...

There are many additional tools you should use when debugging e-mail system issues. Some of them are described in the following sections:

Analyzing mail logs

Your Postfix server sends detailed logs to Syslog's `mail` facility. These messages are usually saved in a file named `/var/log/mail.log`, `/var/log/maillog`, or some such similar name. Refer to the *Viewing and searching through system log files* and *Saving Syslog messages to a file* recipes in *Chapter 5, Monitoring Your System*, for more information.

Every message coming into your server is given a unique ID, which allows you to track it through verbose logs. For instance, a single message sent from `root@mailserver.example.com` to `user@other.example.com` could leave the following log trace as it is picked up, queued, delivered, and removed by your server. Note that the message identifier, `EB0FA2049B`, is contained in every entry.

```
Jan 11 09:35:27 mailserver postfix/pickup[23061]:
  EB0FA2049B: uid=0 from=<root@mailserver.example.com>
Jan 11 09:35:27 mailserver postfix/cleanup[23063]:
  EB0FA2049B: message-id=<1389429314.22675@mailserver.example.com>
Jan 11 09:35:27 mailserver postfix/qmgr[23062]:
  EB0FA2049B: from=<root@mailserver.example.com>,
  size=581, nrcpt=1 (queue active)
Jan 11 09:35:33 mailserver postfix/smtp[23065]:
  EB0FA2049B: to=<user@other.example.com>, relay=
  other.example.com[10.10.10.200]:25, delay=18,
  delays=13/0.03/5.1/0.02, dsn=2.0.0,
  status=sent (250 2.0.0 Ok: queued as 5431B40983)
Jan 11 09:35:33 mailserver postfix/qmgr[23062]:
  EB0FA2049B: removed
```

Testing message sending through Webmin

Webmin provides a convenient way to test whether your mail server is actually able to send e-mail messages. To do that, just follow these steps:

1. Navigate to **Servers | Read User Mail**.
2. Click on the username of the user you would like to send a message as, for instance, **root**.
3. Click the **Compose** button.
4. Use the GUI to enter an e-mail message, subject, and recipient address.
5. Click **Send**.

Sending mail from the command line

A quick way to send e-mail messages to others is to use the `mail` command. You can type the message body manually or pipe it into the `mail` command. For instance, to send a message to user@example.com , you can use the following syntax:

```
$ echo "Message body" | mail -s "Subject" user@example.com
```

If the command is not found on your system, you may need to install a package named `mail` or `mailx`.

Using Telnet to test SMTP authentication

You may test your server's SMTP authentication through a Telnet session. The only tricky part is to encode your username and password combination using Base64. For instance, to encode the username myusername and password mypassword, use the following Perl command:

```
$ perl -MMIME::Base64 -e 'print
  encode_base64("\000myusername\000mypassword");'
```

You should see the following output:

```
AG15dXN1cm5hbWUAbX1wYXNzd29yZA==
```

> Base64 is just a form of encoding; it's not a one-way hash or encryption. The algorithm is fully reversible, for instance, by using the following command:
>
> ```
> $ perl -MMIME::Base64 -e 'print
> decode_base64("AG15dXN1cm5hbWUAbX1wYXNzd29yZA==");
> myusernamemypassword
> ```

Once you have your Base64 encoded username and password, you can use it in the AUTH command of a Telnet SMTP session, as shown in the following commands:

```
$ telnet mailserver.example.com 25
Trying 10.10.10.200...
Connected to mailserver.example.com.
Escape character is '^]'.
220 mailserver.example.com ESMTP Postfix (Debian/GNU)
EHLO localhost.localdomain
250-mailserver.example.com
250-PIPELINING
250-SIZE 10240000
```

```
250-VRFY
```

```
250-ETRN
```

```
250-STARTTLS
```

```
250-ENHANCEDSTATUSCODES
```

```
250-8BITMIME
```

```
250 DSN
```

AUTH PLAIN AG15dXNlcm5hbWUAbXlwYXNzd29yZA==

```
235 2.0.0 Authentication successful
```

If everything went according to the plan, you should see the `Authentication successful` message.

See also

- Take a look at the Postfix manual for more information about configuration and debugging. In particular, take a look at the `http://www.postfix.org/DEBUG_README.html` page, which deals with debugging.

- Other, more advanced Postfix debugging tools include the `qshape` command, which will give you an overview of which messages are getting stuck on your server, and the `XCLIENT` facility, which allows you to pretend to be a user of another system. More information is available in these manual pages:

    - `http://www.postfix.org/qshape.1.html`
    - `http://www.postfix.org/XCLIENT_README.html`

- Also, take a look at the *Controlling the mail queue* recipe in this chapter.

Index

E

echo command 97
EHLO command 344
e-mail
  about 319
  issues, debugging 341-344
  reading, from server 333
  receiving, when service stops
      running 124-126
  writing, on server 333
e-mail aliases
  configuring 334, 335
e-mail notifications
  obtaining. for software availability 37, 38
e-mail receiving functionality
  server, setting up for 320-322
e-mail sending functionality
  server, setting up for 320-322
encrypted websites
  setting up, with SSL 215
errors
  logging 219-222
executable file
  setuid bit, enabling on 144
exim 320
export command 97
Extra Packages for Enterprise Linux (EPEL)
      163, 255, 286, 315

F

facilities 116
facility levels
  * 117
  about 116
  auth 116
  authpriv 116
  cron 116
  daemon 116
  ftp 116
  kern 116
  local0 117
  local7 117
  lpr 117
  mail 117
  mark 117
  news 117
  syslog 117
  user 117
  uucp 117
Fedora 11
field
  adding, to database table 282
  deleting 283
files
  copying 138
  creating, on server 139
  deleting 138
  downloading, from server 134
  downloading, from Web directly
      onto server 136
  downloading, from Web in background 136
  editing, on server 138
  extracting, from compressed archive 140
  managing, on server 137
  moving 138
  options, setting for 201-203
  ownership, modifying 141-144
  permissions, modifying 141-144
  renaming 138
  restoring, from backup archive 177
  SQL script, executing from 278
  Syslog messages, saving to 118
  uploading, to server 135, 136
files list
  displaying, in directory 210, 211
filesystem alias
  creating 214
File Transfer Protocol. *See* **FTP**
firewall
  building, around system 70
  FTP access, opening in 164, 165
  service, accessing through 78, 79
  verifying, by port scanning 80-82
formatted CSV file
  database table, restoring from 280
FreeBSD
  URL 15
FreeDNS
  URL 88
FTP
  about 133, 163
  access, restricting to users' home
      directories 166

R

recent logins
listing 123, 124

records
editing, in database 284

RedirectMatch directive 213

REFERENCES privilege 274

remote host
backing up to 182-184

remote NFS volume
mounting 159, 160

remote server
monitoring 130, 131

repository
module, installing from 22

RFC2142 document
URL, for info 334

RHEL 11

rkhunter
URL 71

root login
disabling, over SSH 86

Roundcube
about 322
URL 323

row
adding, to database table 284
deleting, in database table 285
editing, in database table 284

RPM-based system
Webmin, installing on 11, 12

Rsyslog 116

rule 73

RULE privilege 273

Running Processes module
about 99
command, executing as another user 99

S

Samba
debugging 152
home directories, sharing 151

Samba shared network folder
creating 149

Samba user accounts
creating 149

Samba users access
granting, to shared folder 150

SASL (Simple Authentication and Security
Layer) 326

schemas 274

Secure File Transfer Protocol (SFTP) 133

secure IMAP access, to mailboxes
setting up 322-325

secure SMTP relay
setting up, for users 326

Security Enhanced Linux (SELinux) 150, 287

security flaw 70

SELECT privilege 273

self-signed certificate
creating 215

sendmail 320

series, of command
executing 97

server
command, executing on 96
directories, managing on 137
directory, creating on 139
Drupal, installing on 311-313
e-mails, reading from 333
e-mails, writing on 333
files, downloading from 134
files, editing on 138
files, managing on 137
files, uploading to 135, 136
MySQL, setting up on 227
netstat command, executing on 96
new file, creating on 139
Postfix, setting up on 321, 322
setting up, for receiving e-mail 320-322
setting up, for sending e-mail 320-322
symbolic link, creating on 139
WordPress, installing on 307

server configuration files, PostgreSQL
locating 262, 263

Server Name Indication (SNI) 214

server security checklist 70

service
accessing, through firewall 78, 79
restarting, automatically 129

service accessible
creating, from internal network 80

U

UDP (User Datagram Protocol) 146
UNIX pseudo user
  creating 147
Unix sockets 260
Unix users 42
unnecessary services
  turning off 70, 83, 84
UPDATE privilege 273
user account
  disabling, temporarily 58
Usermin
  about 42
  installing 66, 67
user privileges
  granting, on database table 273
users
  about 42
  cloning 45
  creating 43, 45, 272
  creating, based on system accounts 52, 53
  exporting 61, 62
  importing, into another system 61, 62
  options 45
  password, modifying 59, 60
  secure SMTP relay, setting up for 326
  SMTP relay, setting up for 327-330
  specifying, based on ability for
     scheduling cron jobs 106
  UID, modifying 56, 57

V

virtual host
  creating 198-308
virtual server 166
vi text editor 8

W

Web 190
Web2Py 314
Webalizer
  about 222
  used, for analyzing logfiles 222, 223

Webmin
  about 7
  access, restricting to specific IP 86, 87
  connecting to 16-18
  connecting to, over SSH tunnel 89, 90
  enabling, for sending e-mail 36
  installing, on another system 13-15
  installing, on Debian-based system 8, 9
  installing, on RPM-based system 11
  IP address, specifying 20
  listening port, modifying 18, 19
  logfiles, adding to 119
  logfiles, monitoring through 120
  logging in 50, 51
  message sending, testing through 345
  modules, installing 20-22
  monitoring 23, 24
  used, for restarting Apache 193
  user log, controlling 54
Webmin group
  about 42
  creating, with access to modules 46-48
web.py 314
Web Server Gateway Interface (WSGI) 317
Werkzeug 314
who command 124
wildcard certificate 216
Windows
  network shared folders, setting up for 146
  tunnel, creating on 91, 92
Windows shared folder
  mounting 154
WordPress
  about 306
  installing 308-310
  installing, on server 307

Y

yum utility 11

Z

Zope 314
zypper utility 11

Thank you for buying
Webmin Administrator's Cookbook

About Packt Publishing

Packt, pronounced 'packed', published its first book "*Mastering phpMyAdmin for Effective MySQL Management*" in April 2004 and subsequently continued to specialize in publishing highly focused books on specific technologies and solutions.

Our books and publications share the experiences of your fellow IT professionals in adapting and customizing today's systems, applications, and frameworks. Our solution based books give you the knowledge and power to customize the software and technologies you're using to get the job done. Packt books are more specific and less general than the IT books you have seen in the past. Our unique business model allows us to bring you more focused information, giving you more of what you need to know, and less of what you don't.

Packt is a modern, yet unique publishing company, which focuses on producing quality, cutting-edge books for communities of developers, administrators, and newbies alike. For more information, please visit our website: www.packtpub.com.

About Packt Open Source

In 2010, Packt launched two new brands, Packt Open Source and Packt Enterprise, in order to continue its focus on specialization. This book is part of the Packt Open Source brand, home to books published on software built around Open Source licenses, and offering information to anybody from advanced developers to budding web designers. The Open Source brand also runs Packt's Open Source Royalty Scheme, by which Packt gives a royalty to each Open Source project about whose software a book is sold.

Writing for Packt

We welcome all inquiries from people who are interested in authoring. Book proposals should be sent to author@packtpub.com. If your book idea is still at an early stage and you would like to discuss it first before writing a formal book proposal, contact us; one of our commissioning editors will get in touch with you.

We're not just looking for published authors; if you have strong technical skills but no writing experience, our experienced editors can help you develop a writing career, or simply get some additional reward for your expertise.

SELinux System Administration

ISBN: 978-1-78328-317-0   Paperback: 120 pages

A comprehensive guide to walk you through SELinux access controls

1. Use SELinux to further control network communications.

2. Enhance your system's security through SELinux access controls.

3. Set up SELinux roles, users, and their sensitivity levels.

Web Penetration Testing with Kali Linux

ISBN: 978-1-78216-316-9   Paperback: 342 pages

A practical guide to implementing penetration testing strategies on websites, web applications, and standard web protocols with Kali Linux

1. Learn key reconnaissance concepts needed as a penetration tester.

2. Attack and exploit key features, authentication, and sessions on web applications.

3. Learn how to protect systems, write reports, and sell web penetration testing services.

Please check **www.PacktPub.com** for information on our titles

open source*
community experience distilled

PUBLISHING

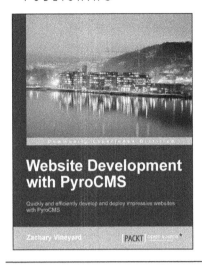

Website Development
with PyroCMS

Quickly and efficiently develop and deploy impressive websites
with PyroCMS

Zachary Vineyard

PACKT open source*

Website Development with PyroCMS

ISBN: 978-1-78328-223-4   Paperback: 104 pages

Quickly and efficiently develop and deploy impressive
websites with PyroCMS

1. Learn how to build websites quickly,
   thus saving time.

2. Effectively use the advanced system
   features of PyroCMS.

3. Acquire in-depth explanations on how to
   use data and themes in PyroCMS.

Getting Started with
PhantomJS

Harness the strength and capabilities of PhantomJS to
interact with the web and perform website testing with a
headless browser based on WebKit

Aries Beltran

PACKT open source*

Getting Started with PhantomJS

ISBN: 978-1-78216-422-7   Paperback: 140 pages

Harness the strength and capabilities of PhantomJS to
interact with the web and perform website testing with a
headless browser based on WebKit

1. Writing scripts that can interact directly with
   web services and pages.

2. Interacting with social media websites using
   PhantomJS scripts.

3. Creating web-based test scripts and running
   them in a headless browser.

Please check **www.PacktPub.com** for information on our titles